The Inca Empire

*The Formation and Disintegration
of a Pre-Capitalist State*

The Inca Empire

The Formation and Disintegration of a
Pre-Capitalist State

Thomas C. Patterson

Oxford • New York

First published in 1991 by
Berg Publishers
Editorial offices:
150 Cowley Road, Oxford, OX4 1JJ, UK
70 Washington Square South, New York, NY 10012, USA

Berg is the imprint of Oxford International Publishers Ltd.

British Library Cataloguing-in-Publication Data

Patterson, Thomas C.
  The Inca empire: The formation and disintegration of a pre-
  capitalist state. — (Explorations in anthropology)
  I. Title II. Series
  985
ISBN 0–85496–714–1   0–85496–348–0 (pbk)

Library of Congress Cataloging-in-Publication Data

Patterson, Thomas Carl.
    The inca empire : the Formation and disintegration of a
  pre-capitalist state/Thomas C. Patterson.
      p. cm. — (Explorations in anthropology)
    Includes bibliographical references.
    ISBN 0–85496–714–1   0–85496–348–0 (pbk)
    1. Incas—Politics and government. 2. Incas—History
    3. Incas—Social conditions. I. Title II. Series
  F3429.3.P65P38   1991
948´01—dc20   90-27115

Printed in the United Kingdom by WBC Book Manufacturers,
Bridgend, Mid Glamorgan.

For
Richard Burger and Lucy Salazar-Burger,
who rekindled my interest;

and
Peter Gran, Peter Rigby, Christine Gailey, and Phil
Yannella, who helped me to explore the relations
between theory and practice and generally made
life interesting while I toiled over the manuscript.

EXPLORATIONS IN ANTHROPOLOGY
A University College London Series
Series Editors: Barbara Bender, John Gledhill and Bruce
Kapferer

Jadran Mimica, *Intimations of Infinity: The Cultural Meaning of the Iqwaye Counting System and Number*

Tim Ingold, David Riches and James Woodburn (eds.),
Hunters and Gatherers
   Volume 1. *History, Evolution and Social Change*
   Volume 2. *Property, Power and Ideology*

Barry Morris, *Domesticating Resistance: The Dhan-Gadi Aborigines and the Australian State*

Bruce Kapferer, *A Celebration of Demons*

Alfred Gell, *The Anthropology of Time: Cultural Constructions of Temporal Maps and Images*

Max and Eleanor Rimoldi, *Hahalis and the Labour of Love: A Social Movement on Buka Island*

Henk Driessen, *On the Spanish-Moroccan Frontier*

Joan Bestard-Camps, *What's in a Relative? Household and Family in Formentera*

Pnina Werbner, *The Migration Process: Capital, Gifts and Offerings among Pakistanis in Britain*

Contents

Preface   ix

Introduction   1

1. **The Historical Landscape**   9
   1.1 Pre-State Societies in the Andes
   1.2 Class and State Formation: Some Theoretical
   Considerations
   1.3 Class and State Formation in the Andes

2. **Inca Society Before the Empire**   42
   2.1 The Creation of Inca Society
   2.2 The Prelude to Empire
   2.3 The Constitution of the Empire

3. **The Impact of Empire**   69
   3.1 The Formation and Organization of the
   Imperial State
   3.2 Conquest, Succession, and the Changing
   Composition of the Imperial Ruling Class

4. **Quiescence, Resistance, and Rebellion**   98
   4.1 Border Wars and Imperial Expansion
   4.2 Rebellions and Civil Wars

5. **The Clash of Empires and the Formation of
   Colonial Society**   129
   5.1 The Plunder Economy: War, Resistance, and
   Immigration
   5.2 The Crisis of the 1560s
   5.3 The Formation of Colonial Society

Conclusions   157

Notes   166

Figures   170

Glossary   173

Bibliography   175

Index   204

Preface

This book marks a resting place on an odyssey, a time and place to collect thoughts and to reflect on their meaning. Like many of my contemporaries who went through the U.S. public school system in the 1940s and 1950s, I grew up in an environment in which people perceived their lives, and, by extension, the modern world, as rooted in fairly recent events – World War II, the Depression, or twentieth-century immigration from the old country. They were largely unconcerned with the more distant past or with faraway places, unless events there impinged on them in some direct way. Time and space were often fused, so that a visit to the old country – rural Quebec and one of Montreal's older working class neighborhoods in my family's case – or to some place even more exotic, like those portrayed in *National Geographic*, also became a journey through time, a trip back to the past. The fusion and journeys always evoked a sense of disconnectedness I found both intriguing and disturbing.

Although other societies may have seemed distant and remote in the southern California town where I attended school, the influence of the U.S. government was pervasive and obvious. Aerospace companies that built jet fighters and guided missiles for the military dominated the economy in very visible ways. This was no illusion; it was reality. I found this, too, intriguing and disturbing.

My initial explorations of this illusion and reality were closely related to my first exposure to the Andean world. In an undergraduate "Peoples of the Andes" course, I read about the Incas and the empire they erected. What I remember more vividly than the Incas were the Araucanians and the Chiriguanas, peoples who lived on the margins of the imperial state and whose resolve halted the imperial march into their land and lives. Through lectures and readings, I gradually became aware

that anthropology, history, and archaeology could be inter-
woven to make sense of the imagery that shaped my views
about the world and to reconstitute the connections between
past, present, and U.S. societies in a more informative way. I
also realized that the boundaries and distinctions between anthropology, archaeology, and history were intellectually meaningless.

In 1961 I went to Peru for the first time. It was a long flight,
and the sky was still dark when we landed. We disembarked
into an airport swarming with heavily armed soldiers. Soon after
leaving the airport, we came to a shanty town, where people
huddled around fires built in oil drums to drink their morning
coffee on one side of the road, and garbage trucks were already
dumping their loads on the other. Further on, painted political
slogans covered the walls. I was seeing Peru close up for the first
time, and it was not exactly what I expected. I returned a year
later to do archaeological research for a doctoral dissertation,
and, for the next thirteen months, I found myself in the middle
of a civil war, alleged election fraud, curfews, a military junta,
and police attacks on political demonstrations and university
students.

By the late 1960s I had already realized that the analysts who
gave the most validation and meaning to my perceptions of
contemporary Peru were leftists. In 1966 I bought a copy of Karl
Marx's (1965) *Pre-Capitalist Economic Formations* in a Lima book-
store, and began to read Marx and contemporary left commen-
tators to understand their theoretical frameworks. Although this
enhanced my appreciation of what was happening in modern
Peru and the rest of the world, I was not able to transfer what I
was learning to archaeology. I could not yet elaborate a theoretically grounded and informed understanding of the pre-Incaic
societies, the refuse and remains of which I had been excavating.

By the mid-1970s I knew the linkage of anthropology, archaeology, and history only became meaningful when their prac-
titioners shared a clearly formed theory of society and could
pose questions in ways that were relevant given the limitations
imposed by the diverse kinds of evidence each of them used. By
the end of the decade I had begun to explore the relevance of
Marxist social theory in conjunction with a number of friends,
most notably Karen Spalding, Peter Rigby, and Peter Gran.

I have had wonderful traveling companions on this journey
and have met interesting people in the process. They have

shared their company and food, prodded me when I was moving too slowly or wandering off in wrong directions, and pointed out new paths to follow. This book could not have been written without their support. I have been heavily influenced by historians who have described the Andean world, especially John Rowe, John Murra, María Rostworowski de Diez Canseco, Craig Morris, Dorothy Menzel, Tom Zuidema, Luis Valcarcel, Waldemar Espinoza, Frank Salomon, Irene Silverblatt, Steve Stern, and, above all, Karen Spalding. My colleagues at Temple University – Peter Gran, Peter Rigby, and Phil Yannella – provided different and diverse kinds of advice and inspiration before and after I began to write. Talal Asad, Brigitte Boehm de Lameiras, John Gledhill, Katherine Hagedorn, Mogens Trolle Larsen, Stanley Diamond, Don Nonini, Richard Lee, Nan Woodruff, and Bob Paynter forced me to clarify my thoughts with their insights, comparisons, and questions. Christine Gailey took on a difficult and dangerous task; she became a sounding board, and provided almost instantaneous criticism and encouragement for what I was thinking and writing. I thank all of them.

Philadelphia, PA
21 January 1991

Introduction

This book is about the Inca state that dominated the Andean peoples of western South America during the fifteenth and sixteenth centuries. It tells two stories. One is about the appearance of the state, its rapid rise to dominance, and its even quicker disintegration; the other is an account of the unequal and oppressive social relations it created. However, the book is more than a narrative account of the rise and fall of the Inca state or of its relations with subject populations and neighboring peoples; it is also a contribution to anthropological theory on the formation and dissolution of states. This topic is of considerable importance in a world where people must confront every day the effects of decolonization, nation building, military coups, civil wars, invasions, and the highly exploitative new international economic order.

The Incas, their subjects, and their neighbors have been implicated almost continuously in discussions about politics and culture since the 1530s, when the first accounts of this civilization began to filter back to Europe. While Inca society is mentioned specifically by social theorists, critics, and writers as diverse as Michel de Montaigne (1958), François de Voltaire (1963), Corneille de Pauw (1768), and Karl Marx (1965), its involvement in the development of social thought since the sixteenth century has more often been implied and unacknowledged.[1] Knowledge and comprehension of the Inca state unfolded in a milieu shaped by the development of absolutist states and characterized by polemical arguments about the assets and liabilities of different forms of government. These understandings were incorporated in perspectives that extolled the virtues of civic republicanism or monarchy and explored the dangers (dissension and revolt) inherent in societies, presumably widespread outside Europe, whose despotic rulers lived in luxury, reduced the vast majority of their subjects to the same

1

base level, and governed arbitrarily with little or no regard for law. Social and political theorists called these despotic states oriental societies (Krader 1975; Springborg 1987).

Contrary to popular opinion, Andean peoples contributed in more than one way to various debates about the nature of human society and good government. Various social theorists appropriated their society and culture for dissection and analysis, and Andean writers – like Inca Garcilaso de la Vega, whose mother belonged to the Inca ruling class – did much to shape the contours of those debates with their widely read and translated descriptions of the Inca state.

The Inca state – *tawantinsuyu*, or the Land of the Four Quarters, as the Incas themselves called it – was an empire based on conquest. It stretched nearly three thousand miles along the Andes Mountains. From Cuzco, the imperial capital located in one of the mountain valleys of southern Peru, the Incas exerted varying degrees of control over the peoples from the Ecuadorian-Colombian frontier in the north to central Chile and the uplands of northwestern Argentina in the south. Their empire was short-lived; it took shape in the 1430s and grew explosively during the middle of the fifteenth century, when, in quick succession, the Incas subjugated one group after another. It was still expanding on the eve of the Spanish invasion in 1532 even as it was beginning to unravel and disintegrate under the weight of its own contradictions. These facts are supported by the testimony of various sixteenth-century Andean peoples, former Inca state officials, and archaeological evidence.[2]

The Inca empire was neither the earliest state in the Andes nor the first one to raid and conquer neighboring peoples. In fact, it was merely a single, late episode – and a short one at that – in the development of native Andean states. While there may have been a small state or two in the Andes as early as the second millennium B.C., it existed only briefly before it was destroyed or collapsed. Consequently, there existed no continuous tradition of class-stratified, state-based societies – i.e., civilization. In this sense, Andean civilization arose in the closing centuries of the first millennium B.C., when the social relations that constituted the fabric of numerous kin-based tribal communities were broken down and reconstituted in terms of stratified social classes and state institutions. The Inca empire was built on the foundations erected by these earlier class-stratified states;

it gained prominence because it was the latest representative of the tradition of Andean civilization – which Francisco Pizarro and his followers encountered when they arrived in the early 1530s.

The Spaniards quickly learned that the Inca state was in the throes of a devastating civil war that had begun about five years earlier in the mid-1520s as a successional dispute between rival claimants to the throne. The fighting spread rapidly as the leading contenders eliminated their rivals, forged alliances, and brought their allies into the fray, and as other groups, tired of Inca rule, seized the opportunities created by the struggle and by a weakened and distracted state apparatus to rebel and reclaim their autonomy. As they gained a clearer understanding of the war, the Spaniards recognized the opportunities it afforded. Using Cortés's invasion of Mexico as a blueprint for action, they kidnapped one contender and held him hostage, and demanded an enormous ransom payment. With gold and silver currently hovering around \$380US and \$4US per ounce (respectively) in the world market, the precious metals they extorted as ransom and melted down into bullion was worth about \$83,000,000US.[3]

The Spaniards had inserted themselves into the political dynamics of the Andean peoples. To secure their position, they enmeshed themselves in the successional dispute, first supporting one faction and then another, and, more importantly, establishing close ties with powerful groups that were disenchanted with Inca rule. However, their capacity to control and their position of dominance were both limited until the 1570s because of the continued fighting, new revolts, and banditry that ravaged the land after Inca rule began to disintegrate. The ability of the colonial elite to extract surplus goods from the native population during this period depended on establishing good working relations with its traditional leaders and keeping the traditional modes of production intact.

The next forty years witnessed new levels of extortion, violence, and destruction, as the Spanish ruling class in the colony attempted to impose its will, and the Andean peoples along with slaves imported from the Caribbean and Africa resisted. In the late 1540s, about the time the plunder began to decline, vast quantities of silver were discovered at Potosí, and the colonial economy was reorganized. Most areas of the old Inca state were reintegrated into the economic space it created; however, areas like Paraguay, which lay beyond the imperial frontiers and was never subject to Inca rule, were also incorporated into the political economic space dominated by Potosí and Lima. Even though the colonial ruling class, with the support of the Spanish crown, steadily chipped away at the key institutions and practices of Andean society during these years, they were not able to dismantle them effectively until the 1570s, when the state apparatus of the colony was strengthened significantly. This did not, however, mark the end of Andean resistance to state domination; it merely shifted the conflict onto new terrain and gave rise to new forms of opposition.

Inca civilization, its predecessors, and the social relations that emerged as it disintegrated illustrate various aspects of class and state formation. Any account of class and state formative processes involves selecting and emphasizing certain categories of information. It necessarily builds on and explores issues framed in terms of a particular theoretical framework. It must confront questions and problems provoked by dialogues with other perspectives.[4] And it must be historical.

The theoretical framework I have adopted is Marxist, and thus links the historical appearance of the state with the emergence of social classes. It views the state as an instrument of repression necessary for the maintenance of exploitation. Most important, it recognizes that class and state formation are historically and sociologically contingent. This contingency neither denies "determination in the last instance by the economic level" nor overlooks causality situated in other levels or "the complex intertwining of causal connections between the various levels" (van Binsbergen and Raatgever 1985:13). It means, in specific instances, that class and state formation are diverse, complex, social processes rather than the inevitable outcomes of universal, metaphysical, evolutionary potentials or voluntaristic action.

In this perspective, the common thread of human society – life in the relatively undifferentiated community, where the members are bound to each other by shared interests and practices – is broken when social classes appear (Krader 1976:223–226). Everyday life is disrupted as one part of the population begins to pursue its own interests, rather than the consensual ones of the community as a whole, in the context of the continuing institutions and practices of the heretofore classless and predominantly kin-organized community. The traditional social relations of the community become distorted and are ultimately reconstituted and reorganized to accommodate the private interests of that group. Thus, class formation, when it succeeds, involves the suppression of at least one way of life.

Social classes never exist alone but always within a hierarchical structure, in which each class is opposed to the others and is defined by its relations with them. Class is a social relation constructed in terms of the degree of control over the means of production – raw materials, the instruments required to transform them into useful objects, and labor power. A class structure composed of social classes with different relations to the conditions of production has been called "the collective social expression of the fact of exploitation, the way in which exploitation is embodied in a social structure" (Ste. Croix 1984:100). It determines who, through control over labor power and the means of production, can consistently extract labor or goods from the direct producers.

State formation is intimately linked with the conditions that underlie the constitution of class structures and the reproduction of class relations. When a class structure is erected, a state is born. The authority vested in the community as a whole is seized by the newly emergent dominant class, consolidated, and transformed into power. The state becomes organized partly in terms of the social categories that compose the class structure and partly in terms of the institutions and practices of the community. The state subsumes the administration of justice, the conduct of diplomacy and war, and other activities that were previously carried out by the society for the benefit of the community as a whole. It becomes simultaneously the representative of the dominant class in whose interests it was organized and the mediator of the struggles between that class and the members of opposing groups in the wider society.

The fundamental relationship between the existing kin community and the emerging dominant class is antagonistic and conflictual, since it is based on exploitation and extortion. As a consequence, class and state formation creates contradictions, as the collective institutions and customary practices of the kin-based community are distorted, expanded, and transformed to incorporate the appropriation of tribute by the dominant class. Stanley Diamond (1951) has coined the phrase "kin/civil

conflict" to describe the contradictions between the priorities of
the dominant class, the state, and the subject peoples and how
the dynamics they engender are played out in everyday life and
social relations.

In this perspective, attention is focused on the dialectical
relationship between the actions of the state and the dominant
class, on the one hand, and those of their subject peoples, on
the other. The state and the dominant class selectively appropriate and repress, refine and eliminate, the customary practices
and relations of the community to further their own goals, to
rationalize what they have attempted to do. At the same time,
subject populations, with identities imposed on them by virtue
of their position in the state-based system of exploitation and
oppression, continuously devise ways to evade and resist the
demands of the state and the alienation these demands promote. No state, however, has ever exerted total control over its
subjects' lives, and because of the creativity people continually
display in devising new ways to oppose the demands and
exactions of states, no state has ever been able to take everything it wanted (Gailey 1991).

This perspective raises the issues of articulation and reproduction. How did the dominant mode of production become dominant? How did the relations of production of the old modes
facilitate or oppose articulation with the new dominant mode of
production? How were the emergent class structures and contradictions constituted and reproduced? Such processes are
always contingent on the forms of the modes of production as
well as on the form of their presence in the particular society
under investigation (Gailey and Patterson 1988). The outcomes
of these processes varied from one part of the Inca state to
another.

Chapter One uses archaeological evidence and a theoretical
framework that owes much to recent elaborations of structural
Marxism to reconstruct the political-economic structures and
praxis of successive forms of pre-state societies in coastal Peru
and to examine several of the major episodes of class and state
formation that preceded the emergence and subsequent development of the Inca state. Although inequalities existed in some
of the non-state or pre-state societies, these were transcended
because of the cooperation required for social reproduction and
the ambiguities inherent in authority structures. There can be no

general theory of class and state formation, but only one that deals with the conditions in which class and state formation can occur. In the Andean area, states appeared toward the end of the first millennium B.C., when one group began to reproduce itself by appropriating the surplus labor and products of others.

Chapter Two makes use of Inca dynastic traditions to investigate the conditions and processes that led to the consolidation of the imperial state. The dynastic accounts do not necessarily tell the true story, but they do describe the crystallization of political-economic structures and praxis that were familiar to the Andean peoples and would be familiar to those peoples living elsewhere who also had to confront the exactions of tributary states that derived their revenues largely from the expropriation of land and labor power. In this and subsequent chapters the Marxist analytical categories and framework are retained, but there is an emphasis on historical rather than archaeological evidence. The shift represents a change in the kinds of evidence that are available. Documentary information appears and is relatively abundant, while available archaeological data are less substantial from the Inca homeland region for this period than for earlier times. Examining the different kinds of evidence through the same theoretical lens enhances the range of information that can be brought to bear to explain the historical development and transformation of Andean societies.

Chapter Three considers how the Incas attempted to impose and maintain their will, and thus examines the contradictions that shaped imperial society and the largely unsuccessful attempts of the ruling class to resolve the resulting structural and practical problems. The fragility of the Inca state stems from contradictions that increased the levels of surplus extraction, left local economies and traditional political structures largely intact, and continually transformed the composition of the imperial ruling class to minimize the effects of successional disputes and local rebellions.

Chapter Four examines how the Andean peoples defied and resisted the state's attempts to expropriate their means of production and to seize their labor power as it attempted to assert its control over the production and reproduction of everyday life. Neither a continued imperial expansion nor the incipient construction of a professional bureaucracy and army in the waning years of the empire was able to stem the effects of the contradictions inherent in the Inca state. In its attempt to assert a *pax incaica* throughout its domain, the imperial state was almost continuously at war. It had to suppress civil wars resulting from successional disputes, border wars resulting from inconsistent control over recently conquered or encapsulated frontier populations, and local revolts by peoples who wished to reassert their autonomy. These were several of the ongoing crises of the Inca state.

Chapter Five traces the events that followed the disintegration and collapse of the Inca state. Important continuities in the organization of the production and the reproduction of everyday life persisted from pre-Columbian times into the early Colonial Period. To periodize history in a way that diminishes or minimizes their significance is to deny Andean peoples the contributions they made to the development of European civilization through the precious metals they mined and the taxes they paid.

Chapter 1

The Historical Landscape

> The relationship between human groups and their environment is basic to any understanding of the patterns of Andean society. (Karen Spalding, *Huarochirí*)

The Inca state was constituted in one of the most ecologically diverse parts of the world. The Andes mountains, its backbone, rise abruptly out of the Pacific ocean. Jagged peaks, many continually capped with snow and ice, tower above high plateaus and mountain valleys. The land trembles almost continuously from earthquakes and tectonic shocks, the pains of a world that is still being born. The sixteenth-century inhabitants of the coastal regions of the empire recognized this connection and attributed it to Pachacamac, a powerful deity who was both the creator of the world and the earthshaker (Patterson 1985a).

The seismic activity of this world is the product of plate tectonics. The Andes are still being thrust upwards, a few centimeters each year, by the collision of two enormous plates that slide slowly but inexorably over the earth's surface. As the westward-moving South American continental plate overrides the eastward-moving Nazca Oceanic Plate, the continental land mass buckles and the mountains rise. This process has been going on for several million years and has produced a vertical landscape with one of the steepest gradients in the world (Dollfus 1965, 1978; Moseley 1983; Tosi 1960).

Because of their height, the mountains form an effective meteorological barrier and have combined with the prevailing patterns of atmospheric and oceanic circulation to produce the world's driest desert on the coastal plain and the Pacific slopes below the 2000 meter contour (Patterson and Lanning 1968).

9

When the rains come to the high Andean landscapes in November, the rivers swell. Those rising on the upper western slopes rush through narrow rocky gorges and flow across the desert coastal plain before emptying into the Pacific ocean; those of the Atlantic watershed, trapped and channeled by parallel mountain ranges, typically flow north or south until their contents escape eastward through deep canyons and eventually merge to form the Amazon. Further south, the rivers that rise on the *altiplano* in Bolivia and in the mountains of northwestern Argentina are ultimately tributaries of the Parana.

Virtually the entire coastal region of the Inca state, with the exception of Ecuador and the most northern part of Peru, is bathed by cold waters that upwell from the ocean's bottom. These cold currents bring enormous quantities of microplankton to the surface, creating the conditions for one of the world's richest fishing grounds. As a result, the marine resources are abundant and diverse (Koepcke 1961:55–59, 103–235; Moseley and Feldman 1988; Schweigger 1964).

The grandeur of the Andean landscape makes human beings seem insignificant. The bleak windswept tundra of the high plateaus, the barren coastal desert, as well as the steep slopes of the mountains themselves seem harsh and forbidding. They appear to erect formidable obstacles that would inhibit social development or prevent it altogether. Crop failures, that still occur three out of every five years at high elevations, make even life itself precarious. These difficulties are compounded by the frequent, but always unanticipated, floods, earthquakes, or other natural disasters. These calamities, as well as those created by peoples themselves, prove that life was never easy in the Andes, heightening the ever-present sense of desolation, imminent danger, and vulnerability.

While the perception of the Andes as a dangerous world is partly true, it is also partly an illusion, for the area was one of the few places in the world where people produced surpluses, where civilization developed autochthonously. Archaeological sites, recognized as an integral part of the landscape, stand like sentinels, bearing silent yet eloquent testimony to the changes wrought by the Incas and their predecessors.

As harsh and forbidding as the Andes can be, the diverse ecological habitats of the landscape and the ocean waters that sweep along the shore provided the raw materials used by the

ancient inhabitants to create surpluses and construct civilization. By extracting materials for consumption or use, by con-
verting land into pasture and arable field, the Andean peoples
transformed the landscape and its raw materials into means of
production. The banks of the irrigation canals they dug into the
coastal desert and across dry valley bottoms were colonized by
trees, bushes, and weeds; the llamas, alpacas, and guinea pigs
they domesticated provided wool and food; the agricultural
fields and settlements they sculpted on mountain slopes and
hilltops altered the local topography; mollusk beds were destroyed by overharvesting and vast tracts of bushes and trees
were denuded as they sought fuel and construction materials;
and the quarries and mine shafts they dug into the landscape
yielded building materials and a variety of minerals.

In the process of creating their world, the Andean peoples
also changed themselves. The transformations that occurred
were not uniform throughout the entire area. Instead, they
manifest the subtle but significant variations that result when
peoples live in a diverse environment, have complex historical
pasts and varied relations with their neighbors, and emphasize
different elements of the forces and relations of production.
Even slight differences of emphasis in the forces of production –
the raw materials taken from the environment and the implements and labor power employed to transform them into useful
items – can yield significant variations in the details of the
organization of labor. They can affect the labor processes by
introducing new forms of specialization and technical divisions
of labor. Differences in the relations of production – whether the
producers themselves own or control their means of production
and labor power, or whether these are controlled by another
class that extracts goods or labor from them – constitute another
source of variability.

Production is necessary for the maintenance and reproduction
of the conditions necessary for life. This means not only the
reproduction of labor power, in the demographic sense, but also
the social relations that organize work and other activities.
Needless to say, there is nothing intrinsic in the activities associated with fishing, shellfish harvesting, hunting, foraging, or
even farming that specifies particular forms of social organization. These activities can and have been organized in a variety
of different ways. The social conditions of production in the

various Andean societies were diverse. This complexity was manifested not only in the economic aspects of these societies but also in political, ideological, and cultural ways.

1.1. Pre-State Societies in the Andes

"Modes of production" are simply the bare bones of a Marxist analysis of historical process. (Rodney Hilton, Introduction, *The Brenner Debate*)

The system of production relations [is]. . .the "skeleton" of socio-economic formations, which is always clothed in the "flesh and blood" of other social relations. (Yuri Semenov, "The Theory of Socio-Economic Formations and World History")

People have certainly lived in the Andes for the last fifteen thousand to eighteen thousand years (Dillehay 1985; MacNeish, Patterson, and Browman 1975). There is some evidence indicating that they may already have been living there as early as thirty-two or thirty-three thousand years ago, though not all archaeologists accept this interpretation (Benditt 1988; Bray 1986; Dillehay 1988). The archaeological evidence comes from the deepest layers of a cave in eastern Brazil and from a stratum beneath an open campsite in southern Chile that was occupied about thirteen thousand years ago (Dillehay 1984; Guidon and Delibrias 1986). In both instances, small assemblages of flaked and unflaked stones were found near hearths or lenses of charcoal, which have yielded radiocarbon measurements. Since the results of the excavations are largely unpublished, it is difficult to comment extensively on the culture, activities, and social relations of the groups that produced the two early assemblages.

Interpreting social relations and culture from the objects and associations preserved in the archaeological record entails moving beyond the objects and associations themselves in order to comprehend, construct, and clarify the patterns they encode and the circumstances that led to their formation. Such procedures necessitate moving back and forth between the phenomena and appearance of the archaeological record, on the one hand, and the conditions of their creation, on the other. The phenomena of the archaeological record refract, rather than mirror precisely, the social relations and cultures of that past society (Patterson 1983a).

All societies manifest one or more modes of production. The mode of production itself is an abstraction concerned with elements that structure everyday life in all societies: the forces of production, the relations of production, and associated juridical-political and ideological dimensions. While these elements are always present, they vary, of course, from one concrete, historically specific society to another. The forces of production consist of the raw materials people transform into useful items, the implements and knowledge they employ in the process, and their labor power. The relations of production express the form of control that the direct producers exercise over the productive forces and the relations between the owners and them when they have been separated from their means of production and/or labor power. The forces and relations of production constitute a society's economic structure and provide a grounding for the associated juridical-political and ideological dimensions and forms of social consciousness. Modes of production refer to the political-economic structures of society and to the material conditions under which the social relations and forms of consciousness they engender are reproduced or transformed in the course of everyday life.

The earliest Andean societies for which there are significant amounts of evidence are based on variants of the communal mode of production. In these societies, there is collective control and appropriation of the means of production. Individuals belong to the community by virtue of their regular participation in activities and practices that give meaning to their interdependence. There are no structural differences between producers and non-producers, since such a distinction can only exist from the perspective of a given individual in relation to a particular labor process; this distinction disappears when the focus is extended beyond that event to other instances in which the producer becomes a consumer, and vice versa. The absence of a social division of labor implies that there is no exploitation. This absence, however, does not mean that there is no social differentiation, that social relations may not be oppressive, or that there exist no differences in levels of wealth. In kin-based communal societies, individuals and groups occasionally do withdraw from direct labor and depend on the labor of others.

modes of production

RECIPROCITY.

However, their ability to appropriate the labor of others depends on the continued goodwill of the community, since their authority to do so is based on age, societal status, gender, or kin connections rather than on force or control over the community's means of production. This dependency or authority is fragile and must be continually renegotiated (Leacock 1982:159; Patterson 1987d; Siskind 1978).

Paloma was one of the early societies that manifested a communal mode of production. It was a coastal society in central Peru that began before 6000 B.C. and came to a close about 3250 B.C. (Benfer 1984, 1986; Donnan 1964; Moseley 1978; Patterson 1971, 1983b, 1989a; Quilter 1980). Some of the Paloma communities lived in year-round settlements if the resources they used were in close proximity, while others seem to have moved from place to place according to the seasonal availability of resources. The settlement at the Paloma site exhibits both residence patterns: an earlier phase characterized by seasonal occupancy, and a later one, beginning around 4400 B.C., which exhibited sedentary habitation (Benfer 1984:536). While Paloma society had an economic base that was dominated by fishing, littoral harvesting, hunting, and foraging, there is nothing intrinsic in these activities that expresses how work was organized. However, analyses of coprolites and intestinal contents, as well as the low strontium content of skeletal remains from Paloma, attest to the dietary importance of marine life (Benfer 1986:66; Quilter and Stocker 1983; Weir and Dering 1986:38).

The household was the basic production and consumption unit in Paloma society, judging by the burials of men, women, and children beneath the floors of houses that were still being used and by the presence of storage pits near these structures. The division of labor, as indicated by the skeletal remains and grave goods, was based on gender and age. Adolescent and adult males frequently exhibit exostoses on the external auditory meatus, while females do not (Quilter 1980:49–51; Quilter and Stocker 1983:547–548). One circumstance that promotes the growth of these lesions is immersion in water with temperatures below 17.5° C, which are typical of the ocean-bottom waters that bathe coastal Peru (Tattersall 1985). This strongly suggests that adolescent boys and young men engaged in deepwater swimming and diving for mollusks, while girls and women did not. The presence of weaving implements in the graves of women and older men indicates that some tasks were not specific to a particular gender but related to age.

The division of labor based on age and gender meant that no individual in the community was able to procure or produce all of the goods essential for life. It necessitated cooperation – sharing the products of one's labor with one or more members of the opposite sex and different generations in return for a portion of the products of their labor. Kinship expresses the linkage between sharing and the division of labor (Siskind 1978). Each item that was produced or acquired potentially moved through a circuit of individuals before it was used or consumed. In Paloma, the circuit through which some subsistence goods moved apparently involved the members of households: adult men, adult women, and children.

The presence of infants and children among the burials beneath the floors of houses still in use, as well as the reuse or rebuilding of domestic structures, suggests that sharing occurred in the context of relatively permanent relations that involved not only men and women of the same generation but also members of successive generations. Marriage and filiation defined the membership and place of an individual in the domestic group and determined his or her share of its production. The burials and the reoccupation of houses imply that the connections between the domestic groups of a village or camp were also relatively enduring. The apparent permanency of the domestic groups in a settlement also implies that the individuals who participated in any collective, settlement-wide labor activities were drawn repeatedly from the same relatively small labor pool.

The small numbers of people who resided in Paloma settlements – estimated between twenty-five and seventy-five individuals – meant that the camps and villages were not autonomous, independent demographic entities. There was matrimonial mobility of men and women between settlements; the social composition of the villages and camps likely would have mirrored this practice. If only men moved, the settlement population would have consisted of women with kin ties, their children, and husbands from outside; if only women moved, the community would have been composed of men who were related to each other, their offspring, and women from other settlements.

Toward the end of the fourth millennium B.C., the members

of Paloma society adopted agricultural techniques and plants that had been domesticated elsewhere. Land was gradually transformed from an object of labor provisioned by nature that provided immediate returns to an instrument of labor (a major means of production) that yielded returns only after considerable labor investments over an extended period of time. The productivity of the initial agricultural endeavors in Paloma society was low, judging by the paucity of domesticated plants in archaeological deposits. Agriculture was merely one of a number of economic practices; it could be adopted because the productivity of other subsistence activities was sufficient and reliable enough to permit individuals to engage in activities characterized by delayed consumption, such as those associated with farming.

The economy of the Conchas society, which followed the Paloma on the central Peruvian coast and lasted from roughly 3250 to 2350 B.C., was dominated by fishing and littoral harvesting. The new forms of production that provided the foundations of the economy included: the reorganization and increased productivity of labor processes associated with the extraction of marine resources (likely to have been men's work, given the gender division of labor in Paloma society); the development of new labor processes associated with agricultural production – especially of two inedible plants, cotton and gourds; the manufacture of cotton nets, fish lines, and textiles (activities associated with women and elderly men in Paloma society); the crystallization of collective labor processes associated with the construction of platform mounds and architectural complexes; and the circulation of economically important subsistence and industrial goods between specialized farming and fishing settlements (Feldman 1980, 1985, 1987; Moseley 1975; Moseley and Feldman 1988; Patterson 1983b, 1990).

Production and its spatial organization were transformed. Permanently occupied villages were established on the coast near rich fishing grounds. However, since agriculture was impossible or only marginally feasible around some of the fishing villages, the cultivation of cotton, gourds, and a few food plants was often carried out at some distance from the villages. This led to the formation of economically specialized farming and fishing villages. On the central Peruvian coast, it meant that, for at least part of the year, farmers resided and worked in hamlets that were located between fifteen and twenty kilometers from fishing villages, like Ancón, where agriculture was either marginal or impossible. They grew gourds and cotton that the fishing villagers spun to make fish lines, nets, and clothes. In return, they received fish and marine mollusks from the fishermen. This challenged the self-sufficiency of both farmers and fishermen, since neither produced the whole range of goods they used and consumed.

This new territorial organization of production was not merely superimposed on the existing age- and gender-based division of labor characteristic of Paloma society, nor did it completely supplant and transform that arrangement by creating a new technical division of labor between farming and fishing villages. In those localities, where farming and fishing could be carried out by residents of the same village, the traditional division of labor may have persisted. Adolescent boys and men likely continued to fish and dive for mollusks, while women probably continued to forage and cultivate. However, in those communities where the loci of farming and fishing activities were spatially separated, the gender-based division of labor was transformed. In economically specialized fishing communities, like Huaca Prieta, both men and women engaged in activities centering around the sea, judging by the fact that both sexes suffered from exostoses of the auditory meatus (Tattersall 1985). By extension, the gender-based division of labor in the economically specialized farming hamlets may also have diminished, as the labor practices of men and women converged. At the same time, the differences between the labor practices carried out in fishing and farming hamlets were intensified.

The relations of production that developed in Conchas society did not merely replicate the earlier division of labor. Rather, they involved the elaboration of community-level relations and their articulation with the domestic level, where the real appropriation of raw materials still occurred. The community-level relations linked a spatially organized, technical division of labor with the age- and gender-based divisions of labor in both the traditional and the new economically specialized settlements. They facilitated the regular acquisition of the raw materials and resources from distant localities. Their importance is particularly evident in those labor processes and activities that were clearly beyond the capabilities of a single domestic group or even a small number of cooperating households – like the construction of fish-drying terraces, platform mounds, and the early stages of the large architectural complex at El Paraíso. The labor required for building each of the handful of platform mounds at Aspero or Río Seco exceeded sixty thousand person-days, feasible for a few households with large numbers of productive members; however, the minimum of almost two million person-days of labor necessary to build the stone structures at El Paraíso certainly surpassed that capacity (Feldman 1985, 1987; Patterson 1983b, 1990; Quilter 1985). Community-level relations of production and their linkage with domestic-level relations are important because they constitute the conditions for the reproduction of the society. This means that social reproduction is embedded in and conceived through ideological institutions, such as kinship and ritual (Rigby 1985:15–22; 1987).

The shift to a truly agrarian economy in coastal Peru, in which the cultivation of food plants, rather than fishing, played the determinant role, occurred in the La Florida Social Formation, which lasted from 2350 to roughly 400 B.C. Agricultural production, previously concerned mainly with cotton and gourds, was expanded to include a greater variety and quantities of cultivated plant foods. This laid the foundations for new forms of production and appropriation that built on the existing community-level relations and territorially organized division of labor. The reproduction of La Florida society depended on the continued participation of households in community-level structures and activities.

The shift involved establishing additional economically specialized farming hamlets in localities with ecological conditions suited to the production of particular food crops as well as the construction of water management systems in the midvalleys and U-shaped platform mounds at inland localities. These pyramids served as the loci for social practices – rituals, predictions, and offerings – that established and maintained the conditions necessary for successful farming (Burger 1987; Patterson 1983b:33, 1985b, 1990; Ravines and Isbell 1976; Salazar-Burger and Burger 1983). These pyramids required many millions of person-days of labor to build, an amount that could only have been appropriated at the community level. The rate of labor appropriation for such projects, defined in person-days of labor per year, was two to four times greater than it had been in

Conchas society (Patterson 1983b).

The real appropriation of nature continued to occur at the household level. Storage pits and refuse deposits associated with residential structures and tool kits placed in the graves of different individuals attest to the continued importance of domestic production-consumption units in everyday life. However, the composition of the household units changed, given the evidence for a threefold increase in the size of consumption units at the Ancón fishing village during the early part of the second millennium B.C. (Patterson 1984). By that time, the production units were not simply nuclear families, even if they had been so previously. Whatever their composition, the production-consumption units were clearly both more extensive and more inclusive than they had been earlier. Furthermore, not all of the goods produced were circulated at the level of the community. Pottery was manufactured by several individuals in each settlement, indicated by intrasite variability, which reflects different levels of skill, time, and concern with the final appearance of the objects, and by intersite variations, which reflect the limits of circulation (Burger 1987:371; Patterson 1987d).

Like Paloma, the Conchas and La Florida societies were not stratified. There is no evidence for inequalities exhibited by artifacts with restricted distributions in the societies; there is no evidence for a class-based distinction between center and countryside; and there is no evidence for centralization, settlement hierarchies, or multiple levels of decision making of the kind posited for class-stratified, state-based societies (Patterson 1983b, 1990; Burger 1987:373). While there were economically specialized settlements in La Florida society, there is no evidence for a social division of labor in which the members of one social class exploited those of another by permanently appropriating either their labor or products. Nor is there any archaeological evidence for the resistance of one group against another.

The primary means of production in Conchas and La Florida society seem to have been appropriated collectively by the community. Each individual was dependent on the group as a whole, and all adults participated directly but differently in the production, distribution, circulation, and consumption of social product. In other words, like Paloma society, the La Florida communities manifested the social relations characteristic of a communal, kin-based mode of production. But there were some differences. La Florida society was determined by a variant of the communal mode of production with elaborated community-level relations of production. Conchas society represented an articulation of two forms of the communal mode of production: an egalitarian form that conforms with Eleanor Leacock's (1983) description of primitive communism and one with elaborated community-level relations (Patterson 1987d).

1.2. Class and State Formation: Some Theoretical Considerations

There is an alternative to this explanation. Several archaeologists, who advocate an evolutionary model of state formation, claim that Conchas society was a chiefdom and that sections of La Florida society on the central and north-central coasts of Peru were state-based (Haas 1987a, 1987b; Pozorski 1987). Their claim is based on lineal developmentalist notions of state formation: chiefdoms follow tribes and precede states. Furthermore, this theory asserts that monumental architecture is erected only in the context of class-stratified, state-based societies (Haas 1987a:31). While chiefdoms build moderate-sized structures,

> the construction of significantly larger monumental architecture. . .marks the appearance of the first state-level polities [because it]. . .requires the exercise of a much higher order of coercive power than is found in chiefdom-level societies and therefore signals a new and different form of power relationship between the ruler and subordinate populations (Haas 1987b:3).

This statement implies that more is involved in state formation than just the construction of large buildings. The extraction of goods, class stratification, the concentration of surplus, exploitation, oppression, resistance, specialization, and the existence of a state apparatus are only a few concomitants of state formation that one might expect to find manifested in the archaeological record. However, by placing so much emphasis on monumental structures, they neglect, to some extent, how and in what ways the archaeological record is indicative of other aspects of state formation.

Viewing the roughly fifty platform mounds, built along the Peruvian coast during La Florida times as temples, has permitted archaeologists to adopt a self-contained theory of state formation, the central premises and implications of which have remained largely unexplored. This is the theory of the theocratic state and the temple economy (Falkenstein 1974; Foster 1981; Gelb 1969; Webster 1976). This theory assumes not only that the coastal social formation was state-based, but that the polities composing it were theocratic, dominated by religion (Pozorski 1987:18–21; Steward 1950:103–104; Willey and Corbett 1954: 163–164). They depended on an intellectual and artistic elite whose creative genius was immortalized in the architectural monuments that reflected the religious fervor of the people (Carrión Cachot 1948:169–172). Religious practices, centered at the temples, provided the ideological glue that cemented together the various economically specialized villages in each region. Religious specialists – associated with the temples and typically assumed in the absence of evidence to be men – supervised the production, accumulation, and redistribution of foodstuffs, subsistence goods, and craft items in the spatially separated and economically specialized hamlets and villages that formed the larger community. These religious specialists were supported by the surplus production and labor of direct producers and constituted the ruling class in the emerging social division of labor.

If La Florida society is to be characterized as a series of theocratic polities, then it is necessary to specify in more detail how the transformation from kin community to state actually occurred, especially in relation to the reconstructions of Paloma and Conchas society. Under what conditions did class and state formation occur? How was the ruling class able to acquire and usurp authority that originally resided in the community as a whole, and to transform it into power? What was the locus of this authority; was it vested originally in administrative, war, or ritual specialists? What processes and circumstances led specifically to the development of a theocratic as opposed to some other kind of state apparatus? What traces of these conditions and processes of the non-state/state transition might one expect to find in the archaeological record?

Many descriptions of kin-based communities emphasize that experience and inventiveness are pooled. When there arise tasks requiring organization and supervision or crises, the community selects organizers and persuades them to serve. It grants authority to them for a limited period of time, until the task is completed or the crisis resolved (Gearing 1958, 1961, 1962). The authority of the leaders is ad hoc and provisional. Tendencies toward state formation occur when these temporary and provisional leaders are not inclined to relinquish their authority; when they attempt to transform it into power. Any attempt to consolidate and concentrate authority requires the support of others in the community for the seizure to be success-ful. If and when this happens, a class structure is formed and the state is born. If the would-be rulers are unable to establish and assert their claims, neither a class structure nor a state apparatus is imposed: class and state formation fail. In this sense, both class and state formation are historically contingent. They are one lane of a two-way street that also involves the dissolution of class structures and the state – in Marc Abélès's terminology, the state/non-state transition (1981:12–13).

Thorkild Jacobsen (1943, 1957) and Ignace Gelb (1972) view the non-state/state transition in early Mesopotamian society in terms of the concentration of political – legislative, administrat-ive, and judicial – power in as few hands as possible. They examine how authority, granted for limited periods of time by the community, was usurped. Igor Diakonoff (1972) focuses attention on the relation between the community and potential or would-be rulers in Early Dynastic society. He discusses the economy in terms of two sectors: the communal-and-private and the state. The former comprised the lands and activities of family communes that were linked together into hierarchical lineage groups that formed territorial communities. The latter

> embrace[d] the economies of the palace and temple; both are based on the unconditional property of the state (whether ideationally conceived as property of the god of the community, or of the king, or in any other way). The land of the palace and temples belong originally to the community as a whole, but at a very early period it got sequestered from it, becoming to all practical purposes the direct property of the temple or palace. The original aim of such economies was to create a fund for exchange between communities and as insurance for the community against emergencies, but later they become mainly sources of income for the king and royal bureaucracy (both secular and spiritual) (Diakonoff 1972:43).

Diakonoff then shows that the importance of the community

and state sectors varied, but that in no instance did the state sector encompass the whole society.

While Diakonoff, Gelb, and Jacobsen place the original extortion of the community and the impetus for class and state formation in the political realm, Aidan Southall (1988) situates them in the realm of ritual. In kin-based societies with no hereditary differences in rank, the original extortion resides in the custodians of ancestor shrines who become "the focus for flows of prestations which are, in turn, almost entirely consumed by the congregation offering them" (Southall 1988:74–75). Subsequently, these ritual personages arrogated or were granted further privileges, powers, and restrictions that distinguished them from the rest of the population; under certain, unspecified circumstances, these ritual figures, together with their kin or entourages were "tempted and able to exploit their position, crystallizing differences of rank and privilege between themselves and the rest of the population and adding political elements to the ritual office" (Southall 1988:75). He proceeds to show that economic changes underlie these developments:

> The ability to extract tribute presupposes higher productivity and a larger extractable surplus than, as well as improved means of enforcement. . . .The direct producers remain in autonomous communities, but the ruler and his close family, kin, and retainers become a ruling class of parasitic consumers, with a relationship to the means of production quite distinct from that of the direct producers. . . .There is always a tendency to increase the pressure on direct producers for more extractable surplus, which leads to disaffection and possible secession, especially on the borders of states. Repressing and preventing these disintegrative current requires a greater, more permanent, and therefore better organized mobilization of control and coercion through both administration and standing armies. Such measures in turn also raise costs, demand more taxes, and further increase pressure on direct producers to the breaking point where they must either flee or rebel, leading to a vicious cycle and eventual collapse. . . .To escape this there is great incentive to increase productivity by more direct and detailed control of direct producers and of the economy as a whole (Southall 1988:76–77).

When class and state formative processes dominate, the tensions of kin-based authority coupled with the potential for power become disengaged from the constraints of kinship.

Christine Gailey (1984:3) has noted that "class structures and institutions of surplus generation and extraction develop out of, and fundamentally in opposition to, the kin relations that order the communal holding of property, and that organize work, the allocation of products, and the continuous creation of cultural meanings." Kin relations do not disappear with the development of social classes; they are transformed and increasingly politicized.

> On the one hand, kinship within the emerging ruling class becomes "kingship" – the absorption of effective sharing and prior authority into the person(s) of the ruler(s). On the other hand, local kin communities become districts of producers, at least with regard to tribute extraction. . .an institutionalized negative reciprocity, in the form of tribute or labour provided to the politically dominant class(es) (Gailey 1984:3–4).

Class and state formation generate contradictions, that Allen Zagarell (1986:157–160) has viewed in terms of conflicts between the demands of the state on the community, on the one hand, and the rights and obligations of community leaders who are interposed between the head of state and the various subject populations, on the other. These traditional leaders are caught on the horns of a dilemma. They must be generous in order to retain the support of their subjects; at the same time, they must appropriate goods from their followers to satisfy the demands of the state. Their position is fraught with contradictions: they can find themselves pitted against the head of state and his entourage; they can become pitted against their kin from whom they appropriate goods and labor for the state; they may pit their kin against other kin groups in the same society; the subordinate classes in the various, localized kin communities can oppose both the state and their own leaders, the local representatives of the state; or one tribe or ethnic group, may be pitted against another. These oppositions present possibilities for creating different alliances. The contradictions and the alliances they engender constitute the historical contingency of both the non-state/state and state/non-state transitions.

The appearance of state-based societies in the Andes indicates the development of class structures and of a class-based division of labor, in which the members of the dominant class appropriate goods and services from the direct producers. To survive as nonproducers and to ensure the reproduction of class relations, the dominant class must create institutions and practices that promote and disguise their attempts to control production (Gailey and Patterson 1987). Class and state formation also imply a transition from kin-based societies shaped by communal mode of productions to those rooted in a tributary mode of production. The transition involves a shift from the collective control and use of surplus product, regulated by kin relations, to instances where labor and goods are appropriated from the producers by an exploiting class.

State-based societies manifesting the tributary mode of production have several distinctive features. The most important is that kin-organized communities continue to be the dominant units of production in the society, even though their survival is continually threatened by the claims and exactions of a state that is unable to reorganize production on non-kin basis. While the state is able to intervene in the production and reproduction of the local kin communities, its survival depends on their continued existence (Krader 1975:286–339). In these societies, production is organized for use rather than exchange; the items and goods kept by producers as well as those appropriated from them by the state and the dominant class are used or consumed. Tribute is not extracted exclusively by force, since the direct producers might acquiesce or even agree to these exactions, especially when they are threatened with coercion or violence. Since exploitation is the most distinctive feature of any class-based society, then resistance, its mirror image, is equally symptomatic; therefore, class conflict or struggle comprises the fundamental relationship between the constituent classes of tributary states. When the kin or village communities of tribute-based states retain effective control over their lands and labor, over their own subsistence production and social reproduction, they deprive the ruling classes of some of the goods and services their members demand and consume. When the dominant classes are unable to exact tribute consistently from their own subjects, their members often seek the goods and services they have lost or desire by following expansionist policies that exploit or subjugate neighboring peoples (Amin 1976:13–58, 1980:37–55; Gailey and Patterson 1988).

The development of new relations of production is an integral feature of state formation. In the Andes, the first major

transformation of the production relations occurs at the end of
La Florida society rather than in its formative phases. The
community-level relations of production – which developed in
Conchas society, ensured the maintenance and reproduction of
a spatially organized economy, and mobilized labor for communal construction projects – broke down between about 400 and
200 B.C. Labor was no longer appropriated at the community
level for the construction of platform mounds that guaranteed
the agricultural success for the community as a whole. Surplus
product and labor were redirected into new channels: the construction of forts, raiding, and the assertion of class, status, and
regional differences.

The episode of class and state formation that occurred during
the closing centuries of the first millennium B.C. was seminal. It
marked the appearance and consolidation of a continuous tradition of state-based societies in the Andes, which includes the
Inca Empire and persists to the present day (Schaedel 1985a,
1985b). However, it should not be viewed as either the first or
the only attempt to impose civilization on Andean peoples.
There is evidence of an earlier, unsuccessful episode of class and
state formation centered at Cerro Sechin in the Casma Valley
toward the end of the second millenium B.C. (Pozorski and
Pozorski 1987:79–82, 121; Samaniego, Vergara and Bischof 1985).
"Failed states," like the one at Cerro Sechin, are of great importance because they challenge the validity of linear developmentalist assertions that state formation is a unidirectional process
and that the state is the highest form of social development.

1.3. Class and State Formation in the Andes

The collapse of community-level relations of production in coastal
Peruvian societies was accompanied by other changes. Fortified
hilltop villages and retreats were built along seven hundred
miles of the Peruvian coast (Daggett 1987; Rowe 1962; Willey
1953:92–100; Wilson 1987:61–62). Burials contained headless individuals and persons entombed with additional human skulls
or trophy heads, stone-headed maces, and spearthrowers. Individuals with depressed skull fractures or dart points embedded
in vital areas are not uncommon. When taken in concert, these
evidences indicate that raiding was rampant and permit us to

infer that "war leaders" had acquired prominence (Patterson 1973:98–105). This configuration coalesced about the same time skillfully made pottery styles with marked, largely non-overlapping regional distributions appeared. These developments suggest the elaboration of craft specialization, the restricted circulation of certain kinds of goods, and the use of cultural elements, like art styles, to mark the boundaries between communities that participated in different production-consumption systems. Roughly a century later, there were tombs with markedly different arrays and quantities of grave goods and individuals interred with retainers. In this context, such a configuration suggests the emergence of class-based social differences.

Thus, the appearance of state-based societies, the rise of civilization, began, as Stanley Diamond (1974:1) suggested, with "conquest abroad and repression at home." The process of state formation was rooted in the transformation of classless societies into class-based societies. In the classless, kin-organized societies, goods and labor were used collectively for the benefit of the community as a whole. By contrast, in the state-based societies, they were appropriated by an exploiting class or classes that controlled the conditions of production and used the surplus they exacted to ensure their own leisured existence (Ste. Croix 1981:52).

State formation, as archaeologists have observed, is a regional process that affects several societies simultaneously. The spatial structures produced by the rise of civilization has been described in various ways. Barbara Price (1977) has called it "cluster interaction," while Colin Renfrew (1977, 1986) has used the term "peer polity interaction." They consider the region, rather than individual societies, to be of primary importance and argue that the autonomous societies found there are linked in complex ways. One effect of the almost continuous interactions among these societies is that when state institutions appear they spread rapidly. This produces a kind of regional homogeneity in forms of sociopolitical organization. Civilization, for the proponents of this position, is a spatially organized cluster of interconnected self-governing, politically autonomous state-based societies.

However, this is only one spatial arrangement that state formation can take. Other forms also occur and are probably more common than instances in which all of the societies have

the same kind of political structure. These forms are characterized by uneven development (Gailey and Patterson 1988).
Emerging states are unable to consolidate control over a region,
because neighboring and less-stratified societies successfully
resist annexation. This means that state formation produces a
mosaic of different kinds of societies, each characterized by
distinct social, political, and economic structures. Some are
class-stratified societies, while in others the kin communities
retain significant use-rights and control over their land and
labor. The ruling classes of emergent states extract goods and
labor not only from their own kin and subjects, but from the
kin-organized communities on their peripheries. The form of
tribute extraction shapes the structures of the social, political,
and economic relations that develop not only within the state-
based societies themselves, but within the encapsulated societies on their peripheries and between them and the state
(Patterson 1987a). From this perspective, civilization is a con-
stellation of societies with different political forms; it is structured
by continually shifting relations of dominance and subordination.

The rise of Andean civilization in the waning years of the first
millennium B.C. was characterized by uneven development,
engendered by the articulation of different forms of the tributary
and communal modes of production. However, this statement
is not sufficient. Since modes of production are always manifested in the productive forces and social relations of historically
specific societies, it is essential to consider how the class structures of those societies were constituted and what configurations of class power existed. This demands a degree of
specificity that archaeologists are just beginning to provide for
the early state-based societies of the Andes. We do not yet have
a great deal of information about the characteristics of particular
early states. The evidence we do have, however, suggests that
there were important differences among them. The diversity of
early state forms reflects the historic specificity of the circumstances surrounding their formation and development. The
historically constituted differences among them were probably
of the same magnitude as those that existed among the various
state-based societies of the Aegean during the fifth century B.C.
or of coastal Peru prior to its incorporation into the Inca Empire
during the fifteenth century (Menzel 1959; Wood 1988:83–87,
112–119).

Two thousand years ago, almost all of the Andean peoples must have been involved in subsistence production, given the relatively low level of development of the productive forces. They were peasants, pastoralists, or fisherfolk who devoted part of their time to spatially organized subsistence production and the rest of it to crafts, communal work, trading, and a variety of tasks that would have been performed by full-time specialists in societies that extracted greater amounts of labor and produce to support their activities. They accomplished these activities with the cooperation of their households, kin, and neighbors.

Given the enormous number of direct producers, many of the early Andean states seem to have lacked massive infrastructures and large, leisured privileged classes; there were apparently not great disparities of wealth between the direct producers and their rulers. This must have been especially true in those societies where the burden of tribute was light – either the direct producers had successfully resisted the attempted extortions of their rulers, or they had joined with them in military adventures against neighboring peoples. Such attacks provided an alternative to subsistence production, a way of making up deficits in the combatants' own supplies. The participation of peasants, pastoralists, or fisherfolk in these raids limited the extent to which they could be exploited. It protected them from certain forms of surplus extraction by the dominant class or the state, and also mitigated against the formation of a warrior elite supported by either plunder or the tribute payments of a subordinated class of direct producers.

This perspective emphasizes the relations between tributary states, the dominant classes of which frequently were unable to appropriate goods and labor in sufficient amounts from their own direct producers and neighboring communities. Some were probably class-stratified communities, but others – perhaps the vast majority – were kin-organized groups that were relatively autonomous, or allied, to varying degrees, with communities that were quite similar to themselves. The states focused their attention on these villages and local communities when they attempted to exact goods and labor from their members. Tribute extraction deformed the kin organization of the communities, as their members and the state struggled to control the conditions of production and distribution. Social relations within the communities were transformed and enmeshed in new forms of social reproduction and resistance (Gailey and Patterson 1988; Scott 1985).

This perspective focuses attention on "articulation," a concept elaborated in the 1970s, to describe the linkage of societies, the structures of which were shaped by different modes of production (Althusser and Balibar 1970; Bettelheim 1972; Rey 1982; van Binsbergen and Geschiere 1985; Wolpe 1980). The concept of articulation indicates that the two modes of production do not simply coexist, but are combined in a dialectical relationship. Thus, articulation is not static; it is a process that involves both linkages and contradictions. It has been described as "combat between the two modes of production, with the confrontations and alliances which such combat implies: confrontation and alliances between the *classes* which these modes of production define" (Foster-Carter 1978:56).

By conceptualizing articulation as a process, it is possible to distinguish stages in its development. The initial phase involves societies, the structures of which are determined by different modes of production; they are linked at the level of the exchange sphere in ways that reinforce and possibly deform the existing relations of production. This stage is followed by a phase in which one society has established dominance, subordinating the other while simultaneously making use of its structures. The processes of social reproduction characteristic of the subordinate community become distorted, progressively restricted, and increasingly dependent on those of the dominant group. In the third phase, the structures of the subordinated community are disassembled and reconstituted (Rey 1982; Wolpe 1985:93). This does not mean that articulation is a uni-directional process that involves the simple, unilinear destruction of the subordinate modes of production and the immediate subsumption of their agents into the social relations of the tributary states. Rather, since articulation involves structural contradictions that become manifested in various ways, its development is not necessarily smooth; it is historically reversible.

Articulation directs attention to phenomena that are readily observed in the archaeological record: the emergence and consolidation of discrete "cultures" in particular regions, their development, and their eventual disruption or disappearance. It brings into focus questions about the processes that underlie these phenomena. For example, what is involved in the consolidation of a distinctive culture in a village or local community; how are these integrated into larger social units; and what produces sudden shifts in the trajectories of their development?

Ethnogenesis is clearly one process involved in the emergence and consolidation of distinctive local or regional archaeological cultures. Ethnogenesis is the historical creation of a people with a sense of their collective identity, a consciousness that is shaped and constrained by their interdependence in producing and reproducing the conditions necessary for everyday life (Moore 1988; Sider 1976). When these relatively autonomous local communities become enmeshed in the webs of tributary relations created by state-based societies, the conditions of everyday life are altered. The members of these communities begin to participate in new spheres of production, distribution, and exchange. Their culture is modified to express the new circumstances of their lives and to give voice to the new sentiments and sensibilities engendered and empowered by these conditions. At one level, this cultural transformation may involve hybridization, fusion, or even replacement by state-imposed forms; at another, it may manifest itself in resistance or attempts to assert or invent tradition (Hobsbawm and Ranger 1983). The creation of culture is perhaps most explosive and diverse when structural contradictions – like those engendered by class struggle, encapsulation, or conquest – intensify.

The south coast of Peru is one region that provides information about the interrelations of state formation and ethnogenesis. The data permit us to gain some appreciation of the complexity of these connections. During the second century B.C. (Early Horizon Epoch 9), the inhabitants of the Ica and Nazca Valleys were subject to influences from two state-based societies: the Pucará state, centered far to the south in the northern part of the Lake Titicaca Basin, and the Topará state, located immediately north of Ica in the Pisco, Chincha, and Cañete Valleys (Franquemont 1986; Massey 1986; Menzel 1960a; Wallace 1986; Wheeler and Mujica 1981).[1] Judging by shared iconographic themes and artistic preferences, the populations of Ica and Nazca were more closely involved at this time with the distant Pucará polity than they were with their neighbors to the north. A mythical figure called the oculate being was depicted in the art styles of the south coast communities and in the contemporary materials from the Titicaca Basin and Marajo Island at the mouth of the Amazon River (Menzel, Rowe, and Dawson 1964:171–172, 196–198, 239–244; Ponce Sanginés 1961:22 top; Willey 1971, fig. 6-48); however, it was not found in the Topará styles. The polychrome pottery used in the Pucará polity and by the inhabitants of Nazca and Ica are easily distinguished from each other and contrast markedly with the monochrome Topará ceramics.

This does not mean that the pottery styles of the Ica and Nazca Valleys were homogeneous. They were not; two regionally distinct variants of pottery were produced and used in Ica. The vessels manufactured at one center circulated through the lower and middle portions of the valley and were used by the inhabitants of large fortified villages; the other regional style was used by local groups residing in the upper Ica and Pisco Valleys (Massey 1986:289–297; Menzel, Rowe, Dawson 1964:175–208). During the first century B.C. (Early Horizon Epoch 10 and Early Intermediate Period Epoch 1), the communities of the upper Ica and Pisco Valleys shifted their affiliations as they became enmeshed in the tributary relations of the Topará state. They began to use monochrome Topará pottery. The pottery used by their neighbors in the middle and lower portions of the Ica Valley, but not in Nazca, was also heavily influenced by the Topará styles. This situation persisted until the beginning of the second century A.D. (Early Intermediate Period Epoch 3), when the local communities of the Ica and Pisco Valleys were incorporated into a state-based society centered in Nazca, which emerged in the wake of the collapse of the Pucará polity (Proulx 1966). For more than a century, the residents of Pisco used a kind of pottery associated with the Nazca state; it was indistinguishable from that used by their contemporaries living three hundred fifty kilometers to the south. The Nazca-based state apparently collapsed about A.D. 250. During the next century (Early Intermediate Period Epochs 4 and 5), the local communities of Pisco were once again allied with or incorporated into the Topará state (Menzel 1960a; Peters 1986).

Topará enveloped but apparently did not completely subordinate the inhabitants of the coastal plain of central Peru between the Lurín Valley and Lachay during the second century B.C. (Early Horizon Epoch 9). The local communities of the region amalgamated into a single group, which persisted until the closing decades of the first century B.C. (Early Intermediate

Period Epoch 1), when they reasserted their autonomy. As the social and historical conditions that formed the basis for their unification weakened, the alliance was reworked. New communities were constituted, and new patterns of land and resource use appeared. Members of two or more groups began to occupy and make use of the same region. The community that emerged in lower portions of the Lurín Valley shared land and resources with another group, whose core territories were situated in the upper reaches of the valley and in the neighboring alpine grasslands (Patterson, McCarthy, and Dunn 1982). Herders from the uplands pastured their llamas and alpacas in grazing areas along the coast during the highland dry season, and farmers from both communities lived next to each other in a series of mid-elevation hamlets and villages. Precisely how they accommodated or adjusted their activities to the presence of others was the result of specific historical circumstances (Albers and Kay 1987).

A major episode of class and state formation began about A.D. 350 (Early Intermediate Period Epoch 6). It coincided with the collapse of Topará and witnessed the consolidation of agrarian tributary states centered in Nazca, around Lima on the central coast where the inhabitants of the lower Lurín Valley reestablished links with their former allies, and in the Nepeña-Moche-Lambayeque region of the north coast. Evidence for both raiding and class stratification is more pronounced than it had been earlier. An elaborately furnished tomb dating to this period was recently discovered on the north coast and, at Pachacamac on the central coast, an individual was interred with more than one hundred retainers (Alva 1988; Patterson 1974; Strong and Corbett 1943:41).

The class-stratified states that appeared in the fifth and sixth centuries A.D. derived their revenues from the labor of peasants, pastoralists, and fisherfolk and from the goods they produced as part-time craft workers. Since the wealth of their ruling classes depended on the control of labor and, ultimately, on extending the agricultural base, the administrative and economic restructuring that occurred during the formation and subsequent development of these states was organized primarily to assess and collect tribute from subject communities. Some of the labor appropriated was employed to weave textiles that were placed in storehouses, to build pyramids, to dig irrigation canals, and to expand existing water management systems.

The class-stratified Moche, Lima, and Nazca societies that flourished in coastal Peru are usually portrayed as being relatively homogeneous entities. Such representations implicitly accept the "dominant ideology thesis": the idea that social order is promoted and maintained when all layers of a class-stratified society have the same beliefs, values, and culture. There are two versions of this thesis. One is that the beliefs of the dominant class have swamped and infected the consciousness of the subordinate groups so that the culture of the society constitutes a seamless whole. The other is that the dominant class, while its members are unable to promote a homogeneous culture shared by all classes, can prevent the subordinate groups from fully developing counter cultures and ideologies (Abercrombie, Hill, and Turner 1980:1–58; Patterson 1986).

Characterizations that create illusions about the uniformity of the archaeological records left by these tributary states are misleading. For example, different arrays of pottery were produced and used in the northern and southern regions of Moche society during the fourth and fifth centuries; this diversity has led some archaeologists to question whether the two regions had common political institutions and practices or whether they constituted separate states, a northern one centered in Lambayeque and a southern one centered in Moche. On the central coast, there were at least four, and possibly as many as eight, centers of pottery production, each of which produced a distinct variant of Lima pottery style that was used mainly by the communities of a particular region.

Acceptance of the dominant ideology thesis also promotes the view that the various state and religious institutions and practices of society were necessary for the reproduction of the existing class relations. This implies that there were strong linkages between the two sets of institutions and practices and that religion functioned to safeguard class and state interests. It also implies that religious institutions and practices were uniform throughout the society, and that they reflected in some mediated way the interests of both the state and the dominant class.

Yuri Berezkin (1978a, 1978b) provides an alternative to this orthodox view. He suggest that Moche religions during the fifth and sixth centuries consisted of a pantheon of supernatural beings, each of which corresponded or gave voice to the sentiments of a particular class or group in Moche society. In this view, Moche religious institutions and practices involved a loosely articulated network of cults. Different classes, kin-based communities, and perhaps even regional groups or blocs supported shrines or cults dedicated to particular supernatural beings. Cults like these are documented historically and were widespread among those societies that were incorporated into the Inca Empire (Spalding 1984:64–71). The state and the various cults constituted distinct centers of gravity that competed for power.

In class-stratified societies, like Moche, where there may have been kin-based groups within the ruling class that competed for political power and control of the state apparatus, one would expect to find evidence of attempts by these groups to legitimate their claims by evoking historical depth and continuity. In fact, Moche Valley potters imitated earlier representations of particular cult-associated, supernatural beings to create or promote an illusion about the continuity of old institutions and practices. They did this not once but twice: first in the late fourth or early fifth century (Early Intermediate Periods Epoch 6 and 7A) and again during the sixth century (Middle Horizon Epoch 1). The imitation of something old, or the incorporation of the old into new contexts, is called archaism. Archaism is especially common during major episodes of class and state formation, when people are making their own histories while the existing social order is being decomposed and reconstituted (Patterson 1987b).

Archaeologists investigating ancient Peru have documented several instances in which preliterate peoples employed archaisms. The earliest archaisms known so far occurred during the second century B.C. (Early Horizon Epoch 9), when the inhabitants of the fortified villages in the middle Ica Valley revived stylistic features from pottery vessels that had been used two centuries earlier (Early Horizon Epochs 6–8); this occurred at the time when their neighbors in the upper valley were being encapsulated by the Topará state (Massey, personal communication 1986). Archaisms, involving reinterpretations of Pucará mythical beings, were also prominent features in the formation of the Huari and Tiwanaku states in the Ayacucho area and the southern Lake Titicaca Basin during the sixth century (Cook 1983).

The tributary state that coalesced in the Nazca-Ica region of the south coast during the fifth century (Early Intermediate Period Epochs 6–7) also had an agrarian economic base. Men are depicted on pottery vessels as farmers and warriors, and the number of headless individuals and trophy heads encountered in tombs seems significantly greater than in the preceding century. This suggests that raiding continued to be an important activity, a way of making up deficits in goods and labor.

Pottery vessels manufactured in the Ica-Nasca region during this period were traded and commonly emulated by the apparently unstratified communities of Pisco and Chincha, which had reasserted their autonomy when the Topará state collapsed; pottery manufactured by the inhabitants of Pisco or Chincha has also been found in the refuse deposits of a village in Ica (Menzel 1960a:123–129). Pottery produced in the Nazca-Ica region also appeared occasionally in Cañete, which was a buffer area between the class-stratified polities of the central and south coasts (Patterson 1966:102). The Nazca-Ica state also had linkages with the kin-based communities of the mountainous Ayacucho area to the east, judging by very specific stylistic similarities in the pottery produced in the two regions (Isbell 1985; Menzel 1964, 1968; Paulsen 1983).

The tributary states that developed during the fifth and sixth centuries – both on the Peruvian coast and in highland areas like Huamachuco, Ayacucho, and Tiahuanaco at the southern end of the Lake Titicaca Basin – were based on production for local use or consumption. Their subsistence economies were dominated by the agriculture sector, while the pastoralism and fishing varied in importance from one state to another (Browman 1976, 1978, 1981; Kolata 1986, 1987). They were organized to collect tribute in either labor or kind, and they appropriated narrow ranges of goods. For example, when the pastoral communities of the upper Mantaro Valley were incorporated into the Ayacucho-centered Huari state during the early seventh century (Middle Horizon Epochs 1B–2A), pastoral production was disrupted, and its importance diminished significantly as the herders were transformed into farmers (Browman 1976). That taxes were levied on their agricultural production or labor suggests that the state was less concerned with gaining access to something that was not readily available in its core area than with reorganizing the subsistence economy of subject populations to provide greater quantities of the goods it already produced. The state was not intent on creating a highly differentiated, regionally interdependent subsistence economy in which surplus moved toward the core area, since the goods produced by the encapsulated communities were apparently used or consumed locally. This meant that the regions incorporated into the state were economically autonomous (Thapar 1981). It also implies that they had the potential of being politically self-sufficient, especially when "local strong men and disgruntled peasants threatened, or actually dissolved, the thin film of state hegemony that bound them to the central power" (Fox 1971:8; Lathrap, Gebhard-Sayer, and Mester 1985:90). The political economies of states like Huari were easily fragmented and could be reconstituted around autonomous productive regions (Menzel 1977), which partially explains why Andean states, including the Inca Empire, were so short-lived.

Several archaeologists have argued that long-distance trade was an important motor of state formation in the Andes during the fifth and sixth centuries (Browman 1978; Shady and Ruiz 1979). However, the better-known pre-Incaic states seem to have been based on the control of subsistence production rather than commerce. The political economies of these states tended to extend the agricultural base of the communities they enveloped and to reorganize their populations to facilitate levying and collecting tribute. Under these circumstances, any production of goods for trade must have been grafted onto production for local consumption. Agrarian tributary states had political economies that were significantly different from those of the mercantile states that controlled trade and derived their incomes from taxation. Mercantile states were organized to exert military control over trade routes and administrative control over those groups involved in the production and circulation of goods. They were integrated into wider networks of social relations, and the form of this integration was affected by processes that emanated from outside the mercantile states themselves, in the agrarian civilizations (Amin 1976:37–52; Thapar 1981:410–411).

Mercantile states are constituted on very different grounds from agrarian ones. Their ruling classes exploit the direct producers of other societies rather than their own. Merchants are intermediary agents in the process of surplus extraction; they transfer to their own state and ruling class the surplus appropriated by the ruling classes of other societies or goods that they themselves have extracted directly from producers. By itself, trade does not cause state formation; however, "monopolies over imported prestige goods can play an important role in the growth of social stratification and centralisation of political-economic control" (Gledhill 1978:241). Since subsistence production is not a major source of state revenues, local peasant, pastoral, and fishing communities retain a great deal of autonomy and are only weakly linked with the state. Mercantile states are frequently urban-based. Their cities are inhabited by the ruling class, various state officials, merchants, and artisans engaged in the production of commodities – i.e., goods for exchange. Different consumption patterns occur between the city and the hamlets and villages of the surrounding countryside.

Following the line of argument developed by Samir Amin (1976:37–52; 1978:10–21), mercantile tributary states develop and exist on the margins of agrarian states or civilizations. They cannot exist without other tribute-based states. In the Andes, this meant that mercantile states may have been more readily discerned in areas like the north coast of Ecuador (on the periphery of the Inca Empire) or perhaps the Atacama Desert of northern Chile and the Hualfin Valley of northwestern Argentina (on the margins of the Tiwanaku state in the sixth and seventh centuries) (González 1961; Isbell 1983; Patterson 1987c; Salomon 1978a; 1978b; 1986). If the agrarian states were expanding, continually extending new patterns of social relations into the communities along their frontiers, then the actual geographical locations of the mercantile states may have been displaced outward from the core areas.

This draws attention to two questions about mercantile states: how was production for exchange organized and controlled, and how were the conditions that permitted trade secured and maintained? Talal Asad (1980) has observed that the relationship of a state to trade is quite different from the relationship of merchants to the transit trade they control. The former acquires its revenues from taxation; the latter derive their income from profit. Taxation "requires the presence of institutions of force and a continuous threat that it will be effectively used. . .[commercial profit] may require the very absence of force – at least at certain crucial points in the process of economic development" (Asad 1980:453–54).

To argue that the central Andean states were based on the control of labor rather than commerce does not mean that trade was nonexistent. The members of various communities clearly trafficked in goods, sometimes far beyond their boundaries. What has not been satisfactorily demonstrated in these instances is that they trafficked in commodities – i.e., goods that were deliberately produced for exchange. What appears more certain about the circulation of goods and ideas within and among pre-Incaic states are some of the conditions in which it occurred. Cults, shrines, and, in some instances, perhaps even pilgrimages provided one framework that permitted this kind of horizontal integration. The observation of classicists, that "gods travel on the backs of people who are also engaged in other activities," is appropriate for Andean societies as well.

Some of the cults and shrines that existed just before the formation of the Inca Empire were local and devoted to particular deities. Others were official and closely linked with states; however, they may not have been especially important in the everyday life of particular communities. Other cults were widespread; while shrines devoted to their deities existed in many communities, the rituals and practices may have varied from one community to another because different attributes or features of the deities were emphasized. The connections between these widespread cults and states were complex. Their relations with other cults and shrines were flexible, reflecting multiple layers of interpretation and alternative explanations. The various cults and shrines developed historically to meet the changing conditions of everyday life. At least some shrines and their cults were corporations that held lands and collected revenues; the caretakers, who looked after their affairs and ensured that the appropriate rituals were performed and practices observed, came from particular kin groups or communities (Patterson 1985a).

The Incas appeared as a recognizable community during the thirteenth and fourteenth centuries. This was a period of considerable regional diversity. It is often portrayed as a time when kin-based communities existed in the interstices of a number of relatively small, weak states that were less centralized and controlled fewer subjects than those that existed five or six hundred years earlier. These successor states, which arose out of the ashes of earlier empires, coexisted when the balance of forces dictated that they do so and struggled for power when the scales seemed to tip in their favor. For those who profess admiration for empires and strongly centralized states over societies that lack state institutions or have only weakly developed ones, this was truly a "dark age," analogous to those that followed the collapse of the Mycenaean city-states in the Aegean, the Old Kingdom in Egypt, the Western Roman Empire, or the Teotihuacán and Classic Maya civilizations in Mesoamerica (Drews 1983; Janssen 1978; Millon 1988; Wickham 1984; Wood 1988:92–96). More often than not, their subjects played prominent roles in the events that led to their reorganization or demise. State institutions were decentralized and reconstituted along new lines. Local lords reasserted their independence or emerged as autonomous agents. Tribute extraction frequently became erratic, reflecting the struggle between the capacity of the lord to levy and collect tribute and the ability of the local producing communities to resist his demands.

The history of Andean civilization – the rise of states – was not a simple, linear progression from kin-based to class-stratified societies punctuated by regular, irreversible transformations in the forces and relations of production. Nor was it characterized, à la Oswald Spengler (1918–1922) or Arnold Toynbee (1933–1954), by regular cycles of growth and collapse. The Inca state and its predecessors were also not stagnant oriental despotisms or Asiatic societies, forever stuck in a particular stage of social development (Mann 1986:121–124, 525; Wittfogel 1957). They lacked the homogeneous bureaucratic structures and processes of encapsulation often attributed to such states. They did not exhibit the systemic rationality ascribed to such societies, since there were fissures within and outside their bureaucratic structures, and since the power of their ruling coalitions – ambiguously structured by ethnicity, class, and gender – was reconstituted or shifted during times of succession when the composition of the ruling class was transformed (Weber 1951:33–149; 1978:217–240, 966–1005). Furthermore, the idea that state formation represents increased rationality seems to be less what happened in practice than the ideology of a bureaucratic intelligentsia seeking to impose rule by law and replace the order or custom (Weber 1958, 1978:941–955).

Instead, class and state formation in Andean America were ongoing processes, constrained by existing social relations and shaped by the actions of dominant classes attempting to assert their hegemony and control, and by those of local communities and subject populations struggling to retain or reassert their autonomy. This dynamism yielded uneven development – a mosaic of societies characterized by different cultures and structures that merged and interlocked in various combinations. Changes occurred as people made history, their actions conditioned by the social relations that existed within and among historically specific societies. It is true that states coalesced, were transformed, and even disappeared. The motor for these changes was that class structures could not be reproduced successfully for extended periods of time. The composition of the various classes was neither homogeneous nor stable. Commoners were ennobled, and nobles and officials became commoners. The interrelations of the various classes were also transformed because deposed individuals and groups frequently retained power. In these circumstances, states lost the basis for appropriation and their capacity to extract goods and labor from the producing classes.

Chapter 2

Inca Society Before the Empire

> Inca historical reconstructions – regardless of their constraint by certain structural definitions – should not be confused with the history-making processes that shaped the Andes. (Irene Silverblatt, *Imperial Dilemmas, the Politics of Kinship, and Inca Constructions of History*)

According to traditions recorded by sixteenth-century Andean and Spanish writers, the Inca empire came into being in the 1430s (Rowe 1945). Many of the same authors also indicate that the Incas – as a distinct, named social entity – had already existed for several centuries. According to their accounts, pre-imperial Inca society appeared during a period when everyday life was shaped by a number of small states, chieftainships, tribes, and autonomous local communities (Menzel 1959; Murra 1967, 1968; Rostworowski de Diez Canseco 1972a, 1972b; Rowe 1948). The archaeological record corroborates the broad outlines, if not the details, of the information they preserved from interviews with various functionaries after 1532.

These officials, collectively called *khipukamayoq*, were memorizers who kept track of information required by the state, local groups, and shrines. They employed a system of recording and notation based on the use of *khipus*, a series of knotted strings attached to a main cord. Some were bookkeepers who kept track of numerical information. They resided in each district and, according to William Prescott (1968, vol. 1:134),

> were required to furnish the government with information on various important matters. One had charge of the revenues, reported the quantity of raw materials distributed among the laborers, the quality and quantity of the fabrics made from it, and the amount of stores, of

various kinds, paid into the royal magazines. Another exhibited the register of births and deaths, the marriages, the number of those qualified to bear arms, and the like details in reference to the population of the kingdom. These returns were annually forwarded to the capital, where they were submitted to the inspection of officers acquainted with the art of deciphering these mystic records. The government was thus provided with a valuable mass of statistical information, and the skeins of many-colored threads, collected and carefully preserved, constituted what might be called the national archives.

There were also other kinds of *khipukamayoq*. Some were annalists, entrusted with remembering the important things that had happened in each province or during the reign of each dynasty. Others were troubadours, who performed ballads and recited poems at various public gatherings (Murra and Morris 1976; Prescott 1968, vol. 1:135–136; Rowe 1945, 1946:201, 326). Their narratives and ballads were more than popular entertainment that evoked images and memories of past deeds and events, for they also explained why particular relationships existed and furnished guidelines for appropriate personal and social behavior.

The use of *khipus* was not confined to the Inca state. It was an ancient and widespread tradition among Andean peoples. The earliest objects now recognized as *khipus* date from the eighth and ninth centuries, a period that witnessed a major episode of state formation in ancient Peru (Christopher Donnan, personal communication, 1984). Sixteenth-century writers like Blas Valera recorded the testimony of *khipukamayoq* who were retained by different individuals, corporate groups, shrines, and communities – for example, Huarochirí, Pachacamac, Chincha, and Tarma (Markham 1920:8). One consequence is that the accounts of different *khipukamayoq* were often at odds with one another. In some instances, the differences appear insignificant; in others, they are quite substantial. This was especially true when the annalists were called upon to testify for various parties in lawsuits that pitted one community or lord against another (Rostworowski de Diez Canseco 1988a).

It is clear that sixteenth-century European and Andean peoples held different views about the meaning of history. For Europeans, history was linear, the unfolding of a chain of events, each of which was produced by the events that preceded it and each of which produced the events that followed. For their

Andean contemporaries, history was cyclical and composed of a configuration rather than a chain of events. The Andean peoples viewed their history as an alternation of imperial and antipolitical ages that followed one another in a succession; the transitions from one age to the next were marked by cataclysms (Earls and Silverblatt 1978; Salomon 1982:10–11). Thus, the crystallization of Inca society or the construction of the Inca Empire implied profound transformations in the content and function of the pre-existing modes of everyday life, intensified by the introduction of radically new structures that gave expression to new practices and social relations. Events such as these had the property of "eternal return"; they were "renewed sightings of constant points [that]. . .stand in fixed relation to each other behind and beyond the flux of experience" (Salomon 1982:11). Dynastic oral traditions, ancestor cults, and ritual calendars involving spatially organized networks of shrines gave history meaning and thereby made it usable. But the Andean peoples also possessed a sense that they, too, made history as they continually recreated and transformed the conditions of everyday life.

Thus, various Andean accounts concerned with the formation and historical development of pre-imperial Inca society diverge from each other; these differences, the meaning of which we may not yet fully comprehend, reflect in complex, mediated ways the position and interests of different groups both within and outside Inca society. To paraphrase an argument made by Jacques Derrida (1983), the hidden contracts that exist between bodies of knowledge, social institutions, and power are inscribed in texts, like the various accounts of Inca origins and history. He implies that the creation of culture is contested in class-stratified societies; this quest for power is not confined to texts alone, but resides also in the practices and social relations of the society as a whole. Different communities or classes have alternative understandings of existing social realities in class-stratified societies and how these circumstances came to be. They construct different explanations of the history of that reality, creating heritages – usable pasts – that account for their own position in that totality.

The existence of diverse Inca and Andean origin myths is merely one aspect of the struggle for power that occurred during the sixteenth century; control of the historical past was a central aspect of this struggle, but not the only one (Adorno 1986:5; Ossio 1977). The contradictory world views and historical perspectives characteristic of class-stratified societies reflect the perspectives of groups with different relations to power. Thus, various origin myths express in subtle or blatant ways the power relations that prevailed when the various accounts were constituted, when they were told in public, and when they were finally recorded in the sixteenth century. The multiplicity of narratives generated uncertainty by furnishing alternative explanations of Andean history. It created opportunities for reinterpreting tradition and reconstituting it in new ways.

Andean scholars have viewed the oral historical traditions of the *khipukamayoq* through different theoretical lenses (Godelier 1977; Katz 1966:263–266; Kirchkoff 1949; Murra 1961, 1980; Olsen 1986; Rowe 1945, 1946:201–210, 1979a; Schaedel 1978; Sherbondy 1977, 1982; Silverblatt 1987, 1988a; Zuidema 1964, 1973, 1983a). One of the contested issues in Andean studies is whether the Inca dynastic traditions are historical. Do they describe a succession of Inca rulers and their deeds? Or do they describe structural relationships within Inca society and between its members and neighboring peoples in the Cuzco Valley? Some have treated the accounts as narratives that approximate historical reality. Others have viewed them as constructions, constituted in the early years of the empire to explain and legitimate the practices and patterns of social relations that had been instituted. They are just now beginning to pay attention to what the differences between the various accounts may actually indicate about the social conditions that existed before and after the empire was organized.

2.1. The Creation of Inca Society

Let us begin our discussion of the formation and development of pre-imperial Inca society by relating what has come to be viewed, by some modern students, as the standard version of Inca dynastic history. It is actually a composite of several, slightly divergent accounts that were told around Cuzco in the sixteenth century (Acosta 1954; Betanzos 1924; Cieza de León 1967; Las Casas 1948; Molina 1943; Pachakuti Yamqui 1927; Polo de Ondegardo 1916a, 1916b, 1916c, 1940; Sarmiento de Gamboa

1960). According to Inca Garcilaso de la Vega (1960 vol. 1:30), this version was common among the Indians living north and east of the capital city, while Pedro Cieza de León (1967:8–23) said he heard it from one of the descendants of Wayna Qhapaq, the Inca king who died in the 1520s. Several writers, most notably Pedro Sarmiento de Gamboa (1960:211–220), provide fairly detailed accounts of the standard history.

A number of Andean peoples trace their ancestries to mythical figures who emerged from holes in the ground. These places of origin, or *paqarina*, were shrines where rituals had to be performed. The Inca *paqarina* was at Paqaritampu, three caves located about fifteen miles south of Cuzco. The founders of the Inca dynasty emerged from the middle cave and assumed leadership over the *ayllus*, groups of people or kindreds, that came out of the neighboring caves. The different versions of the standard account begin to diverge at this point. They disagree over the number of Incas involved, their names, their birth sequence, and the motivations behind some of their actions. Manqo Qhapaq and his sisters, Mama Huaco and Mama Oqllo, are central characters in these accounts.

According to Sarmiento de Gamboa, eight Incas, the three just mentioned and their three brothers and two sisters, led the ten clans that emerged from the side caves on a journey, moving from village to village in search of arable land. Mama Huaco was as important as her brother during the journey. She was the one who proclaimed that the Incas were strong, wise, and powerful; that they would go forth from Paqaritampu in search of fertile lands; and that they would subjugate people, take their lands, and make war on those who would not receive the Incas as their lords. She and her brother were the war chiefs who led the clans on their quest for land, plunder, and power. She and Manqo Qhapaq played central roles in the conspiracy to murder their brother, Ayar Cachi, whose cruel and outrageous conduct toward the villagers they subjugated as well as toward their own followers threatened the very basis of Inca domination. During the trek, Mama Oqllo bore Manqo Qhapaq's son, whom they called Zinchi Roq'a. After the Incas and their followers established themselves in Cuzco, Mama Oqllo, Mama Huaco, and Manqo Qhapaq began to terrorize the original inhabitants of the valley. As Manqo Qhapaq grew old, he began to worry about his son's future. Fearing that the things he had done might undermine the legitimacy of Zinchi Roq'a's rule, the old man ordered that the ten *ayllus* that had come with him and his siblings from Paqaritampu should form a guard to protect the Incas and that "they were to elect the successor when he was named by the father or succeeded him upon his death" (Sarmiento de Gamboa 1960:219). When Manqo Qhapaq died, his son became the next Inca leader.

Another Inca origin myth, probably recorded by Blas Valera in the sixteenth century and copied by Fernando Montesinos (1930:63–86), is a genealogy that lists the names and deeds of ninety rulers before the Incas inserted themselves in the Peruvian monarchy. According to this account, the monarchy was virtually destroyed, and each province erected its own ruler. However, the kings of Cuzco were kings in name only, since they had almost no control at all over their barbarian neighbors. There was a woman of high rank, Mama Huaco, who listened with compassion to the complaints of her kin and neighbors about the misfortunes that afflicted the kingdom. The people respected her as an oracle; those who deplored the situation gathered together and vowed to do everything in their power to restore the kingdom to its former grandeur. They were led by her son, a man called 'Inka Roq'a. Mama Huaco conspired with her sister, a great sorceress, to put her son on the throne and to restore the city and kingdom to its ancient condition. After certain rituals and sacrifices were performed, Inca Roq'a appeared before the people, proclaimed himself king, and repeated his desire to return Cuzco to its ancient splendor. He did this with so much authority that no one doubted the authenticity of his claims, except the kings of Vilcas, Huaytará, and Tiahuanaco, who were skeptical about the whole affair. In this version, 'Inka Roq'a was the first Inca king.

Tiahuanaco, the archaeological site on the southern shores of Lake Titicaca, is implicated in a third set of origin myths, versions of which are related by Garcilaso de la Vega and Pachakuti Yamqui (Rowe 1960b). These frequently precede some version of the standard account of Inca dynastic history. Garcilaso de la Vega (1960 vol. 1:27–31) actually recorded two versions. In one account, told by people living south of Cuzco, a man appeared at Tiahuanaco and divided the world into four parts. He gave each part to a king and ordered the kings to go into the areas assigned to them to conquer and govern the people found there. Manqo Qhapaq went to Cuzco. In the other version, the Sun placed his son and daughter, Manqo Qhapaq and Coya Mama Oqllo Huaco, on earth at Tiahuanaco to indoctrinate the barbarians. They journeyed to Huanacauri near Cuzco, where they split up to teach and aid the local peoples. Manqo became king and the leader of men; his wife, the queen, became the mistress of women. Pachakuti Yamqui (1927) claimed that Viracocha appeared at Tiahuanaco and subsequently turned its inhabitants into stone. He then left on a long journey and encountered a number of communities that were not impressed by his claims. His travels ended at Paqaritampu with the birth of his son, Manqo 'Inka.

The various Inca origin myths have several premises in common. The first is that Cuzco Valley was inhabited by small, relatively autonomous communities of farmers and herders. The economy, described or implied by the chroniclers, was agrarian, in which land, water, and herds were the major means of production. Control over the means of production and the means by which people reproduced themselves as a social group was vested in the community, or *ayllu*. Every man and woman had access to the land, water, and herds by virtue of their membership in a community and participation in its activities. Kinship was the idiom of their membership in the community, the matrix in terms of which their work was organized. In addition to providing them with access to the means of production, kinship defined a circumscribed set of mutually recognized expectations and obligations. The origin myths also presume that the members of these communities, including even the Incas themselves, engaged in farming, weaving, herding, and other productive activities that provided the subsistence goods necessary for life, work that was essential for reproducing labor claims and obligations.

Several chroniclers, including Sarmiento de Gamboa (1960:221–228), indicate that there was also another, more fragile sector involved in these village economies. The Incas battled with their neighbors for centuries before the empire was organized. These struggles were waged over access to land and water, the theft of goods, and kidnaping. Thus, looting and pillaging also constituted an important sector of the pre-imperial economy. This plunder economy was built on the expropriation of goods produced by neighboring communities for their own use; it also may have involved taking captives to hold as hostages against reprisals or to perform labor.

The second premise shared by the various origin myths is that the Incas viewed themselves as outsiders who came to Cuzco to live among, subjugate, or civilize the native communities – aims that were not necessarily mutually exclusive. This premise has a number of dimensions, involving the Incas' establishment of themselves as a ruling class, the creation of a state apparatus, and the construction of a usable past that explained and legitimated their dominance before and after the empire was organized. The genealogy of the Peruvian monarchy recorded by Montesinos incorporates the view that history was repetitive. The splendor of a highly civilized empire was terminated abruptly by cataclysmic events that plunged the world into the barbarism of a dark age characterized by small, politically autonomous communities, whose members lacked proper respect for authority and advocated a variety of practices the Incas viewed as typical of animals rather than of civilized, cultivated human beings. The impressive ruins and stone sculpture still visible at Tiahuanaco were incorporated into some Inca constructions of a usable past as evidence of a prior civilization.

The Incas were able to portray their early history in a variety of ways that they did not necessarily perceive to be contradictory. They could represent themselves as the descendants of a ruling elite that came from Tiahuanaco to settle and rule Cuzco; their ancestors were trapped there when the empire collapsed and the world was plunged into the darkness of barbarism. Not surprisingly, however, the myths are silent on the processes involved in the fall of civilization. It is not clear whether regional administrators of the old empire disappeared, government circles became increasingly divided between opposing factions, public institutions were weakened and localized so that the responsibilities of the state could no longer be met, authority was transferred to local officials as society and the political economy became more localized, or village communities merely stopped paying tribute to the state and its ruling class.

Whatever the cause, the local communities went their separate ways during this dark age, which archaeologists today call the Late Intermediate Period. As a result, the ancestors of the Incas wielded little, if any, real power beyond the boundaries of their own village community and feuded continually with their neighbors.

Alternatively, the Incas could argue that they were new-
comers – an emergent, recently created people – that came to
Cuzco bearing the gifts of civilization and the state; this por-
trayal implied that they were not the direct descendants of an
old ruling class, whose abilities to control were localized and
diminished when the old state collapsed. They were, instead, a
new group, the creation of which carried with it the promise of
bringing the dark age to a close. They were created, so the story
goes, to be the new ruling class, and their origins were separate
from those of the Inca-speaking peoples they led from the caves
at Paqaritampu and from the village communities around Cuzco
that they subjugated. In this construction, they had no linkages,
direct or otherwise, with Tiahuanaco or any other ancient state-
based society.

The third premise of the usable past constructed and acknowledged by the Incas was that they viewed themselves as an
integral part of a wider social entity that included other communities in the Cuzco Valley and its environs. The area was a
complex ethnic mixture, in which kin-defined communities provided the horizontal linkages important for everyday life and
support. The Incas' assertions that they were created separately
from the rest of humanity suggests that this wider Cuzco social
formation was also estate-ordered or even class-stratified (Rousseau 1978a, 1978b). This hypothesis does not mean that the
entire social formation exhibited class stratification; in fact,
some local communities may have been characterized by relatively egalitarian relations. What it does mean is that the class
structure was unstable; the ruling groups in the class-stratified
communities had failed to consolidate their position successfully, their capacity to extract goods or labor on a regular basis
from kin and neighbors had diminished, or the state institutions
and practices that supported and masked this exploitation had
broken down. The various communities were locked in a struggle
for power, but the control they were able to exert over the economies of their neighbors was minimal and short-lived. A community that exploited its neighbors one moment might be exploited
by them a few years later. Stanley Diamond's (1951:15) description
of the Dahomey protostate captures the dynamics and turmoil of
pre-imperial Inca society and the Cuzco social formation as well:
"the kin-civil conflict was locked in equilibrium. The State was in
process of birth; it had not yet been fully conceived." It had not yet

entrenched itself in the everyday life of local village communities.

The fourth feature embedded in the oral traditions expresses a recognition and constitution of the gender system in early Inca society. There were clearly defined spheres of men's and women's production – men plow and women weave – that provided the foundations for a gender-based division of labor. Of course, men and women did more than just plow and weave; these activities merely symbolized their production (Murra 1980; Silverblatt 1987:9–14). However, there were also spheres of activity that were not so intimately linked with gender. For instance, in Sarmiento de Gamboa's account, Mama Huaco, one of the founders of Inca society, was characterized as a ferocious war leader. In another recorded by Montesinos, her persona was merged with that of her sister, and she was portrayed as a ritual specialist, an oracle, who connived with her kin to place her son on the throne. These accounts indicate that women played important, perhaps central, roles in spheres like raiding and ritual, which are frequently assumed to have been the exclusive domains of men. They also assert the centrality of women in questions of succession and, hence, with the reproduction of existing social relations. Women bestowed power on kings. The various traditions demonstrate the indissoluble linkage between gender systems and ideologies, on the one hand, and the constitution of class and state structures, on the other. As Irene Silverblatt (1976, 1978, 1987) and others have convincingly shown, changes in gender relations are not mere reflections of more profound political and economic transformations; they are instead the very essence of those processes (Gailey 1987; Muller 1977, 1985, 1987, 1988).

The fifth premise of the various dynastic traditions, including Montesinos's, is a dual one. They acknowledge the presence of earlier state-based societies, shrouded by the mists of time, and they indicate that the imperial state organized by the Incas was recent and short-lived. When read as historical annals, the origin myths show that imperial expansion occurred during the reign of Pachakuti 'Inka Yupanki, whose great grandsons, Washkar and Ataw Wallpa, were rivals for the throne when the Spaniards arrived. This perspective indicates that the formation and expansion of the empire took place almost entirely during the reigns of three rulers; thus, the calendrical dates assigned to their reigns by Miguel Cabello Valboa (1951) appear to be accurate or at least reasonable approximations (Rowe 1945). When the dynastic traditions are read as statements that map structural relations between the Inca royal corporations, or *panaqa*, and their non-noble kin and neighbors in Cuzco, the origin myths suggest that Inca society reduced the socially significant, usable past to a period of five generations before the present (Duviols 1977; Zuidema 1973). Thus, a structuralist reading of the myths also supports the idea that the imperial state had a brief duration.

2.2. The Prelude to Empire

Using the standard account of Inca dynastic history as a vehicle, let us continue examining the pre-imperial Cuzco social formation and focus our attention on the conditions that preceded and surrounded the consolidation of the empire in the 1430s. The different versions of this tradition agree that the empire was formed during the reign of the quasi-legendary reformer, Pachakuti, whose name means "cataclysm." Furthermore, several of them indicate that eight rulers followed Manqo Qhapaq, one of the mythical founders of Inca society, before Pachakuti 'Inka Yupanki consolidated his power and established the foundations of the empire.

Each of the pre-imperial leaders was the focus of an ancestor cult, or *panaqa*, that existed when the Spaniards arrived. Briefly, the *panaqas* were corporate landholding groups composed of brothers and sisters who claimed descent from the same ruler. According to the traditions, the various corporations were created when a king died. His sons and daughters used the property and the servants he had accumulated to support themselves and his mummy bundle and to maintain a cult in his honor (Cieza de León 1967:29–33, 154–155; Pizarro 1963; Rostworowski de Diez Canseco 1960; Rowe 1967:60–61, 67–68; Sancho de la Hoz 1938). Whether the *panaqas* of Pachakuti's predecessors were constituted before the empire existed or whether they were created *en masse* after its inception is not relevant for this discussion, but it is an interesting question and we shall consider later.

Zinchi Roq'a and his son, Lloq'e Yupanki, were the second and third Inca leaders. The traditions said little about either of them, except that both were peaceful men who added nothing to the domain established in the upper part of the Cuzco Valley by Manqo 'Inka. Perhaps the most notable thing about Lloq'e Yupanki was that he had an older brother who did not become the Inca leader. Thus, Zinchi Roq'a did not follow his father's lead in naming his eldest son as his successor (Cieza de León 1967:108–113; Sarmiento de Gamboa 1960:220–221).

Mayta Qhapaq, the fourth Inca leader, was portrayed differently. In contrast to his father and grandfather, he was described as a large, aggressive youth who began fighting with the Alcavizas, a neighboring community that also had lands in the Cuzco Valley. The fight erupted because the Incas were taking Alcaviza water. By the time Mayta Qhapaq was an adult, the quarrel had become a full-scale feud. The two communities raided each other's villages, but eventually the Incas crushed the Alcavizas, many of whom were killed. After the victory, the Incas offered sacrifices to their oracles. Mayta Qhapaq took possession of the fields and the inheritances of the Alcavizas who were slain in battle and divided them among the people of Cuzco (Cieza de León 1967:114–115; Sarmiento de Gamboa 1960:221–223).

Qhapaq Yupanki became the next Inca chieftain, when his older brother, described as being very ugly, was designated high priest. Qhapaq Yupanki led the first attacks on communities outside the Cuzco Valley. After defeating the people of Cuyumarca and Ancasmarca, the Incas sacrificed both men and women. Lavish feasts were held when they returned to Cuzco. The Inca leader married the daughter of a local strongman, or *zinchi*, from the neighboring community of Ayarmaka (Cieza de León 1967:116–119; Sarmiento de Gamboa 1960:223).

Three events stand out in accounts of the reign of his successor, 'Inka Roq'a. The first was that 'Inka Roq'a channeled rivers around Cuzco to irrigate fields that still benefited his descendants in the 1570s. The second was that the warriors he led defeated the people of Pomatambo and forced them to become tribute-paying subjects. The third involved his marriage to Mama Miqay, who was the daughter of a strongman from Huayllacan (Cieza de León 1967:120–122; Sarmiento de Gamboa 1960:223–228). After their marriage, it became evident that she had also been betrothed to an Ayarmaka strongman who demanded compensation for his bridewealth payment. After feuding for several years, the two communities agreed on an appropriate compensation: the young son of Mama Miqay and 'Inka Roq'a, a boy called Yawar Waqaq. The payment of bride-wealth apparently established the affiliation and identity of the woman's children.

According to Sarmiento de Gamboa (1960:225–227), a brother of the Inca leader who resided near the Huayllacan invited his nephew to visit so he could become acquainted with his maternal relatives. During the visit, the Huayllacan told the Ayarmaka where the boy would be at a certain time and he was kidnaped. Another version related by Sarmiento de Gamboa indicated that the Yawar Waqaq was turned over to the Ayarmaka by his uncle's sons. In any event, the boy was held captive for several years, and the Inca leader was unable to learn who kidnaped him or where he was being held. During his captivity, part of which was spent with herders, the boy was befriended by a woman who was a concubine of the Ayarmaka strongman as well as the daughter of a *zinchi* from Anta. The Anta then abducted the boy and held him for a year before they informed 'Inka Roq'a of his son's whereabouts. Their condition for returning Yawar Waqaq was to become "relatives" of the Incas in order to prevent retaliation.

Yawar Waqaq succeeded his father as the Inca leader. His brothers, Wika-k'iraw and 'Apu Mayta, were skilled war leaders who incorporated lands east and south of Cuzco into the Inca domain. His principal wife was an Ayarmaka woman who bore three sons. He wanted their second son to succeed him as leader; however, the heir apparent was killed by the Huayllacan kin of another wife who wanted to install her own on the throne. Yawar Waqaq himself may have been assassinated shortly thereafter as part of a plot by communities in Condesuyu to rid themselves of Inca domination (Cieza de León 1967:125–127). The elders chose Wiraqocha 'Inka as his successor (Sarmiento de Gamboa 1960:227–228).

The standard dynastic histories provide opportunities for insights into the dynamics of class and state formation prior to the consolidation of the imperial state. The origin myths characterized the founders of the Inca dynasty as a foreign ruling class that led groups of commoners to Cuzco, where they collaborated to steal land and plunder the indigenous communities. Accounts describing subsequent Inca leaders did not portray them as foreigners, but as residents of the Cuzco Valley who interacted both with their followers and with non-Inca local communities. At times, the relations among the Incas, their followers, and their neighbors were peaceful. At other times, the Incas feuded with their neighbors, stole their property, kidnaped them, and attempted to extort tribute from them. The dynastic accounts of pre-imperial Cuzco describe a time and set of conditions in which the institutions and practices normally associated with the state were weakly developed at best, if at all.

Two terms were used to refer to the leaders of the Inca and indigenous, non-Inca communities of Cuzco. Some were called *zinchis*, or strong men; others were referred to as *qhapaqs*, men who were both powerful and wealthy because of the large numbers of people they could call upon for assistance. An obvious question is what were the political-economic relationships that existed within and among the Incas, their followers, and other indigenous communities. Were the Inca leaders "big men," whose "authority derived from personal efforts and abilities [to build followings] through the allocation and reallocation of private resources" (van Bakel, Hagesteijn, and van de Velde 1986:1)? Were they tribal chieftains whose authority was embedded in the systems of customary expectations and obligations characteristic of kin-stratified, estate-ordered societies? Or were they kings, responding to the demands of class stratification, who laid the foundations for and oversaw the development and elaboration of various state institutions and practices?

The dynastic traditions suggest that the history of pre-imperial Inca society can be periodized. During one phase, at least, they described Inca society in terms that imply that it was an estate-ordered chieftainship (Gailey 1987:54–59; Rousseau 1978a). The Incas constituted the chiefly estate, and the *ayllus* that accompanied them from Paqaritambo were the commoners. The two estates were created separately. The Incas were leaders who depended on the good will of the commoners for prestations of labor service; the only kind of labor service mentioned, however, was soldiering. The commoners gave their labor power only so long as the chiefs responded generously with gifts of food and clothing. Zinchi Roq'a, the second Inca leader, was said to have been responsible for initiating the pattern of chiefly generosity and reciprocity.

This one established the style of attracting and entertaining these nations so that his court and house never angered anyone. His way was to keep the table set and the goblets full for whoever wished to come, and natives as well as strangers were there always, day and night, occupied with dancing and music in their own style (Cabello Valboa 1951:274).

The chiefly Inca estate consisted of a small number of *panaqas*, or corporate landholding groups, each of which had a founding patriarch and property to support both his descendants and a cult dedicated to his memory. The men, women, and children who constituted a *panaqa* held joint use-rights to its land, water, herds, labor, and other resources. This property was not divided, for to do so would have threatened the continued existence of the group and the capacity of its members to produce what they needed for themselves, for the cult honoring the founder, and for the gifts given to and expected by the commoners. This meant that the chiefly men and women of the Inca *panaqas* engaged in direct production. Given the gender division of labor, the *panaqa* men plowed the fields and the women made the beer and wove the cloth that was lavished willingly or begrudgingly to satisfy the customary expectations of non-chiefly people and neighbors. Thus, it was chiefly women who produced those items, the circulation of which ensured the social reproduction of the estate structure characteristic of this phase in the development of Inca society.

The chiefly peoples were not the only ones grouped into localized landholding groups. Their non-chiefly followers were also grouped into *ayllus* with landed property, water rights, and herds. As Janet Sherbondy (1977, 1982:16–30) observed, the patterns of land ownership and water rights of the various chiefly and non-chiefly corporate groups inscribed the social organization of production on the Cuzco landscape. The spatial dimensions of production also help to explain two other features of Cuzco social organization. The first is that the various *panaqas* were internally ranked; the second is that each was linked or paired with a particular non-chiefly *ayllu*. Tom Zuidema (1973:737–740; 1983a) has explored how they were connected. The highest ranking *panaqa* was that of the current ruler; the next highest was his father's group; the third ranking *panaqa* was the one dedicated to his grandfather; and so forth. Each *panaqa*

was paired for ritual purposes with a non-chiefly group, whose
members were still called Incas; however, they were not Incas
by birth or blood but rather commoners who had been granted
the status of "Incas by privilege." The commoner *ayllus* were
also localized corporate groups that held land and water rights.
Sherbondy (1977) has shown that each group in a particular
panaqa-ayllu pair held land and water rights in close proximity to
each other. Zuidema (1973) has argued that the members of the
non-chiefly *ayllu* were distant relatives of the *panaqa*'s founder –
six generations removed at best – or they were indigenous
peoples who were adopted and then granted the status. The
consolidation of class and state institutions provided the Inca
ruling class with a mechanism for getting rid of distant kin and
for retaining those who served their needs.

The Inca chieftains – Zinchi Roq'a and Lloq'e Yupanki – did
not challenge the traditional use-rights of the non-chiefly groups
in Cuzco. To do so would not only have jeopardized their
prestations of labor service but also adversely affected or
weakened the capacities of the Inca chiefs to negotiate with
neighboring communities and to defend themselves against the
exactions or predations of societies with more elaborated techniques of tribute extraction. It would, in effect, have eroded the
conditions for maintaining the estate structure of pre-imperial
Inca society.

The next two Inca leaders – Mayta Qhapaq and Qhapaq
Yupanki – set in operation practices and institutions that distorted the earlier estate structure and gender relations of Cuzco
society. Their reigns are described as ones in which raiding
occurred with increased intensity and ferocity. Sacrifices to Inca
wak'as and the oracular responses given through their priests
and caretakers attested to the appropriateness of past actions
and of those that were planned for the future. Lavish feasts
were held to celebrate victories and to encourage or compel
non-chiefly men, by playing on customary expectations of
generosity and reciprocity, to serve once again as soldiers in the
Inca's armies. Mayta Qhapaq, it seems, shared the land and loot
acquired during the raids he led on nearby communities with
his followers in Cuzco. This seems to mean that these shares
were gifts to the men who followed him into battle.

The accounts that describe their reigns suggest a series of
changes. These were subtle shifts in emphasis rather than struc-

tural transformations. The activities of ritual specialists, the caretakers of cults and shrines (especially the ones closely linked with the Inca ruler), seem more important than they had been during earlier reigns. The activities of non-chiefly men as soldiers following the Inca leaders into battle seem to offer opportunities for obtaining gifts of land – a new avenue for the acquisition and accumulation of wealth that was apparently not open to the women of their *ayllus* or to men who did not participate. The possibility of accumulating wealth outside the *ayllu* was a class formative process. For soldiers, it had the potential of diminishing the importance of the customary rights and obligations associated with *ayllu* membership or even eliminating them altogether. Thus, the new avenue of wealth accumulation available to soldiers also threatened the integrity and continued existence of the non-chiefly *ayllus*.

Increased raiding suggests the possibility, at least, that non-chiefly women bore more of the burden of direct subsistence production as their men were away and engaged in combat promoted by the chiefs. It suggests that there was an increased demand for the cloth, beer, and other goods produced by chiefly women – goods that were distributed at the lavish banquets and feasts that celebrated the victories of the chiefly people and their commoner allies over their non-Inca foes in neighboring communities. The plunder economy that was emerging may have created new bonds between chiefs as war leaders and non-chiefly men as the soldiers who accompanied them into combat. As the new conditions and bonds created by the plunder economy began to solidify, the existing system of gender relations and symbols would have been subjected to new stresses and perhaps eventually distorted. Up to this point, however, it appears that the Inca rulers were still unable to extract tribute from their followers. Perhaps they were even unwilling to attempt such extortion, either by direct or indirect means, for fear of the damage it might cause.

While most of the Inca dynastic accounts indicate that Wiraqocha 'Inka was the first ruler to extract regular tribute from subjugated communities, his predecessor, Yawar Waqaq actually laid the foundations of the Inca bureaucracy. The traditional accounts of his reign mention that he was kidnaped as a child. They also mention that his two brothers, Wika-k'iraw and 'Apu Mayta, were skilled war leaders, who gained considerable prestige and power in the future. What Yawar Waqaq elaborated temporarily at least within the chiefly estate was a technical division of labor between war leaders and administrators. This had the potential to create havoc, particularly over succession. While the ruler was the administrator, his chiefly kin – who were never terribly reliable allies – led armies composed of both chiefly and commoner men. While the chief had the customary authority associated with his office, the war leaders had the force of arms.

2.3. The Constitution of the Empire

The reign of Wiraqocha 'Inka marked another turning point in the Inca historical annals. Four themes stand out in the different versions of the standard tradition. They unfolded more or less simultaneously during the first third of the fifteenth century. The first is that Wiraqocha 'Inka laid the foundations for an imperial state apparatus. The second involves the civil unrest sparked by his policies in Cuzco and a series of palace intrigues and assassinations organized by his kin. The third concerns the invasion of the Chancas. The fourth is that Wiraqocha 'Inka and 'Inka Urqon, the successor he designated, were deposed by Pachakuti 'Inka Yupanki in 1438.

Inca imperial expansion began in the early fifteenth century. Up to this time, when the Incas – as well as neighboring groups – attacked and vanquished their enemies, they pillaged shrines and houses, seized fields and streams, and took captives that were incorporated into the community. However, neither the Incas nor their neighbors placed garrisons or officials among the vanquished. This pattern of raiding, plundering, and kidnaping changed during Wiraqocha's reign. He placed resident officials among the peoples subjugated by the Incas to ensure that tribute was delivered at the specified times and that corvée labor was performed; at the same time, the vanquished communities retained their traditional leaders and landholding patterns. The new community relations were cemented with marriages; Inca women were betrothed to the traditional leaders, *kurakas*, of the subject communities, and the Inca ruler apparently married their daughters and took concubines from them. Wiraqocha was ably assisted by his uncles – the two old war leaders, Wika-k'iraw and 'Apu Mayta – who had developed a political-military strategy that allowed them to launch attacks from two directions at the same time. While one would launch a frontal assault on the enemy, the other would attack from the rear (Cieza de León 1967:128–129).

The foundations for the new practices were laid when the Incas expanded their sphere of influence into the northern part of the Urubamba Valley. This occurred when they attacked and subdued the 'Ayarmaka kingdom centered in the southernmost basin of the Cuzco Valley. The Incas crossed over the mountain passes separating the Cuzco and Urubamba drainages to attack the community of Calca. The people of Calca retreated to a hilltop fort that overlooked their fields. After laying siege to the fort, the Incas eventually stormed it and captured its defenders. One of the conditions of defeat imposed on Calca was an Inca governor, who resided there to supervise corvée labor and to ensure that the local leaders remained loyal. At this point, the Incas turned their attention to the 'Ayarmaka, whom they attacked and also defeated (Cieza de León 1967:128–131; Sarmiento de Gamboa 1960:229–230).

The Incas then conquered a series of communities in the Urubamba Valley. These were relatively small-scale campaigns that not only secured the Incas's hold over the Cuzco Valley but also made them an important political force in Urubamba. As a result, the Incas inserted themselves into a conflict between the Colla and Lupaqa, two Aymara-speaking kingdoms located at the northern end of the Lake Titicaca. They allied themselves with the Lupaqa, whose homelands were located on the other side of the Colla territory. However, before the Incas could become active participants in the dispute, the Colla attacked the Lupaqa kingdom and were defeated. By the time the Incas arrived, the battle was over. While they joined the Lupaqa in their victory celebrations, they received none of the spoils – neither land, nor loot, nor captives (Cieza de León 1967:135–147).

The civil unrest that occurred during the reign of Wiraqocha 'Inka had several sources. The first, regarding succession, came from the nobility. While Wiraqocha and his warriors were out of town expanding the imperial domain, one of his brothers seized the opportunity to challenge the legitimacy of his rule and to depose him as leader. This challenge split the Inca nobility into factions; it pitted the members of Yawar Waqaq's *panaqa*, and apparently those of some other corporations as well, against Wiraqocha's descendants and allies outside the city. This dispute within the Inca nobility occurred in the context of ongoing clashes among the Inca commoners and the indigenous, non-Inca inhabitants of nearby villages; the two sets of disputes quickly became intertwined, producing a complex web of alliances and blocs of people that reflected, for the moment at least, perceived shared interests or possibilities for mutual advantage (Sarmiento de Gamboa 1960:229–230). A reign of terror erupted in Cuzco. The pretender and his followers murdered Wiraqocha's son, whom he had appointed governor of the city; they also killed many of Wiraqocha's secondary wives and their children. When Wiraqocha and his warriors returned to the city, they were greeted by some of those who had originally supported the insurrection. The rebellion ultimately failed, and, after his allies deserted him, the usurper, his wives and children, and his loyal supporters committed suicide in order to avoid Wiraqocha's wrath (Cieza de León 1967:132–134).

The other source of civil unrest was Wiraqocha 'Inka's policies toward the indigenous peoples of Cuzco, especially those that involved their deities, shrines, or sacred objects, all of which were called *wak'as*. The local communities believed he had unjustly seized the kingdom from his father and was somehow implicated in his death. They were also angry because he wanted them to worship Teqzi Wiraqocha, a god whose name he taken earlier; they were to give this god precedence over other deities and over *inti*, the Sun, which was specifically linked in some accounts with Manqo Qhapaq, Lloq'e Yupanki, and Mayta Qhapaq (Cobo 1956, vol. 2:107–109; Sarmiento de Gamboa 1960:220, 222). In fact, he planned to destroy their *wak'as* but was prevented from doing so by his wife (Huaman Poma de Ayala 1936:79–80). Earlier in his life, the Inca leader had visited a shrine near Cacha that was dedicated to Teqzi Wiraqocha. He received an oracle from the *wak'a* that promised him and his family good fortunes in the future; he used the oracle to justify imperial conquest. Wiraqocha 'Inka then seized the shrine; his goal was to make it a permanent possession of his own *panaqa* and to appoint its priests and caretakers (Cabello Valboa 1951:301; Cobo 1956, vol. 2:107–109).

The third and fourth themes – the Chancas's invasion and Pachakuti 'Inka Yupanki's seizure of the royal tassel – are closely

linked in all versions of the standard dynastic tradition. The
lands controlled by the Quechuas bordered the western frontier
of the Inca domain. The Chancas resided on the other side of the
Quechuas; their *paqarina* was a lake near Huancavelica. During
the reign of 'Inka Roq'a, the Incas apparently attacked the
Chancas and succeeded in subordinating them to the point
where they were able to extract tribute; however, the Chancas
rebelled a generation later and were able to reassert their autonomy (Cobo 1956, vol. 2:73–75). At the same time Wiraqocha and
his warriors were campaigning in the Urubamba Valley, the
Chancas attacked and defeated the Quechuas who lived between
them and the Incas. They established a capital at Andahuaylas,
which was in the lands of the Quechuas. This brought the Chancas to the edge of the nascent Inca state. They threatened the very
existence of that state, especially when they demanded that the
Incas submit to their domination. This brought into the open a
dispute over succession that was smoldering among the Inca
nobility (Cieza de León 1947:436; 1967:148–155).

Wiraqocha had designated 'Inka 'Urqon, the son of his favorite secondary wife, as his successor. This presumably enraged
the *coya*, his principal wife from the village of Anta, and her
sons, who believed they had more legitimate claims to the royal
tassel than the son of a mere concubine. As the Chancas approached Cuzco, Wiraqocha and the new king, 'Inka 'Urqon,
withdrew to a fort near Calca; they left behind one of the *coya*'s
sons, a man who would later take the name Pachakuti 'Inka
Yupanki, to defend the city. Pachakuti had the support of
several of his brothers as well as that of the two old war leaders –
his great uncles, Wika-k'iraw and 'Apu Mayta, who belonged to
the Wika-k'iraw, the corporation founded by 'Inka Roq'a – and a
few of Wiraqocha's secondary wives and their kin (Betanzos
1924:100–105; Sarmiento de Gamboa 1960:230–232).

Wiraqocha and 'Inka 'Urqon's retreat from Cuzco forced Pachakuti and his supporters into the open. They had to make a
series of decisions in a situation fraught with uncertainties. If
they fled with their royal kin, they would also be implicated in
the consequences. If they remained in Cuzco, they would have
to confront the Chancas, who had the capacity to destroy the
incipient Inca state, and they would also have to deal with the
reprisals of the Calca faction.

The Chancas launched their offensive. Pachakuti and his

partisans successfully repelled two attacks. The fighting was savage; the men and women who defended the city succeeded in wounding or killing a large number of Chanca warriors in house-to-house combat and as they pursued them across the plain outside the city. It took time for both sides to recover from the effects of the initial assault. Because of Wiraqocha's defense of the city, many of his supporters, dismayed and disheartened when the old king and 'Inka 'Urqon fled to Calca, switched their allegiance to Pachakuti. As a result, when Pachakuti launched a counter-offensive later in the year, his forces were larger. The Chancas responded to the Inca assault; the fighting was fierce once again, but the Chancas's resistance collapsed after two of their three war leaders were captured, insulted, tortured, and eventually executed – their heads skewered on pikes, their bodies flayed and turned into drums (Cieza de León 1967:154–155; Sarmiento de Gamboa 1960:232–235).

After the Chancas were defeated, Pachakuti proclaimed himself king, thereby challenging the authority of Wiraqocha and the legitimacy of 'Inka 'Urqon's claim to the royal tassel. This meant there were two Inca states: one in Cuzco and the other in Calca. Pachakuti attempted to negotiate with his father by offering him the most precious spoils from the victory over the Chancas, but the old king refused to act according to customary expectations. Instead of walking on the items, as Pachakuti expected, Wiraqocha said that 'Inka 'Urqon should tread on them. Pachakuti responded by saying that he had not brought the spoils to honor cowards. He then took the riches and returned to Cuzco.

Later, while Pachakuti was attempting to reestablish Inca control and domination over the local communities that had reasserted their autonomy during the wars with the Chancas, 'Inka 'Urqon apparently mounted a campaign to overthrow his brother. His attempt failed when the pretender was murdered by Pachakuti's warriors. He then placed Wiraqocha, if he was not already dead, under house arrest at his retreat; this effectively banished the old king from Cuzco for the rest of his life. Pachakuti also reaffirmed his own claims and those of his sons to the royal tassel when he married both Mama Anahuarque, a woman from Choco whom he took as his principal wife, and the *coya*, the sister-wife, of 'Inka 'Urqon (Cabello Valboa 1951:303–312; Cieza de León 1967:154–155; Sarmiento de Gamboa 1960:232–235,

238–239). These events cleared the way for Pachakuti, the reformer, to consolidate his rule and create the imperial mystique.

While Pachakuti's rise to power was widely portrayed as the
dawn of a new era in the history of Inca society, many of the
reforms unleashed during his reign were built on structures and
practices that were instituted by earlier rulers, most notably
Wiraqocha 'Inka. When viewed from the perspective of the
consolidation of class relations and the expansion of state power,
the most important precedent was the extraction of tribute in the
form of labor service from the members of conquered or subordinated non-Inca communities. This established and situated the
conditions for exploitation on the margins of Cuzco Inca society.

The estate structure of Cuzco society masked or obscured the
processes of class formation set in motion by tribute extraction.
The chiefly and non-chiefly estates in Inca society were categories of people. The members of each estate shared legal rights
and obligations that distinguished them from the people who
belonged to other estates. Thus, the estates were legally defined. The estate system that prevailed in Inca society before
Wiraqocha's reign did not equate precisely with the class structure that began to develop after the initiation of the wars of
conquest and the appropriation of labor. The class structure that
emerged was the collective expression of this exploitation. It
crosscut the estate system of Cuzco Inca society in important
ways.

While the members of the Inca chiefly estate may have retained their authority, which was embedded in kinship and
rested on customary expectations of generosity, the power to
dominate belonged to the emerging ruling class that was centered
around the ruler, the members of his *panaqa*, and those collateral
kin who were either war leaders, the overseers of subject populations, or priests at shrines that served the interests of this group –
such as the one dedicated to Teqzi Wiraqocha. Linked with this
group presumably in a subordinate way were the *kurakas* of the
subjugated communities. They served as intermediaries between
the Inca ruling class and state, on the one hand, and between their
own kin and community, on the other; thus, their position and
relations were ambiguous and conflicting.

Thus, the class structure that began to develop under Wiraqocha distorted the internal ranking of the *panaqas* that composed the chiefly estate. It gave greater emphasis to the primacy

$396

$76.03

Phone

$36.29

of the ruler's *panaqa* and threatened to disconnect it completely from the rest of the chiefly corporate groups. The integrity of those groups was also threatened when some, but not all, of their members were able to establish connections with the ruler or assume positions of power in the developing state apparatus that reduced or eliminated their customary obligations toward kin. The class and state formative processes generated on the margins of Inca society began to elevate and remove Wiraqocha's supporters from the corporate groups to which they belonged. As a result, the Incas who became associated with the ruler or the state had to confront the divided loyalties and contradictions created by their new positions.

What differentiated the chiefly *panaqas* and the Cuzco *ayllus* composed of "Incas by privilege" from the subjugated communities was that their members were exempt from tribute payments or, more precisely, the kinds of labor exactions that were imposed on subject populations (Cobo 1956:119; Huaman Poma de Ayala 1936:118, 455, 740; Murra 1980:101; Polo de Ondegardo 1940:146–147). Individuals from these groups came to fill many of the mid-level positions in an Inca bureaucracy that would expand rapidly in the near future. The fact that the ruling class of the emerging Inca state was unable to exact labor, beyond military service, from the men of *panaqas* and commoner *ayllus* around Cuzco points to the fragility of the political superstructure at this stage in its development. It implies that nonruling-class Inca groups still retained considerable control over their own means of production and social reproduction.

This was not the case in areas that were subjugated and more firmly controlled, at least temporarily, by the developing imperial state. While these communities retained traditional use rights over their land and water resources, their members were required to engage simultaneously in subsistence production that ensured their own reproduction as corporate landholding groups, in production for local chieftains who were both kin and state agents, and in production for the state (Geschiere 1982; Rey 1982). Refusal to contribute the labor demanded by the state potentially had material consequences, not just symbolic ones, especially when the nascent state was able to impose its will and ensure that tribute was paid. Withholding the labor demanded by the state was countered with threats of state-sponsored brigandage, higher levels of tribute extraction, and the replacement of traditional leaders by individuals who were more pliable and responsive to its commands. These could not be perceived as idle threats, because they directly affected the ability of a community to reproduce itself both socially and demographically (Cieza de León 1967:56–61).

However, the Incas were not always able to impose their will on encapsulated communities. There were numerous instances in which communities, like the Chancas or the villages around Cuzco, stopped paying tribute – when the Incas were preoccupied with other matters. Tribute extraction was often erratic, especially when the prevailing conditions prevented direct or effective intervention in the organization of the subsistence sector and the social reproduction of the communities they attempted to control. With few exceptions, the Incas seemed to have imposed their will during this phase either by force or by threat and intimidation.

The fundamental weakness of the state apparatus that became most evident during Wiraqocha's reign was that the collateral kin of the ruler occupied positions of real power. Many of them were not particularly trustworthy allies or subordinates because they all had more or less legitimate claims to the royal tassel. This problem was compounded by a technical division of labor within the ruling class. Two of Wiraqocha's uncles, who belonged to the *panaqa* established by his grandfather, enjoyed reputations as skilled war leaders and presumably had followings among the men of the other *panaqas* and *ayllus*. Other collateral kin of the Inca ruler were governors. Pachakuti himself was a lieutenant left in charge of Cuzco. The other Inca governors must have spent at least part of the year outside of Cuzco in the communities they supervised. They were probably in these communities when labor taxes were assessed and paid. Residing among subject populations afforded them opportunities to forge close relationships with the members of these communities that were independent from those of either the ruler or the state. Just such a connection was established later, during the reign of Pachakuti's successor, when an Inca inspector, who was also the brother of the ruler, attempted to foment a rebellion outside of Cuzco. His efforts were thwarted, however, and he was executed for stirring up trouble among the servants of the ruler.

Wiraqocha and his successors attempted to resolve some of the contradictions that developed within the ruling class through marriage. These were arranged with women of the various Cuzco *panaqa* and *ayllus* and with the daughters of *kurakas* in communities that were on the margins of the state or that had already been enveloped by it. The male children that issued from the various unions, in theory at least, had equally valid claims to the royal tassel, since there was no fixed rule of succession (Rostworowski de Diez Canseco 1960). While the marriages created alliances between the ruler and various Inca groups and subject communities, however, contradictions and tensions resurfaced when a successor was about to be named. These were times of crisis. Some of the ruler's sons were assassinated; there were even attempts on the lives of rulers themselves – some of which, apparently, were successful. It is impossible to understand these struggles without being fully cognizant of the roles played by the wives and concubines of the king, who were, of course, also the mothers of the potential heirs to the throne. They were the links that held together the various elements of the ruling class. The social cement they provided was not durable, however, for when they allied with their sons and natal kin rather than with the ruler and the state, the ruling class came unglued, if only for a moment.

In the context of class and state formation, religion, as Stanley Diamond (1951:51) pointed out many years ago, was transformed into an instrument by means of which the state attempted to secure an elusive power base. Groups no longer venerated just their departed ancestors to reaffirm the solidarity of the collectivities they established; they were also required to pay homage and make prestations to a state cult dedicated to a mysterious force of nature that had be interpreted and explained by priests, who were simultaneously the ruler's kin and agents of the state. Religion was a means for fixing or connecting civil power to the state. In Cuzco society, the state and the state cult developed together. The state cult was a fabric, woven by Wiraqocha, that was embroidered and embellished by Pachakuti and his successors.

In the early phases of its development, before the foundations of the empire, the Inca state built on old institutions and practices that were combined, transformed, and given new meanings in an emerging set of circumstances that were engendered and increasingly characterized by class formation, imperial expansion, successional disputes, factionalism, temporary alliances, and resistance to its exactions. The nascent empire was "a society in conflict, a society divided against itself" (Diamond 1951:124). When Pachakuti seized the tassel – the symbol of royal power – exploitation, alienation, competition, rivalries, conspiracies, and plots were already integral aspects of everyday life, at least within the nobility.

Chapter 3

The Impact of Empire

Men [and women] make their own history, but they do not make it just as they please; they do not make it under circumstances chosen by themselves, but under circumstances directly encountered, given and transmitted from the past. The tradition of all the dead generations weighs like a nightmare on the brain of the living. And just when they seem engaged in revolutionising themselves and things, in creating something that has never yet existed, precisely in such periods of revolutionary crisis they anxiously conjure up the spirits of the past to their service and borrow from them names, battle cries and costumes in order to present the new scene of world history in this time-honoured disguise and borrowed language. (Karl Marx, *The Eighteenth Brumaire of Louis Bonaparte*)

At the time of the war with the Chancas in the 1430s, Inca society was virtually coterminous with the Inca state. However, the historical linkages between them were steadily eroded as the empire expanded and new peoples were brought under imperial rule by Pachakuti and his successors. While the Incas remained the dominant faction in the empire, Inca society and culture were no longer identical with the imperial state itself. Each successive emperor was forced to acquire new allies and to construct new institutions and practices to maintain order and to recreate the conditions necessary for his continued domination and rule. The alliances – forged increasingly across ethnic boundaries – and the gifts of land and servants to non-Inca shrines and individuals cut across pre-imperial Andean social hierarchies. They created the conditions for the emergence of a new class structure that was not identical with earlier forms of stratification. The composition of the imperial ruling class was transformed as non-Inca subjects and allies were incorporated into it and as the emperor's more distant kin were reduced to

Inca-speaking commoners (Patterson 1985c).

The Inca empire was a patchwork of different kinds of societies, each with its own distinctive social, political, and economic structures. The processes of class and state formation associated with the expansion and consolidation of the empire were dialectical. On the one hand, the Incas and the state imposed their will on the encapsulated and subject populations; they acquired both land and labor from them through some combination of intimidation, negotiation, alliance, and cooptation. On the other hand, many Andean peoples opposed the efforts of the Incas and the state to exact land and labor from their members. Frontier populations fought the imperial armies; recalcitrant peasants in many provinces forced the state to place overseers among them to ensure that the tribute demanded was actually paid; and footdragging and other forms of passive resistance occasionally gave way to open insurrection, especially when the hopes and aspirations of peoples who viewed themselves as oppressed were fueled by rumors concerning the ruler's death and the civil unrest that such events provoked.

Culture – the meanings, values, and practices that people continually renew and create to make the events and social relations of everyday life comprehensible – was one arena in which these dialectical processes played themselves out. The state imposed various institutions and practices in an attempt to saturate and homogenize certain aspects of consciousness; it sought to establish the substance and limits of common sense, to constitute and bound socially experienced reality in ways that made it difficult or impossible for subject peoples to construct alternative understandings or to conceptualize reality in different terms altogether (Williams 1980:37–38). The state attempted to organize and represent a dominant culture: a system of values and modes of interpreting reality that claimed to serve universal human interests while actually serving the controlling interests of the imperial state.

Even though the state was the representative of the dominant culture, it could not control all social interactions even if it had controlled all the means of interaction. The interactions that took place within the framework established by the institutions and practices of the dominant culture both reflected and contested the interests of the state and the politically dominant classes. As a result, at the same time that the state was attempting to impose its will and modes of interpretation, subject populations and encapsulated peoples on the frontiers deployed their own understandings of the events and relations that conditioned their lives. Both their acceptance and opposition to the interpretations, signs, and practices of the state were reflected in the trappings of everyday life and in the meanings assigned to them. How they decorated and distributed the articles they used and how they performed traditional rituals reaffirmed their sense of community in new circumstances. This material culture also reflected how they understood the new elements introduced by the state, those that imperial representatives portrayed as unmodified continuations of pre-imperial institutions and practices.

The culture of the Inca state was neither homogeneous nor uniform. The empire incorporated a number of culturally heterogeneous tribes, chiefdoms, and states, each of which shared some features with neighboring groups and possessed distinctive, historically constituted elements that set its members apart. Besides the dominant culture, which was closely linked with the state and the ruling classes and the various subject groups, there were also what Raymond Williams (1980:40–42) called residual and emergent cultures. These provided alternative and potentially oppositional interpretations and practices to those of the dominant culture.

The residual cultural forms were the experiences, meanings, and values that survived when the traditional practices of the various pre-imperial societies were preserved more or less intact. They were not integral elements of the dominant culture, since they could be neither verified nor expressed in terms of the dominant culture. However, certain residual cultural forms, such as the elaborate feasts that preceded imperial requests for labor service, were incorporated into the dominant culture in an attempt to give historically grounded meaning to the new practices and interpretations (Spalding 1984:83). The emergent cultural forms consisted of the meanings and values attached to the new configurations of experiences, institutions, practices, and symbols. At one level, they were represented by the innovative art styles that lacked clear antecedents in any particular tradition. At another, more complicated level, they were manifested in the various attempts of subject peoples to account for their new powerlessness or in the ways traditional leaders tried to resolve the contradictions that resulted when they became officials of the state (Spalding 1973).

Both the state and the ruling class were alert to residual and emergent cultural forms. They realized these were risky practices that potentially undermined the dominant culture, since they afforded alternative forms of explanation and interpretation to those advanced by the state. In some instances, these alternative understandings of everyday life did become oppositional, allowing people not only to conceptualize their lives in a different way but also giving them the will to change the political, economic, and social relations that structured their experience, to elaborate new points of view, and to develop new practices.

3.1. The Formation and Organization of the Imperial State

The standard accounts of Inca dynastic history indicate that imperial expansion began during the reign of Pachakuti 'Inka Yupanki, a heroic figure, who ruled from 1438 to 1471 (Rostworowski de Diez Canseco 1953). Toward the end of his reign, he ruled with his son, Topa 'Inka Yupanki, who ascended to the throne in 1471 and reigned until his death in 1493. A majority of the subject peoples were incorporated into the imperial state and many of its institutions and practices were set in place during this period. Imperial expansion continued on a reduced scale under Wayna Qhapaq, who ruled until his death in 1525. It was probably still taking place during the civil war that was raging when the Spaniards arrived seven years later (Rowe 1945, 1946:201–209).

Pachakuti consolidated his power after the assassination of 'Inka Urqon, establishing an uneasy truce with the Chancas – a balance of forces that allowed both groups to continue raiding, plundering, and conquering as long as they did not attack each other. The Incas were once again reunited under a single ruler. When Pachakuti came to power, the Incas had established control only over the Cuzco Valley, the neighboring valley of Anta, part of the Urubamba Valley, and the hills near Cuyo (Rowe 1945). His forces completed the conquest of the Urubamba Valley and then subjugated polities as far north as Cangallo and Vilcas and as far south as the northern end of the Lake Titicaca Basin.

About 1445, Pachakuti sent a force under the command of his brother, Qhapaq Yupanki from Zukzu *panaqa*, to explore the south coast of Peru (Menzel and Rowe 1966). On their return to Cuzco, the Inca soldiers passed through the territory of the Chancas and captured a few villages. The Chancas retaliated by outflanking the Incas and attacking the Collas in the Lake Titicaca Basin. Tensions increased between the old adversaries but no fighting broke out. Instead, they undertook a joint invasion of the area north of Vilcas. Pachakuti appointed Qhapaq Yupanki to lead the Inca forces; he warned him to watch for any signs of treachery by the Chancas and to proceed no further than Yanamayo. The Chancas distinguished themselves in battle as the combined forces moved northward. This embarrassed Pachakuti, who, fearing that the Chancas might turn on the Incas, ordered his brother to kill their leaders. When the Chancas learned of the assassination plot, they fled into the tropical forests near the headwaters of the Huallaga River before the order could be carried out. Before giving up the chase, Qhapaq Yupanki pursued the Chancas well beyond the limit set by his brother. Seeing that his forces were considerably overextended, he turned his attention toward the rich province of Cajamarca, whose inhabitants were allies of the powerful coastal Kingdom of Chimor (Netherly 1977; Rostworowski de Diez Canseco 1961; Rowe 1948). Qhapaq Yupanki captured Cajamarca and left a small garrison there before he returned to Cuzco (Sarmiento de Gamboa 1960:242–244).

Pachakuti was furious. His orders had been blatantly disregarded and he was apprehensive about Qhapaq Yupanki's intentions. He moved swiftly. Fearing that his brother might attempt to seize the throne, Pachakuti had him killed before he arrived in Cuzco (Sarmiento de Gamboa 1960:244). However, the garrison at Cajamarca was exposed, and both Chimor and the Chancas threatened to attack. He responded to the danger by organizing two expeditions: one to conquer the peoples of the Titicaca Basin and to protect their exposed southern flank, and the other to consolidate and subdue the north. The first expedition was led by two of his sons, who had subjugated the Collas earlier. They turned their attention toward the Lupaqa and their allies; when the expedition was over, the imperial state controlled all of the peoples between Cuzco and the southern end of the Titicaca Basin (Sarmiento de Gamboa 1960:245–247).

The northern expedition was led by Topa 'Inka Yupanki, another of Pachakuti's sons. Topa 'Inka and the forces under his command marched northward toward Cajamarca, pacifying the country as they went. After relieving the garrison at Cajamarca, which was being threatened by forces from Chimor, they conquered as far north as Quito in order to outflank the Chimu armies. Once their control over the inhabitants of the highlands was reasonably secure, they turned their attention toward Chimor and attacked its armies simultaneously from several different directions. The battle was a bitter one, and many members of the Chimu ruling class were executed when the kingdom finally fell. After the battle was over and Chimor was vanquished, Topa 'Inka visited the powerful coastal *wak'a*, the oracle at Pachacamac. He then returned to Cuzco, triumphant and secure in the knowledge that the state he had forged with his father, his kin, and their allies was the most powerful in Peru (Patterson 1985a; Sarmiento de Gamboa 1960:249–252).

During this period, Pachakuti also seized the lands of communities residing in the Cuzco Basin and resettled their members further from the capital city (Rowe 1967). He then used the labor of subject communities from Cuzco to undertake a massive reclamation project in the valley, channeling the rivers and building agricultural terraces on the hills. The productivity of the valley was increased and the newly created agricultural lands were divided among the *panaqas* and Inca *ayllus* (Sherbondy 1977, 1982). These actions were accompanied by the formalization of a calendrical system and the organization of shrines that were located on *ceques* – a series of imaginary lines that radiated outward from Coricancha, the Temple of the Sun, in the center of Cuzco. Both were essential for agricultural production, since the distribution of water was linked with ceremonies that were performed on specific days at one of the shrines located on a particular *ceque* (Cobo 1956 vol. 2:169–186; Rowe 1979a; Zuidema 1964). In the process, Pachakuti created a dozen new *ceque* shrines, and the members of his corporation cared for them, performing the required rituals on the appropriate days. As a result of the reclamation project and the fact that the conquests were carried out by his sons, the lands and estates held by Pachakuti's corporation and by *panaqas* of his predecessors were concentrated around Cuzco (Betanzos 1924:131–153, 173–186; Cobo 1956 vol. 2:169–174; Rostworowski de Diez

Canseco 1966; Sarmiento de Gamboa 1960:235–238, 246–247; Zuidema 1983a, 1983b). It is possible, however, that Pachakuti's *panaqa* also had lands in the area between Cuzco and Lake Titicaca (Cobo 1956 vol. 2:86–88).

Besides the reclamation project, which increased the extent of arable land, there were other construction projects in Cuzco itself. Pachakuti had palaces erected and temples built for the major deities of the state. Coricancha, the Temple of the Sun, which became the focus of the state religious cult, was rebuilt and enlarged. In the process of organizing the administrative and religious apparatus of the state, he established a system of state shrines in provincial areas and alienated lands and assigned servants to maintain them (Anonymous 1906; Betanzos 1924:139–153, 173–177; Rowe 1960b; Sarmiento de Gamboa 1960:235–237).

Catherine Julien (1988:260) has suggested that two viewpoints have dominated recent discussions about the organization and functioning of the Inca state apparatus. One perspective argues that the Incas imposed a bureaucratic structure on subject peoples that ultimately reshaped Andean political organization; this structure was constituted during Pachakuti's reign and included both novel features devised by the Incas themselves and elements derived from other Andean states, such as the Kingdom of Chimor or the lacustrine kingdoms of the Titicaca Basin (Rowe 1945, 1946:204–207; 1960b). The other perspective argues that the Incas enveloped and built on existing political structures, reorienting them to meet their own needs (Morris 1985; Murra 1984). There is truth in both perspectives. Whether the Incas constructed new political organizations, reconstituted existing ones, or merely reoriented them depends on how the state apparatus is conceptualized and on historically specific conditions that existed in different parts of the empire.

The administrative organization of the imperial state is frequently described as pyramidal. The highest official was the emperor, who ruled by divine right and was worshiped as divine during his lifetime. Immediately below the emperor in the administrative hierarchy were the '*apo*, or prefects, of the four quarters, the largest territorial divisions of the imperial state; they were collateral kinsmen of the emperor, close relatives who belonged to the royal corporations and resided in Cuzco. Below them were the governors, the *toqrikoq*, who resided in various provincial capitals that were built at strategically important locations across the empire (Morris 1973; Morris and Thompson 1985). They were also Incas; however, it is not clear whether all of them belonged to the royal corporations or whether some were Incas by privilege. They had judicial and administrative powers and oversaw the activities of the *kurakas*, the leaders of ethnic groups, who were incorporated into the lower echelons of the administrative hierarchy; these non-Inca leaders administered a series of hierarchically organized groups – *chunga*, *pachaca*, *waranga*, and *huno* – that were portrayed as decimal units ranging in size from ten to ten thousand households (Rowe 1946:257–264). The decimal groupings were accounting units defined in the annual census, in terms of which tribute obligations were assessed. The decimal system was an organizational device that did not always correspond precisely with the demographic realities of the situations. In some instances, the accounting units contained more households than they should have; in others, they contained fewer (Julien 1988:262, 266).

Other categories of state officials stood outside the administrative hierarchy. Two of these – the census-takers, *runakhipukamayoqs*, and the inspectors, *tokoyrikoqs* – articulated the Inca and non-Inca layers of the administration. They preserved the new internal order imposed on subject populations by ensuring that the labor demands of the state and the ruling class were met. They were the nexus of what Diamond (1951:32–76) called the "census-tax-conscription" pattern of archaic states. Whether they were Incas or not, they were loyal to the state. The census takers were sent each December to supervise a census of the accounting units constituted for each subject population; their duties also included selecting retainers, *yana*, and chosen women, *aclla*, for the state and punishing individuals who hid from the census and tax assessment (Castro and Ortega Morejón 1936; Julien 1988:266–267). The inspectors visited districts to make secret and public investigations of the activities of provincial governors and *kurakas* and to report their activities to the emperor and his counselors. Their major concerns seem to have to insure that tax obligations were being met satisfactorily and that conspiracies and rebellions were not being planned by dissatisfied officials (Garcilaso de la Vega 1960 vol. 1:63; Moore 1958:112–115; Sarmiento de Gamboa 1960:239–240).

The state had available a series of institutions and practices to ensure the regular and systematic extraction of tribute from the peoples they subjugated. This exploitation was backed up by the army, diplomacy, coercion, and intimidation. The state used the up-to-date census information to levy labor taxes on the subject populations and the households that comprised them. It imposed two kinds of taxes. The first was the *mit'a*, which consisted of a specific number of days of labor in the army, in public works projects, or in personal service to the emperor or various officials and agencies of the state. The other form of labor taxation involved agricultural or pastoral work in fields appropriated by the royal corporations, the state, or the state cult or in caring for the herds of llamas and alpacas they pastured in the territory of their subjects. The tax burden was apparently not equally distributed across the various groups incorporated into the state. Greater demands were placed on some accounting units than others in the same province, and the demands for labor from frontier populations were less than those from groups in the core areas of the state (Julien 1988:263; Patterson 1987c; Salomon 1986:187–218).

The state often broke up ethnic groups and resettled some of their households in other areas of the empire. These resettled populations, the *mitimaes* or *mitmaqkuna*, retained their cultural identities and primary political connections with their natal communities; they were not integrated into the ethnic groups and accounting units among whose members they were settled, nor were they placed under the control and jurisdiction of the local *kurakas* of those areas, who had to provide them with land and partial support during their first two years of residence.There were several categories of *mitimaes*: rebels who were removed from their natal communities and resettled in the center of the state where they were herders or royal attendants; settlers from the center who were relocated among peoples whose loyalty to the state was suspect; groups that were garrisoned in frontier areas and eventually became permanent residents; and farmers who were resettled in underpopulated regions to increase agricultural production for the state (Acosta 1954:191–192; Cieza de León 1947:442–443; 1967:73–78; Garcilaso de la Vega 1960 vol. 1:111–112, 163–165, 187–188, 245–247; Murra 1980:172–182; Rostworowski de Diez Canseco 1963, 1980, 1988b:221–224; Rowe 1946:269–270).

The resettlement policies of the imperial state served various functions. They dispersed groups that were antagonistic or hostile toward the empire, making it more difficult for their members to mount a successful revolt, especially when their members were relocated in areas where the indigenous inhabitants were loyal to the state. They placed settlers from groups allied with the state in areas like the frontiers, where the political conditions were unsettled and the indigenous peoples threatened to resist or revolt against the state. In these instances, the *mitmaqkuna* were charged with setting examples of proper behavior for the indigenous peoples and providing the state with information about their activities and intentions. The settlers were, in effect, spies and potential soldiers in case of rebellion. Since the emperor's kin were also *mitmaqkuna*, the resettlement policies removed collateral relatives but potentially untrustworthy allies from the capital (Huaman Poma de Ayala 1936:312; Murra 1980:179). And, finally, these policies rewarded the loyalty of groups allied with the state by providing them with access to new fields and pastures.

The political economies of polities and peoples incorporated into the empire were often transformed in the process. Large powerful polities – like the Kingdom of Chimor – that opposed Inca imperial expansion were broken up and divided into smaller political entities; their traditional rulers were assassinated and replaced by individuals who were loyal to the imperial state. The Incas also eliminated other *kurakas* whose loyalty was suspect. They created chieftainships among peoples where the institution had not existed earlier. They even combined the members of disparate groups, such as the Collaguas, and assigned leaders to them. They attempted to regularize succession by making the office hereditary; through gifts, marriage, and indoctrination, they sought the loyalty of *kurakas* and incorporated them into the emerging dominant class of the imperial state (Murra 1980:166; Netherly 1977:199–200, 309–310; Patterson 1985c, 1986; Pease 1982:188–189; Rowe 1982:110; Salomon 1986:205–212).

The Incas also employed subtle forms of intimidation and the threat of force to retain the loyalty and obedience of subject peoples. They took the sons of *kurakas*, especially those of large groups, to Cuzco where they were taught the Inca language and trained in the ways of the Inca state. This not only ensured the loyalty of their fathers but also provided the state with a steady flow of loyal, trained personnel for the lower echelons of the bureaucracy. The state also used local religious objects and practices as a means of social control. Once a group was incorporated into the state, the Incas took its most prized *wak'a* to Cuzco, where it was enshrined in the Temple of the Sun or placed in a shrine established and maintained by the subject people. These objects remained under the care of local priests who accompanied them to the imperial capital and performed the appropriate ceremonies when delegations of their kin came to Cuzco. The cult objects of the various subject populations were, in effect, hostages, treated with honor and respect by the Incas as long as those provincial peoples did not conspire against the state or revolt (Cobo 1956 vol. 2:167–168; Polo de Ondegardo 1916a, 1940: 183–184; Rowe 1982:95–96, 108–110).

Polities subordinated and incorporated into the imperial state were no longer able to reproduce pre-Incaic structures of social relations. They became, instead, ethnic groups that occupied particular places in the imperial division of labor and state organization. The state crystallized ethnicity and formed new collective identities that reified and distorted old cultural patterns to provide the illusion of the continuity of old institutions and practices in new contexts. The ethnic groups were territorially based and organized. Their vertical integration emphasized shared cultural features and the linkages between them and the emerging class structure of the imperial state.

Frank Salomon (1978a, 1978b, 1986:187–188, 212–218) has pointed out that, during the reigns of Pachakuti's successors, polities located closer to the center of the empire were more heavily influenced by the state than the less assimilated communities in the frontier areas. He suggests that the gradient reflects different stages in the process of encapsulation. During the early stage of contact, the imperial garrisons did what the local communities did; they acquired goods that moved along trade routes. After the polities were incorporated into the empire, the state demanded the same kind of prestations that their paramount chieftains received. At this point, the traditional economies of the polities were restructured to conform to the imperial model of "vertical archipelagos": closed, self-sufficient communities composed of spatially distinct, economically specialized populations linked together by reciprocity and redistribution (Murra 1972). The merchants that moved along the old established trade routes disappeared and were replaced by specialists from each community who produced different arrays of goods in the various island-like resource areas controlled by their kin. The state simultaneously eliminated the reliance of the encapsulated polities on outside communities and replaced it with a new dependency on the imperial state that had no mandate in local cultural traditions. The state created or preserved the authority of the *kurakas*; their rights and duties became identical to those imposed by the state apparatus in that district. With this change, the state could demand the same kinds of labor service that it demanded from communities and polities residing in other parts of the empire (Patterson 1987c:223).

There was nothing automatic or mechanical about the processes of encapsulation and incorporation that occurred on the margins of the imperial state. Communities confronted with the expanding Inca state resisted the process of expansion, successfully in some instances and not in others. The imperial frontier was porous – an area across which people, goods, and ideas moved back and forth between the more pacified border groups and the less assimilated ones beyond the imperial frontier. By permitting merchants to continue trafficking in the frontier areas, the state was able to acquire goods from peoples that were not under its control. The language and ideas of the empire marched in the vanguard of its troops. This strategy did not always work, because polities in the process of being assimilated retained strong cultural ties and alliances with their less encapsulated and subjugated neighbors. As a result, any Inca defeat in the marginally controlled areas was apt to roll backward as a wave of rebellions. When the frontier was not actively being pushed forward, the processes of cultural and economic transformation could not proceed in the recently secured areas behind the frontier (Murra 1978).

From the perspective of the communities being encapsulated and incorporated into the state, the state would have appeared in different forms at various stages in the process. During the initial phase of contact, its presence was confined to isolated garrisons and its contact with local peoples occurred at fixed places; however, the imperial state posed a threat during this stage. On the one hand, the local communities retained use-rights over their means of production and control over their labor and products. On the other, political authority may have come to reside more firmly in the hands of chieftains, who were able to appropriate increased control over the movement of goods produced outside the subsistence sector through activities associated with raiding and trade and through their enhanced abilities to create and cement alliances with other peoples. Their real control over exchange rested on the control they exerted over their subjects (Gailey and Patterson 1988).

Once exchange relations were established between the local groups and the imperial state, the merchants linked the growing authority and power of the local chieftains – which were based on control over the movement of the labor and products of their subjects – with the power of the imperial state. The autonomy of the local leaders diminished as their alliances with other communities declined and their reliance and dependence on the Inca state increased. The domination of the imperial state was virtually complete when the encapsulated communities became culturally distinct, self-sufficient enclaves within the imperial state. At that point, the merchants moved toward the frontier areas of the state where new opportunities were emerging. The autonomy of the pacified communities was diminished even further as their members began to participate in state-sponsored institutions and practices, such as rituals associated with agricultural production or providing women as *aclla*.

Irene Silverblatt's (1976, 1978, 1987:81–108) investigations of gender show how profoundly the state altered existing social relations when it consolidated imperial rule and attempted to assert control over the social and demographic reproduction of the communities and polities that were incorporated into the empire. When a new territory was incorporated into the empire, the state demanded that a Temple of the Sun be constructed and that *aclla* be selected and assigned to it. Each year, during the December Raymi festival, a state official selected chaste, prepubescent girls from every province of the empire; these *aclla* were sent to the provincial capitals where they lived in the company of women who were dedicated to the service of the state, spinning, weaving, and preparing food and beer. They were taught about the duties of women toward the state. They were maintained by the state and carefully guarded to ensure that they remained virgins. The most esteemed were sent to

Cuzco, while the rest remained in the various provincial capitals. Some were sacrificed; some became the wives of the Sun or were bestowed on other state cults; others, often the daughters of *kurakas*, became secondary wives of the Inca ruler himself; still others were given by the Incas as rewards to men – *kurakas*, officials, and soldiers – who demonstrated their loyalty to the state (Cobo 1956 vol. 2:231–232).

Silverblatt points out that the *aclla* were separated from the natal communities. Their labor, the goods they produced, and even the children some of them eventually bore no longer reverted automatically to these groups. Instead, their labor, their products, even their sexual behavior were controlled instead by the state. The state had removed these provincial girls from their homes and eliminated them as future wives and mothers in their own communities. By claiming the right to appropriate and redistribute *aclla*, the Inca ruler asserted his control, in principal if not in practice, over both the social and the demographic reproduction of the groups incorporated into the empire. The *aclla* were political pawns, emblems of the state's power to control the reproduction of the communities incorporated into the web of social relations it dominated. The ruler and the state used their power to give secondary wives to trusted and valued allies as means of forging a hierarchy of groups based on conquest and cementing political ties. The arranged marriages of the *aclla* functioned simultaneously as punishment, reward, and a symbol of dominance.

The Inca state and its ruling class attempted to control both production and social reproduction. They succeeded to an extent, since they were able to "impose a direction on social life" through coercion and the consent of subject peoples, or at least their acquiescence to the "the values, norms, perceptions, beliefs, sentiments, and prejudices that support and define the existing distribution of goods, the institutions that decide how this distribution occurs, and the permissible range of disagreement about those processes" (Lears 1985:568–569). However, consent was ambiguous at best, and there were often conflicts between the conscious thoughts of peoples and the values expressed in their actions. It was a mixture of "approbation and apathy, resistance and resignation," and the mix varied from one person to another and from one group to the next; some were clearly more accepting of imperial culture than others

(Lears 1985:570). As a result, the state was never completely successful in imposing its will, since the consent of the subjugated peoples was divided and ambiguous.

The religious institutions and practices constructed by the state were important loci of its attempts to impose its culture, and to regulate the production and reproduction of its subjects. John Rowe (1960b, 1982) has pointed out that a series of religious reforms, attributed to Pachakuti, were critical to the consolidation of state power. The reforms included the constitution of a state cult; the construction of sanctuaries for the state cult, and the installation of priests and chosen women in the various provincial capitals of the empire; the creation of state-sponsored rituals and pageants that were performed at regular intervals; and the elaboration of an imperial cosmology that incorporated different local traditions and provided a rational explanation for their diversity.

As soon as a province was incorporated into the empire, the state appropriated labor from the subject populations to build sanctuaries dedicated to the sun and lands to support the priests and women who served the cult (Cieza de León 1947:427; Polo de Ondegardo 1940:154). These Temples of the Sun flourished alongside shrines dedicated to other *wak'as*. Some cults were purely local, while others exerted influence over extensive areas. It was always possible for the subject peoples, as well as for the Incas, to celebrate more than one cult. The imperial cult was an attempt by the Incas and the state to acquire greater and more permanent power. It was a symbol of their dominance and their ability to manipulate local systems for their own purposes and for those of their allies.

The imperial cult was dedicated to the Sun, the ancestor of the Incas and the protector of crops. The myths and practices associated with the state cult prescribed proper behavior, perpetuated socially acceptable explanations, and maintained cohesion and order by asserting the power of ancestors and supernatural beings. Perhaps the cult's most important feature was its annually self-correcting calendar – regulated by the Moon, the wife of the Sun – which established and prescribed the tempo and frequency of various rituals, pageants, and activities. These gave voice to the state's efforts to control production and reproduction; they served as regular reminders of its dominance. The calendar specified when certain kinds of productive work would be carried out, when various gifts would be given to the state, when subject peoples should assent or at least acquiesce to imperial domination, when the census would be taken and taxes assessed, when labor due the state would be performed, when provincial girls and men would be removed forever from their natal communities to serve the state, and even when men and women of the subject communities could marry (Anonymous 1962; Molina 1943; Murúa 1946).

Another important feature of the religious reforms initiated by Pachakuti was the construction of an imperial cosmology. According to this scheme, Teqzi Wiraqochan, the Creator, made the world in total darkness. After a while, he continued his project, creating the sun, the moon, and the stars so he could finish his work in the light. He then modeled people in clay, designing their hair styles and clothing; he gave them life, telling them to go underground and then to emerge in the places where they would live. His assistants went out to teach them how to conduct their lives (Rowe 1960b: 409–410; Sullivan 1985:101–102).

This scheme incorporated various local traditions and provided a rational explanation for their diversity and for everyday experience. John Rowe (1960b) has argued that the content of the imperial cosmology devised by Pachakuti was updated from one reign to the next, continually transformed to deal with new circumstances. While Rowe has emphasized Pachakuti's creativity in organizing the imperial state, Max Weber or Karl Mannheim might have referred to the cosmology he devised in terms of rationality – the quest for orderliness, logical explanation, and calculability. In their view, rationality involved both the creation of knowledge as well as its control. Pachakuti's cosmology was a self-serving guide for structuring social relations and actions at the expense of emotion or traditional views and forms of everyday life. The imperial cosmology had an ambiguity that allowed it to be superimposed on local traditions and to suppress or restrain their significance (Patterson 1991; Poggi 1983:90).

The novelty of Pachakuti's rationality, like that of Aristotle or Confucius, was that its content was attuned to the structural transformations that were taking place in the relations of production – changes that demanded explanation couched in terms of a new world view. His cosmology encapsulated other origin myths; it accounted for their ambiguities – the discrepancies that existed within and between the various local traditions – and diminished their importance. It reduced the richness and diversity of alternative accounts by limiting or diminishing the ways they could be interpreted in different situations. At the same time, the imperial cosmology provided a rational account of the new patterns of social relations that were crystallizing; it invoked divine or supernatural intervention to explain the emerging relationships between peoples and the new state-imposed relationships between a people and the means of production.

Cosmologies or world views emphasizing rationality seem to be symptomatic of an early phase of the process of social transformation. They are not necessarily typical of the transitional phase itself, which is characterized by instability and by the absence of dominant social relations. They seem to be associated with a second phase, the one that immediately follows the instability of the transition, when there is a lack of conformity or correspondence between the new relations of production and the productive forces, when fundamental contradictions involving forms of property and real modes of appropriation still remain. In these circumstances, the continued dominance of the new ruling class is ensured by mediations that attempt to reconcile or explain differences. Pachakuti's new cosmology, with its emphasis on rationality, was one aspect of these mediations – an aspect that was linked to and backed up by other institutions, rituals, and practices, as well as the threat of force (Bettelheim 1975:12–30; Thomson 1961:171–172).

Pachakuti's religious reforms prevented or severely limited the ability of Wiraqocha's *panaqa* to accumulate further wealth. Coricancha, the Temple of the Sun in Cuzco, became the focus of the state religious cult, while a shrine at Urcos – dedicated to a *wak'a* called Teqzi Wiraqocha, which had been supported earlier by the members of Wiraqocha's corporation – was relegated to a less important position. As a result, both the shrine and Wiraqocha's descendants were unable to acquire additional lands and servants in the newly conquered areas of the empire (Earls 1976:218–223; Lehmann-Nitsche 1928; Rowe 1960b:418–423; Zuidema 1964:166–168). The emperor had effectively, if only temporarily, curbed the power of his collateral relatives.

3.2. Conquest, Succession, and the Changing Composition of the Imperial Ruling Class

One of the peculiarities of Inca social structure was that no emperor could inherit the property of his predecessor. The throne passed to one of his sons, all of whom, at least theoretically, had the same rights and could aspire equally to the royal tassel (Rostworowski de Diez Canseco 1960). The remainder of the property passed to his other descendants, who formed a *panaqa* to support themselves and the mummy bundle of the founder and to maintain a cult in his honor (Rowe 1967:60–61, 67–68). Upon ascending to the throne, the new ruler had to establish his own corporation by securing land and servants to support his wives and their children. The early Inca rulers only had estates in Cuzco and its environs, while Pachakuti and his successors had lands not only around the capital but also in the provincial areas of the empire.

The royal corporations wielded considerable power. The men held important positions in the state apparatus; they were generals, administrators of the highest ranks, and influential priests in the state cult. The women were sometimes priestesses in the cult of the Moon, often the wives of the ruler and, hence, the mothers of potential heirs to the throne. The potential for conflict among the royal corporations was heightened during the interregnum periods, when rivals with mothers from different *panaqas* were pitted against one another. These were usually times of crisis, and civil war within the ruling class was always a very real possibility. Women played crucial role in struggles over succession; they held alliances together. Since they were the mothers of rulers as well as their wives, women's relationships with the emperor could increase the power, wealth, and prestige of their own kinsmen. This, in turn, enhanced their position among their kin, especially when they were not noblewomen or even Incas. These relationships also provided the ruler or claimant to the throne with reasonably trustworthy allies.

In order to avoid strife and conflict, Pachakuti designated his successor to the throne. He selected a son born by Mama Anahuarque, a woman from Choco, as his heir. However, after a few years, he changed his mind and nominated Topa 'Inka, the younger son of Mama Anahuarque and the brother of his initial choice. Topa 'Inka reigned for a while with his father before ascending to the throne about 1471 and founding his own corporation, the Qhapaq *panaqa*. During that period, he conquered much of the northern quarter of the empire, extending the frontiers into southern Ecuador and incorporating most of the coastal peoples of Peru into the imperial state. However, relations between Topa 'Inka and his father apparently deteriorated, as Pachakuti became concerned over the exploits of his son. He appointed two of his brothers from Zukzu *panaqa*, Wiraqocha's corporation, to inspect conditions in the lands incorporated into the empire by his son. Later, royal counselors prevented the son of Topa 'Inka's favorite concubine, a Guayro woman, from assuming control of lands north of Lake Titicaca, an area incorporated into the empire when Pachakuti ruled. Topa 'Inka also killed an inspector for fomenting a rebellion among his servants; the man was his brother and, hence, a member of Iñaqa, the corporation established by Pachakuti (Cobo 1956 vol. 2:86–88; Rowe 1945:270; Sarmiento de Gamboa 1960:249–256).

There were two ways that Inca rulers could acquire the lands and servants they needed to support their descendants. The first was to conquer new provinces and incorporate their residents into the imperial state. This required the leader to forge alliances with his collateral kin as well as with at least some of the peoples in the new provinces. The other way Inca rulers could gain wealth, power, and prestige was to take over the care and maintenance of a *wak'a* in order to ensure that the appropriate ceremonies were performed. Pachakuti, who initiated the wars of conquest and who consequently had one of the wealthiest corporations, created nearly a dozen new shrines in the Cuzco area, rebuilt the Temple of the Sun, and organized the entire system of state shrines. There was a close relationship between Pachakuti and the state-sponsored Sun cult. However, the emperor, the Son of the Sun as he was sometimes called, was not the principal spokesman of the state cult. Instead, the top of the imperial religious hierarchy was occupied by a royal kinsman, a collateral relative of the emperor who belonged to a different *panaqa* (Murra 1980:161).

Topa 'Inka seems to have had a very different relationship than that of his father with the *wak'as* of Cuzco and with at least some of the shrines in *chinchaysuyu* – the northern quarter of the empire, which was largely incorporated into the imperial state under his leadership or rule. He apparently neither created nor maintained new *wak'as* in the Cuzco area as his father, his brother, and his son who followed him on the throne had done (Rowe 1979a:10). He was very critical and demanding of the *wak'as* and held them in strict account for what happened (Huaman Poma de Ayala 1936:261; Pachakuti Yamqui 1927:189–190). According to one story, after much fighting in which he could not defeat his enemies, Topa 'Inka called together all of the *wak'as* he had served and given gold, silver, and cloth and asked for their help. When none responded, he became furious and threatened to burn all of their possessions. Finally, one of them – Macahuisa, the son of Pariacaca, a famous *wak'a* in the mountains of Huarochirí – vowed to help the Inca ruler. After the *wak'a* helped him destroy the enemy, Topa 'Inka revered Pariacaca even more, giving him fifty servants, and asked what more he could offer the shrine (Avila 1966:131–135). He established an alliance with a cult that did not have close ties with his father's corporation.

Topa 'Inka developed an especially close relationship with one *wak'a* in *chinchaysuyu* – Pachacamac, which was located in the land of the Ichma. The chroniclers suggest two reasons for this development. One is that the Inca leader, who was attacking the Chimu armies from the north and east, made an alliance with the Ichma, an enemy of the Chanchan rulers, that lived on the southern edge of the Kingdom of Chimor. This was a seasoned Inca battle tactic (Calancha 1638:549–551; Cieza de León 1967:194–197; Bram 1941). The Incas and the Ichma saw themselves as allies fighting a common enemy. After Chimor was defeated, the two remained allies. Topa 'Inka forged an alliance with this frontier kingdom and incorporated it into the imperial state. A provincial capital was established at Pachacamac, and a shrine dedicated to the state-sponsored sun cult was built near the temple dedicated to Pachacamac (Cieza de León 1967:195–196; Strong and Corbett 1943; Uhle 1903).

The other reason concerns the political intrigues of the royal corporations, their noble kinsmen, and their neighbors in Cuzco. This close relationship with the Pachacamac *wak'a* allowed the ruler to distance himself from his collateral kin and to reduce his dependency on them. It also focused attention on the role women played in these intrigues and how they conspired to maintain and assert the interests of sons and kin. One account indicates that Topa 'Inka's mother – Mama Anahuarque, who was from Choco and thus not a member of a *panaqa* – had a revelation while she was pregnant with her son, the future ruler (Cobo 1956 vol. 2:77; Cabello Valboa 1951:303; Santillan 1927:29–31; Sarmiento de Gamboa 1960:238–239). She learned that the oracle, Pachacamac, was the creator of the world. After Topa 'Inka was born, Mama Anahuarque told him about the vision. Later, he was determined to seek out this *wak'a*. He and his retinue spent many days at Pachacamac. They sacrificed llamas and burned many shirts to thank the oracle for his assistance. After fasting for forty days, Topa 'Inka finally spoke with the oracle and asked him what else he could offer. The oracle responded that the Incas could build him a house – in other words, enlarge the Temple of Pachacamac. The oracle also told the Inca leader that he had four sons and that the Incas should also build houses for them.

The sons of Pachacamac were branch oracles. Building shrines for them outside the lands of the Ichma permitted the caretakers of the principal shrine to extend their influence into other areas and to appropriate labor and goods from their inhabitants. The oracle specifically requested that the Inca leader build a house for one son in Mala and another in Chincha. These were coastal valleys south of Ichma, and, at the time the branch oracles were established, neither had been conquered or incorporated into the imperial state (Santillan 1927:29–31; Menzel 1959; Menzel and Rowe 1966). The third son had a house built in the mountains, either at Andahuaylas near the oracle of Apurimac or at Andahuaylillas near the shrine dedicated to Teqzi Wiraqocha, a cult supported by Wiraqocha's corporation. The fourth branch oracle traveled with Topa 'Inka to protect him and to answer any questions he might have.

These were not the only kin of Pachacamac – branch oracles – that had houses outside of Ichma. Pachacamac had wives in Chincha and Mamaq, sons in Huarochirí, and a house near Chanchan, the capital of Chimor (Albornoz 1967:33–35; Dávila Brizeño 1965:163; Avila 1966:113–119; Netherly 1977:32l). One account relates how these branch oracles were established and how they operated in areas that had already been incorporated into the imperial state (Avila 1966:113–119). According to this story, a woman from Huarochirí found an object in a field.

Thinking it might be important, she took it home and showed it to her parents and neighbors. The object identified itself as the son of Pachacamac, and said his father had sent him to protect the people of Huarochirí. They built a shrine and set aside one month each year when they honored him with sacrifices and gifts. After many years, the branch oracle disappeared, and the people were saddened. They went to Pachacamac with gifts of llamas, guinea pigs, and fine cloth and begged him to have his son return to their community. Pachacamac consented and the branch oracle returned. While the people may have been elated with the outcome, the level of tribute extraction had increased. From that moment, the community made sacrifices and gave gifts to the branch oracle on one day and to Pachacamac on the next.

This account is a description of how the caretakers of the principal shrine at Pachacamac and one of the branch oracles began to appropriate the surplus labor and product of others. A kin group from Huarochirí built a shrine dedicated to Pachacamac's son and assumed responsibility for its maintenance and for the performance of the appropriate ceremonies. This action enhanced the prestige of the group, because its members were associating themselves with a *wak'a* whose fortunes were rising as new conditions began to materialize. Some of the surplus labor and gifts they received were undoubtedly used to maintain the local shrine and its staff; another portion was sent to the main temple in the provincial capital on the coast.

Archaeological investigations of the branch oracle at Mamaq indicate that the shrine was controlled and used primarily by local peoples (Patterson 1985a; Spalding 1984:99–102). The presence of a fragments from a few fancy coastal vessels suggests some connection with the Temple of Pachacamac. The absence of Inca pottery vessels or locally made versions of Inca pottery suggests that the branch oracle was not closely tied to the Inca state apparatus. It further indicates that Pachacamac and the Incas were not seen as being closely linked in this province. A different situation prevailed in Chincha, which had a special position in the imperial state; branch oracles were located there and the cult of Pachacamac held lands (Cieza de León 1947:423–424; Menzel and Rowe 1966:88; Rostworowski de Diez Canseco 1977:177, 1980:167–168). Pottery associations found in tombs at La Centinela, the local and Inca administrative center, indicate that the Incas, the Chincha *kurakas*, and Pachacamac had strong ties with one another.

It appears that the caretakers of Pachacamac and the Incas maintained close relations in those areas beyond the imperial frontiers when the branch oracles were established in them. They were less closely identified with each other in those regions of the empire where the branch oracles were established after the local populations had already submitted to imperial rule. At Pachacamac, which was the site of the principal oracle as well as a provincial capital, the connections were not especially close. Objects made to imperial specifications are common around the structures housing the state apparatus; they are not common at the Temple of Pachacamac or in the walled compounds near it.

When the Spaniards arrived, Pachacamac's influence was greatest in the northern and central portions of the empire – the areas subjugated by their ally, Topa 'Inka. The oracle was worshiped by coastal peoples from Huaura to Arica, and origin myths that depicted him as the creator of the world were known as far north as Piura (Calancha 1638:92, 234–236, 407–410). Pilgrims bearing gifts of gold, silver, and cloth journeyed distances of three hundred leagues to consult the oracle at his principal shrine. Traditional leaders from polities located in Mala, Hoar, Gualco, Chincha, Guarva, Colixa, Sallicaimarca, and elsewhere brought gifts of gold and silver to Pachacamac after the Spaniards arrived (Estete 1947:339–340).

The relationship Topa 'Inka established with Pachacamac marked the appearance of a significant new feature in Inca politics. He used the alliances he established with shrines and polities located outside of Cuzco and in the provinces he brought into the imperial state in his ongoing struggle with his collateral relatives. By forging alliances with shrines and polities in the northern quarter of the empire, he was transforming the traditional Inca social hierarchy, defined largely in terms of descent and ethnicity, into social classes. New people, often the traditional leaders of subject or client groups, but occasionally individuals who gained prominence by virtue of their loyalty to the Inca ruler, were incorporated into the ruling class. This potentially diminished the power of his collateral kin in the other royal corporations; it enhanced the ruler's ability, as well as the capacity of his allies, to extract surplus from the Andean peoples. The interests of his allies became linked with those of Topa 'Inka's corporation.

These linkages suggest that the imperial political system was not a stable, fixed structure constructed from the top down by builders following the plan of a distant architect. The state apparatus was like a growth that developed from the continually changing relationships among different groups within Inca society and from shifts in the alliances and rivalries between the members of other Andean polities. It was the product of agreements that were continually tested and modified to bring them into accord with existing conditions and practices.

The alliances forged with shrines and friendly kings – such as the ruler of Chincha – in the border areas of the empire were beneficial to both Topa 'Inka and his allies. They provided the Inca ruler with trustworthy allies that counterbalanced or undermined the power of his collateral relatives, and they provided the allies with a degree of economic, political, and ideological autonomy that was supported – or at least not contested – by the imperial state. For instance, Pachacamac was able to collect tribute from peoples living beyond the imperial frontier in Ecuador, and merchants from Chincha (which was wealthy and occupied a special place in the state) traveled to distant places and traded without the direct control of Incas (Patterson 1987c; Rostworowski de Diez Canseco 1970). These alliances effectively precluded the formation of an imperial state in which all power emanated from the Inca ruling elite, since they created conditions for the formation of an imperial ruling class that included both Inca and non-Inca individuals.

Topa 'Inka died unexpectedly; he may, in fact, have been murdered by members of Iñaqa, his father's corporation, who disagreed with his choice of a successor. His death provoked an open struggle. Originally, he had followed the example of his father and designated as his successor the young prince Wayna Qhapaq – the son of his sister and principal wife, who came from Pachakuti's corporation, and the favorite grandson of the old emperor himself. However, shortly before his death, Topa 'Inka changed his mind and named the son of his favorite concubine, Chiqui Ocllo, as his heir. Chiqui Ocllo plotted with her kin to put her son, Qhapaq Wari, on the throne; however, their plans were soon discovered by Wayna Qhapaq's supporters in Pachakuti's corporation. The leader of the Iñaqa faction that rallied behind Wayna Qhapaq was Waman 'Achachi – the brother of the deceased emperor and his wife and the governor of the northern quarter of the empire. After the attempted usurpation was suppressed, Chiqui Ocllo was executed as a witch and rebel and her son was banished to Chinchero, where he spent the rest of his life (Cobo 1956 vol. 2:88–93; Cabello Valboa 1951:357–361; Sarmiento de Gamboa 1960: 258–259).

The young prince, Wayna Qhapaq, followed the advice of his mother and her relatives. Because of his age, a regent was named to tutor him in the ways of government until he was old enough to rule on his own. The regent was Walpaya – a provincial governor, the son of Pachakuti's brother, and a member of the corporation founded by Wiraqocha. Walpaya's father was Qhapaq Yupanki, who had been executed by the old emperor after he captured Cajamarca. Secretly, Walpaya conspired with his own kin and allies to usurp the crown for himself or for one of his sons. Weapons were smuggled into Cuzco, and plans were made to assassinate the prince. However, the conspiracy was exposed. Waman 'Achachi seized Walpaya and the other conspirators and executed them (Cobo 1956 vol. 2:88–93; Sarmiento de Gamboa 1960:259–260).

Wayna Qhapaq assumed the throne in 1493 at the time of his mother's death. After the funeral, he married his sister, formed the Tumipampa corporation, and assumed control of the government. This involved taking charge of the state cult and assuming the title Shepherd of the Sun; it also entailed purging certain provincial wak'as and diminishing the influence of others (Huaman Poma de Ayala 1936:113; Sarmiento de Gamboa 1960:259–260). As the new king toured the empire, he dismissed governors and punished kurakas who had rebelled against the state (Cobo 1956 vol. 2:88–93). He built forts along the frontiers and oversaw the construction of a "new Cuzco" in Tumipampa, much as his father had done earlier in Cañete (Cieza de León 1947:423, 1967:201; Hyslop 1985). He spent much of his time in Ecuador where he had been born, administering the empire, conquering new territories, and suppressing revolts (Murra 1978).

The new king also appropriated lands in the provinces conquered by his father, creating estates for his corporation, seizing lands for the state, and granting fields to his mother, his sons, and other individuals who were loyal (Rostworowski de Diez Canseco 1977:177). He also seized the traditional lands of polities in the Cochabamba Valley of Bolivia and replaced the indigenous inhabitants with outsiders (members of other ethnic groups) who were permanently resettled there or who worked for given periods of time on the newly acquired state lands (Wachtel 1982:213, 216–218). The crops grown on these lands were used to support an increasingly professionalized army, whose members were full-time soldiers recruited from communities and polities in the north that had recently been incorporated into the state (Murra 1980:158–159, 174; Wachtel 1982:218).

The new ways that Wayna Qhapaq devised to raise revenue represented a departure from the procedures established by his predecessors. They involved the state management of lands seized from conquered polities, the beginnings of private landholdings, and the emergence of conditions of personal servitude to the state (Murra 1980:153–190). The new forms of extracting surplus expanded the role of the state apparatus to include the supervision of production on state-controlled lands. They also created an emerging class of full-time retainers, separated from their natal communities and dependent on the state for ensuring the conditions for their reproduction. While grants of land and servants to individual *kurakas*, the leaders of ethnic groups, or the secondary wives of the emperor may have insulated them from the traditional claims of their kin, these grants obligated them to the emperor, creating ties of dependence similar to those found in feudal or tributary social formations (Espinoza Soriano 1976:254, 259, 262). These grants also may have diminished or removed the obligations of the direct producers toward their traditional leaders. By purging shrines, removing and replacing officials and *kurakas* whose loyalty was suspect, and granting lands to the leaders of the polities in the northern quarter of the empire, Wayna Qhapaq was apparently trying to weaken the alliances made by his father without diminishing the strength of the state. At the same time, he was attempting to consolidate or strengthen his own position. This opened up the possibility for a new balance of forces between disparate factions of an imperial ruling class that was in the process of consolidation.

Wayna Qhapaq died suddenly and unexpectedly about 1525. His death sparked another crisis over succession. His principal wife, who came from Qhapaq *panaqa*, had no sons; however, a number of his secondary wives had born sons, and there were several potential candidates for the throne. The most prominent were Ninan Kuyuchi, 'Ataw Wallpa – whose mother was from Iñaqa – and Washkar – whose mother belonged to Qhapaq. From his deathbed, Wayna Qhapaq designated Ninan Kuyuchi as his heir; however, Ninan Kuyuchi died shortly after his father. Washkar was named to succeed his father in a somewhat unorthodox manner; the priest of the Sun cult, who apparently belonged to the Iñaqa corporation, followed the emperor's wishes and did not perform the required rituals to determine the suitability of the successor. Two members of the Iñaqa corporation accompanied Washkar's mother and the body of the dead ruler as they journeyed to Cuzco to enshrine his body and to inform Washkar that he was the new ruler.

Washkar was furious that 'Ataw Wallpa, his rival, was left in the north with the army, wives, and insignias of the dead emperor. He killed the two members of Iñaqa who arrived with his mother; this infuriated the members of that corporation, and they allied themselves almost immediately with 'Ataw Wallpa, whose mother was one of them. Washkar then sent a messenger from Qhapaq *panaqa* to the north, demanding the immediate return of their father's wives and insignias. When the messenger seized them, 'Ataw Wallpa killed him; this antagonized Washkar and the members of the Qhapaq corporation. This insult also completed the breach between the two rivals, and a civil war ensued with 'Ataw Wallpa being supported by his Iñaqa kin and Washkar being supported by his kin in the Qhapaq corporation and by Pachacamac, the powerful *wak'a* on the central Peruvian coast. Washkar then offended the other *panaqa* by threatening to seize their lands in Cuzco, and they aligned themselves with 'Ataw Wallpa's faction.

At this point, Washkar controlled the southern part of the empire, while 'Ataw Wallpa controlled Ecuador and the northern parts of Peru. Washkar captured his brother in a battle at Tumipampas; however, 'Ataw Wallpa escaped and rallied his forces. He drove his brother out of the Tumipampas area and devastated the fields of the Cañari for supporting his rival. 'Ataw Wallpa's armies moved southward and captured Washkar in a battle near Cuzco in April, 1532. 'Ataw Wallpa then sought to destroy the shrine and the mummy bundle of Topa

'Inka, which was venerated by the members of Qhapaq. He killed the spokesman of the shrine, the members of the Qhapaq corporation, and Washkar's children, pregnant wives, and servants. Washkar and his mother were forced to witness the executions. Shortly afterwards, the Spaniards captured and imprisoned 'Ataw Wallpa at Cajamarca; however, his power was scarcely diminished, and he ordered the execution of Washkar from his prison cell.

During the civil war between Washkar and 'Ataw Wallpa, both granted lands and servants to individual children (Salomon 1978b). Washkar is alleged to have sired eighty children during an eight-year period (Murra 1984:69), which provides some indication of the amount of land and labor appropriated by the two rivals. In other words, both were behaving in the manner of their father; both granted lands and servants to their relatives and to individuals to reward and promote loyalty, which would presumably ensure the conditions required for the reproduction of the class.

The new forms of exploitation that emerged as a result of class formation and the reconstitution of the imperial ruling class initially emphasized control of local shrines and alliances with their spokesmen. Later, the politically dominant elements emphasized the creation of traditional leaders, the replacement of *kurakas* whose loyalty was suspect with allies, and the formation of alliances with powerful shrines in the newly conquered areas of the state. Land was then appropriated not only for the use of the Inca ruling class, but for gifts to be given to individuals who supported the state and its dominant class. The alliances forged across ethnic boundaries and the gifts presented to non-Inca shrines and individuals crosscut traditional social categories and created the conditions for further changes in the composition of the imperial ruling class.

The development of the empire involved the successive recombination of old institutions and practices, which were transformed and given new meanings in the emerging social contexts created by imperial expansion, succession to the throne, and revolts in provincial areas. Old institutions – like the *mit'a* labor obligations of individuals to their community, or the class structures of Andean society based on complexly interrelated hierarchies of landholding corporations, chiefly peoples and commoners, and ruling and subordinate classes – were reworked. Labor was no longer appropriated only by the community; the state, its rulers, and their allies also had access to the labor power of direct producers. The alliances created, maintained, and broken by different factions of the Inca ruling class with non-Inca groups, shrines, and individuals created new conditions for the real appropriation of surplus and for undermining traditional Andean social structures. The transformations engendered by the imperial state involved archaism: deliberate attempts to promote illusions about the continuity of old institutions and practices in a new, historically specific, social context.

The imperial state created and maintained political alliances by continually reworking an unstable class structure, transforming the meaning of traditional institutions and practices. While the alliances clearly involved grants of land and servants and permission to extract surplus from core areas of the state, they also involved continual attempts to transform the culture – the art, language, mythology, and rituals – of both allied and opposing groups in order to link their interests with those of the state. The state constituted and attempted to impose new practices that furthered its ability to organize and control the productive and reproductive capacities of subject peoples. The state was held together by the activities of peoples in various institutions, polities, and communities who were part of the dominant coalition, and who created, shared, and maintained the ideology of the state. Crises developed within the dominant coalition of the ruling class as the state expanded and redefined, and increasingly restrictive class relations began to emerge. The alliances between groups within the dominant coalition were often fragile, especially at times of succession or when the rates of extortion were too high and the subjugated peoples rebelled against the imperial state and its rulers.

Chapter 4

Quiescence, Resistance, and Rebellion

> It is doubtful if very many governments in human history have been considered "legitimate" by the majority of those exploited, oppressed, and maltreated by their governments. . . .[G]overnments tend to be endured, not appreciated or admired or loved or even supported. (Immanuel Wallerstein, *The Modern World System*)

Land and human labor power were the two main sources of wealth in the central Andes, both before and after the Inca conquest. In many areas, agricultural land was owned by kin-based communities, even though it was held by individual households. While there was continuity in family holdings, there were also periodic reallotments of agricultural land to bring its distribution into accord with the changing needs of the various constituent households. Llama and alpaca herds were also owned by the communities and pastured in grazing lands they owned, controlled, shared, or contested with other, similar groups. The animals were sheared for their wool, sacrificed, and occasionally eaten; llamas, the larger of the two camelid species, also served as beasts of burden (Murra 1980:29–30, 51).

Labor-intensive tasks – like agriculture, housebuilding, or the construction and repair of irrigation systems – were carried out by the community as a whole. The beneficiaries of these efforts were "expected to furnish the seeds or cuttings, to feed the workers and to provide them with maize beer" (Murra 1980: 30–31). There were technical divisions of labor that reflected age and gender differences: for example, teenagers typically watched over herds pastured in the *puna*, the high alpine grasslands; men plowed; and women planted seeds, spun thread, and made beer (Murra 1980:50; Rowe 1958:512–513). There was also some degree of craft specialization, as certain households or *ayllus* (kindreds) were renowned as silversmiths, potters, or dancers (Avila 1966; Spalding 1984:86). In many instances, they seem to have practiced their particular skills on a part-time or seasonal basis – after planting or harvesting, before the rainy season in the case of potters, or when dancers were required for ceremonies or other special occasions. Their artisan activities were grafted onto food production; the goods they produced or the services they performed benefited the entire community.

While traditional land tenure practices undoubtedly continued after local communities were encapsulated and incorporated into the imperial state, the Incas immediately imposed liens on the various sources of their wealth. The state expropriated portions of the producers' agricultural fields, pastures, unworked lands, and herds belonging to the communities. These were set aside for the benefit of the state, the imperial sun cult, and the royal corporations (Murra 1980:37, 52, 54).

The Incas also appropriated labor power from the conquered communities. Their demands took several distinct forms, each of which had its own implications for the encapsulated groups. First, the community members were required to cultivate the fields and tend the herds expropriated by the state for itself and the imperial cult. They planted, cared for, and harvested these fields before they worked on their own lands. The produce from these fields and the wool from these herds were destined for separate storehouses in the provincial capital (Murra 1980:54; Rowe 1946:265–267).

Second, the state also demanded other forms of labor service, collectively called the *mit'a* obligation. The needs of the state were both varied and extensive: building and repairing roads, maintaining rest stops, serving in the army, mining, and guarding fields are only a few of the tasks mentioned. Each year, the state requested labor time at one of its monthly feasts. After being feted and honored, the *kurakas*, the local chieftains, returned to their communities, ladened with gifts and tasks to perform. The immediate goal of the chieftains, once they arrived in their villages, was to persuade, cajole, or beg the members of the community for their assistance. Once they consented, the lord assigned the chores equitably across the communities to ensure that enough members in each group remained at home to tend its fields and flocks. When their labor obligation was completed, the workers returned to their homes. When the next call for *mit'a* labor was issued by the state, they were exempt; they were replaced by another group of workers, since the burden shifted or rotated each year through the community. Since some communities were composed of artisans, like miners or silverworkers, the state undoubtedly drew repeatedly on their labor resources to perform certain specialized tasks (Murra 1982; Rowe 1946:267–269; Spalding 1984:86).

The third category consisted of colonists, *mitmaq* or *mitimaes*, who were resettled with their families and leaders in provinces that were scarcely populated, recently incorporated into the empire, or whose inhabitants had rebelled against the state. The colonists were under the authority of the provincial officials in the new location. They were required to retain their own garb and customs; to provide the implements, seeds, and other goods they needed for their livelihood; and to defend frontiers and pacify rebel areas. The resettlement policies of the state were extensive. In some provinces, the colonists apparently outnumbered the original inhabitants, many of whom had been resettled among peoples whose loyalty to the state was not suspect (Rostworowski de Diez Canseco 1988b:221–224; Rowe 1946:269–270, 1982:105–107). The lands settled by the *mitimaes* and the fields they planted had been confiscated by the state from peoples who either resisted its attempts to impose its will or rebelled against its domination (Murra 1980:38). They were detached from their kin and separated from their traditional means of production. Their capacity to produce a livelihood in their new homes was intimately linked with the continued generosity and intervention of the imperial state.

Finally, the state permanently removed certain categories of individuals from their natal communities, thereby depriving the groups of their productive and reproductive capacities. These were the *aclla*, chosen women, and *yana*, retainers. The former were the prepubescent girls selected each year by state officials, who were sequestered in the provincial capitals (Rowe 1946:269, 1982:97–105, 107–108; Silverblatt 1978; 1987:80–108). The latter, described by one chronicler as rebels left out of the census who were spared from death by the queen, worked on royal estates, in the households of local chieftains, and in the shrines of the state cult and other important *wak'as*. They apparently served the rulers, their wives, and families in various capacities that even included chieftainships in Chachapoyas and Collique (Murra 1966; Rostworowski de Diez Canseco 1988b:196–197, 224–226; Sarmiento de Gamboa 1960:256). The practice of removing *aclla* and *yana* from their communities gave the state a measure of control over the demographic and social reproduction of their natal communities. The autonomy of the communities and their ability to control their own destinies were diminished, as their fortunes became inextricably intertwined with those of the state.

The thrust of Inca imperial expansion was to drain the encapsulated communities and polities of their means of production and to obscure the fact that the social relations of production and reproduction were being dramatically transformed in the process. While the Inca state attempted to intervene in the everyday lives of their members to ensure compliance with its demands, its capacity to do so effectively and successfully was hampered in significant ways by the virtual impossibility of rapid communication over the long distances separating the imperial capital from the provincial centers. This capacity was also limited by the political structures the state put together in the provincial areas. Although the governors were close allies and kinsmen of the ruler and members of the dominant class, the layers of provincial administration immediately below them built on the existing local social and political hierarchies, incorporating them into the decimal organization of the state.

The position of the local chieftains, the *kurakas*, in these rapidly erected administrative and social structures was fraught with conflict. On the one hand, there were opportunities for both the chieftains and the communities they represented to benefit materially by supporting the Inca state. On the other hand, the *kurakas* simultaneously represented the interests of their subjects and served as provincial representatives of the state, conveying its requests for labor service to their subjects. Their ability to meet the demands of the state were only as good as their ability to persuade their subjects to provide labor service. To be persuasive, they had to be generous and hospitable. Their requests could not exceed those customarily expected by their subjects and kin. Chieftains whose demands were unreasonable or excessive risked being deposed or murdered by their subjects (Netherly 1977:178–183). Ultimately, the state's claims were backed up by the threat of judicial or military force. The failure of a *kuraka* to respond to the state's request for labor service was a serious matter. It was the first step toward open rebellion, and he could lose his position or even his life (Moore 1958:66–72, 81–82; Murra 1961; Spalding 1984:82–83).

The state sought to retain the loyalty of the *kurakas* and to influence their actions in various ways. It held one lord hostage under the pretext that he fomented a rebellion; he was ultimately replaced by his son, who was loyal to the Incas (Cabello Valboa 1951:330–331). The Inca ruler married the daughters of local chieftains incorporated into the state apparatus of the empire, and accepted these secondary wives into his household (Betanzos 1924:148–153; Cieza de León 1967:109, 201; Cabello Valboa 1951:315). The sons of local chieftains and rulers, especially those responsible for large numbers of people, were taken to Cuzco, where they learned Quechua, Inca traditions, and the behavior expected from a loyal official of the state and a member of the emerging dominant class (Rowe 1982:95–96). High-ranking *kurakas* were forced to maintain a residence in the imperial capital and live there four months each year; this also involved resettling retainers or subjects to act as servants (Rowe 1967:62). The Incas brought provincial *wak'as* to Cuzco for long stays (Cobo 1956 vol. 2:109–111; Spalding 1984:94–95). The presence of the provincial *wak'as* and the sons and heirs of the ethnic lords in Cuzco "made both past and future leaders of their communities hostages to the good behavior of their people, despite the honors with which both wak'as and young people were loaded" (Spalding 1984:95). Gifts of land and servants from the state also ensured the continued loyalty of *kurakas*, shrines, and communities that promoted its well-being (Avila 1966:109–111, 114–119, 131–135; Dávila Brizeño 1965; Rowe 1946: 260–261).

The Inca state demanded obedience from its subjects and employed various institutions and practices to ensure that it received their compliance and submission: the army, loyal *mitima* colonists, and a group of inspectors or overseers called *tokoyrikoq*, a term that can be translated as "those who see all" (Rowe 1946:264). They were sent to the provinces to check local conditions, to ensure that tax obligations were being met, and to determine that rebellions were not being fomented by dissatisfied chieftains or provincial governors. The *tokoyrikoq* were "faithful men whom the Inca could trust"; they may have been members of a royal corporation or personal retainers of the emperor, possibly even *yana* raised in the royal household (Cieza de León 1967:42–44; Goncalez Holguin 1952:38; Murúa 1946:206).

The legal code of the state was repressive, especially toward the lower classes – the members of encapsulated communities. Acquiescence rather than agreement was the desired goal. It attempted to achieve compliance through intimidation and the fear of retaliation for crimes against the state and its ruling class. The penalties were severe. For instance, the penalty for failing to perform work satisfactorily, lying to a census-taker, moving the boundary markers delimiting state fields, traveling without permission, or not wearing clothing that allowed officials to identify an individual's natal community involved corporal punishment; the guilty were beaten with a stone or flogged. Individuals who failed to meet their labor obligations to the state were not only tortured for the first offense but also had their labor assessments increased; those who committed this offense a second time were threatened with execution. Foot-dragging, misrepresentation, deception, false compliance, evasion, desertion, traveling without permission, pilfering, and sabotage – what James Scott (1985:xvi) has called the "weapons of the weak" – were also punishable crimes under the imperial legal code. Death was the penalty for those who stole from the state, the imperial cult, or the fields of the Incas as well as for those who spoke against the Inca, had intercourse with the *aclla*, or committed treason. Rebellious communities were deprived of their lands and herds, and their leaders were taken to Cuzco where they were publicly humiliated by the emperor himself, before they were tortured, skinned, and executed. The emperor then had drinking mugs made from their skulls and drumheads from their skin (Cieza de León 1967:179–182; Cobo 1956:83; Sarmiento de Gamboa 1960:254–256; Moore 1958:165–174).

The state also used more subtle methods to gain the acquiescence of subjects. It attempted to recast the myths and practices of the encapsulated communities, which prescribed proper behavior, perpetuated socially acceptable explanations of everyday life, and maintained cohesion by asserting the power of local *wak'as* and ancestors. These attempts extended the traditional networks of mutual rights and obligations to include new groups. However, the mechanisms for transmitting this new ideology were weak, because its interpretation remained in the hands of traditional intellectuals, the spokespersons of local shrines, rather than in the hands of state functionaries or members of the emerging dominant class. The priests who preserved and transmitted the traditional lore of their communities and interpreted the local *wak'as* belonged to the groups that maintained and served those shrines and that provided labor service to the state (Spalding 1984:63–66). The relation of these traditional intellectuals to the state and the emerging dominant class of the empire varied. Some, like the caretakers and priests of Pachacamac or Pariacaca, saw their shrines derive significant benefits from their relations with the state; others saw the traditional lore of their communities suppressed (Cabello Valboa 1951:319; Patterson 1985a, 1986). Thus, the caretakers and spokespersons of the local *wak'as* were never completely assimilated into or supportive of either the developing class or state structures.

The new ideological forms and practices of the state created new relations of exploitation. They linked together the Incas, the *kurakas* who had allied themselves with the crown and the state, and state functionaries – groups that benefited materially from the labor service of the peasants and artisans. This was not, however, a homogeneous social category characterized by tranquil and harmonious social relations; instead, the relations among the various factions were wracked by competition, conflict, rivalries, and conspiracies. What united them was their exploitation of the peasants and their dependence on them for labor service. This placed their interests and those of the state in opposition to the interests of the peasants. As long as the potential for dispute within the dominant class was minimized, and its demands, along with those of the state, were not too excessive or abusive, the potential for rebellion could be contained. When disputes surfaced or demands were excessive, however, the resentment and hostility of the encapsulated communities could erupt into open dissent or even revolt.

In spite of the state's desire to ensure the loyalty of the *kurakas* as well as the acquiescence of their subjects, it ultimately failed to create the kind of society it wanted. While the settings in which the subject peoples conducted their lives were only partly of their own creation, they were not totally without some degree of power or control over their own lives. If the subject communities acceded to the wishes of the state, then the inspectors and the terror of the harsh legal code would have been unnecessary. That the state found both inspectors and the terror of law necessary indicates how seriously it took threats posed by even petty acts of insubordination.

Everyday forms of passive resistance, regardless of the motivation of those who committed these acts of insubordination, require almost no coordination or planning, since they rely on implicit understandings and informal networks. Passive resistance can also take a variety of forms. Scott (1985:336) has suggested that one way that subjugated classes attempt to penetrate, neutralize, and negate the hegemony of the dominant classes and the state is by using the values and rationale of the earlier social order to press their claims and to disparage those of their opponents. However, they have no monopoly on these techniques, since both states and emerging ruling classes also rework and give new meanings to established institutions and practices to support their new forms of extortion by promoting the illusion of historical continuity. This is why tradition, the past, and heritage are so often contested terrains.

Archaeological evidence from the Ica Valley on the south coast of Peru provides insight into one instance where tradition was decomposed and reconstituted after its inhabitants fell under the sway of the Inca rulers. The local *kurakas* identified with the state and the emerging dominant class and benefited from the association, while their commoner peasant kin created and maintained an oppositional identity rooted in tradition and history. The use of Inca pottery vessels or pottery made locally in the Inca style and to Inca specifications was restricted to the higher levels of the local nobility; this was also true for pottery vessels that combined features of local and Inca styles. These three types of pottery vessels are found exclusively in distinctive structured tombs near Old Ica, the elite residential center of the valley, both before and after it was incorporated into the imperial state. Pottery fragments decorated in these styles are also found scattered on the surface of Old Ica and in nearby refuse deposits. The peasants, however, used only pottery vessels decorated with the traditional local designs rather than ones imitating the Inca style. They also looted tombs for antique pottery vessels of types that were manufactured and used in the valley when it was free of Inca domination; these vessels were used as sources of artistic inspiration, and fragments of them have been found in refuse deposits around the peasant villages and hamlets. They were not only collected and imitated, but used with some regularity during the period of Inca political control. When Inca control collapsed in the mid-1530s, the peasants reasserted the dominance of the local artistic tradition, purging it of all traces of Inca influence. This involved an artistic revival of the old styles – the ones preferred by the peasants, not those adopted by the nobility during the period of foreign domination (Menzel 1959, 1960b, 1976; Patterson 1986).

While acts like this may have had only a marginal impact on the state's capacity to extract labor, even such "protests within compliance" or "working the system to minimize disadvantage" issued challenges that were more than merely symbolic (Scott, 1985). They mitigated or denied the claims of the state and its dominant class. What is ultimately threatening and dangerous about the "weapons of the weak" is that, under the right conditions, they can be transformed into a rallying point for more open defiance of authority or even direct confrontation against it. Such conditions did develop with some regularity in the Inca state, and not all opposition to its policies and practices was passive.

Border wars were a persistent feature of imperial expansion into new territories; rebellions erupted unexpectedly; and civil wars seem to have been an integral part of everyday life, especially after the death of an emperor. Clearly, not all of the communities on the margins of the state or even those already incorporated into it recognized the value of *pax incaica*, acknowledged the superiority of Inca beliefs and norms, viewed imperial demands in the same way as those of their traditional leaders, or were even particularly intimidated by the force the state could muster or the severity of its legal code. The consequence of the border wars and revolts engendered by imperial expansion and conquests, the civil wars produced by disputes over succession to the throne, and the rebellions and uprisings resulting from the desire of subject populations to reassert their autonomy was that the Inca state was engaged almost continuously in armed struggle from its inception in 1438 through the Spanish invasion in 1532 to its collapse in the 1570s.[1] Revolts in the frontier regions and rebellions in the core areas of the state were often sparked by rumors of the emperor's death and the civil disruption caused by the successional disputes that inevitably followed such an event. As a result, the state frequently had to reconquer peoples that had already been incorporated into the empire (Murra 1978:930).

4.1. Border Wars and Imperial Expansion

Through military conquest and negotiated incorporation, the Incas brought different kinds of societies into the imperial state. These included class-stratified kingdoms, such as Chimor or the Lupaqa; kin-based communities with unstable or ambiguously defined social hierarchies such as the peoples of Huarochirí; and kin-based communities, such as the Pastos, which showed no evidence for any overarching political authority before their encapsulation by the imperial state (Patterson 1987a; Pease 1982). The Inca state was clearly more interested in some peoples and areas than others. Rich, well-populated countries were particularly intriguing because of their human and natural resources. It was considerably more cautious with groups, like the Chiriguana, who were "poor and warlike" (Cabello Valboa 1951:383–384). While its policies toward subject peoples may have been uniform in theory, they varied in practice,

> depending on the economic and political importance of a given region, the circumstances under which it had been incorporated into the realm and, particularly, its existing organization at the time of incorporation (Morris and Thompson 1985:24).

The Incas frequently intervened in frontier areas because local social and political dynamics created changes in existing arrangements, which they viewed as affecting their interests. The initial goal of the state was usually to establish cordial relations with at least one local group in order to gain and secure a foothold in the region.

Imperial expansion created continually shifting frontier areas and border societies. However, there was nothing automatic about the processes of encapsulation and incorporation that occurred on the frontiers of the Inca state. Communities confronted the expanding empire in various ways. Some abandoned their villages and fields, retreating to more remote, inaccessible locations where they reestablished their lives away from the immediate threat posed by the state. Other communities, finding it beneficial or desirable to establish or confirm relations with the Incas, received the imperial envoys, presented them with gifts, and negotiated their incorporation into the empire (Cieza de León 1967:177). Some, like the Kingdom of Chimor, Huarco, or the inhabitants of Chachapoyas, waged war on the imperial armies sent to pacify them and were subdued only after a series of military campaigns spread over a number of years (Cieza de León 1967:162–164, 216; Garcilaso de la Vega 1960 vol. 1:291–303; Rostworowski de Diez Canseco 1980: 187–188; Rowe 1948). Others, like the Pastos in northern Ecuador, were more tentative in their response; they exchanged gifts with the state – cane tubes filled with lice for llamas – but continued to maintain close ties with their neighbors and kin who resided outside the frontier and still retained their autonomy and independence (Cieza de León 1947:385–386).

From the perspective of the communities being encapsulated, the Inca state appeared in different forms at various stages in the process. During the initial stage, gift-bearing strangers – "spies and harbingers" to use Cieza de León's (1967:177) words – began to appear on the frontier and establish contact with them; they came with llamas laden with food and other goods. These entourages of outsiders represented the state and, in some instances during and after the 1470s, represented its allies as well. For example, Topa 'Inka helped the caretakers of Pachacamac, the great oracle on the central coast, establish branch oracles in Mala and Chincha before those regions were incorporated into the state, and merchants from the coastal kingdom of Chincha were active on the northern frontiers of the empire in the 1520s (Patterson 1985a; Rostworowski de Diez Canseco 1970, 1975; Salomon 1978a). Besides their gifts, the strangers brought news about the aims of the Inca state. Some stayed to trade, talk further with the local peoples, and establish more intimate contact with their representatives or with the individuals who put themselves forward as important and influential personages; other from the entourage eventually left with information about local conditions and the prestations they had received for their gifts.

While the local peoples exchanged gifts and food with the outsiders, they retained firm control over their means of production, their labor power, and the goods they produced. But interpersonal relations were not quite the same as they had been earlier. In some instances, political authority came to reside more firmly in the hands of privileged members, chieftains, or self-proclaimed powerful individuals, who were able to gain increased control over the movement of goods created outside the subsistence sector through raiding and trade or through their enhanced ability to create and cement alliances with other peoples. Sometimes this consolidation of authority was accomplished subtly within the terms of the customary rights and obligations that prevailed in the community; their ability to make alliances and their control over exchange rested on their legitimacy, the authority they possessed in the eyes of their kin or subjects. In other instances, individuals who had gained prominence and followings through activities that were disconnected from customary practices of the community were able to propel themselves into positions of influence with the foreigners. Their capacity to make arrangements rested on both their relations with the foreigners and their ability to retain the loyalty of their followers in a milieu where some of the old constraints on action had been removed and new avenues for mobility were being paved (Patterson 1987d).

Soon, more strangers arrived. Some were refugees fleeing from the imperial army and the threat of Inca domination; others were deserters from the army, who were unable to return to their natal communities because of the death sentences that hung over their heads. Still another group of outsiders came from the region itself; they were transient merchants, the *mindaláes* or "those with the tattooed faces" in northern Ecuador, who brought food, raw materials, and finished goods from the region and beyond to trade with the local peoples, the new arrivals, and the remaining members of the imperial entourage (Patterson 1987a:121, 1987c; Salomon 1978a, 1986). The traders's presence benefited the local chieftains and persons of influence as well as the imperial state. In some instances, local leaders or individuals of renown were able to gain or consolidate control over the distribution of goods in circumstances where the local social structures and relations were slowly being distorted, deformed, and modified by the growing interference of the state. The presence of the *mindalá* traders also permitted the imperial state to acquire goods from people who were not under its direct control, and to spread its ideology and language to the independent communities beyond the frontier.

After a while, more strangers arrived from the empire. This time, its envoys came at the head of a column of soldiers, and a moment of decision had arrived for the inhabitants of the region. Should they accept the offers of the gift-bearing strangers and all that implied? Should they resist the invaders and fight them from *pucaras*, the hilltop fortresses and strongholds, that had been prepared earlier? Or should they attempt to avoid the threat altogether by retreating to remote, relatively inaccessible areas or by fleeing across the frontier to lands and peoples whose lives were still unaffected by imperial control?

If they chose to resist, as the Huarco of coastal Peru did, then the state established garrisons, provisioned from the nearest provincial capital, to pacify the region (Cieza de León 1967: 194–197; Hyslop 1985; Rostworowski de Diez Canseco 1980). Once resistance was crushed or the inhabitants acquiesced, acknowledging the balance of forces that prevailed, governors and *mitimae* colonists moved in and settled on lands expropriated from the indigenous peoples by the state. At first, the officials and colonists were also sustained by provisions from the provincial capital, but, after the first harvests, they began to establish their self-sufficiency. They often fortified their settlements to ensure their own safety, and they brought whole hamlets and isolated homesteads down from the mountains and resettled their inhabitants in villages where they could be watched more easily (Morris 1972, 1982; Spalding 1984: 99–101). The state did not want to deal with a potential enemy in relatively unknown terrain, where it would be almost impossible to prevent or defend against ambushes, hit-and-run attacks, or the destruction of isolated farmsteads initiated by rebel bands living in remote fortresses.

Pacification and incorporation into the imperial state meant that the local communities had to provide labor. Their members had to cultivate the fields expropriated by the empire and the imperial cult, and, during their *mit'a* obligation, they had to manufacture finished goods, according to imperial specifications, from raw materials provided by the state (Morris 1974, Rowe 1979b). The authority of the local leaders or persons of influence no longer rested solely on their abilities to distribute goods acquired from the *mindalá* traders, but rather on their connections with the imperial state and their abilities to provide the labor power required to produce the goods and services it demanded. Incorporation into the state diminished the autonomy of the local communities and their leaders, the importance of their contacts with other communities, and the role of local traders as the middlemen of frontier trade. Inca domination would be complete when the encapsulated communities became easily recognized, self-sufficient dependencies of the imperial state. The autonomy of these communities was even further diminished as they began to participate in state-sponsored institutions and practices, like the rituals associated with agricultural production or the *aclla*, which linked their reproduction with that of the empire.

At the same time, the connections between the frontier merchants and the communities and chieftains they once served were severed as the Inca state restructured the traditional economies and became the main source of goods produced by distant peoples. The fate of the merchants now depended on their rather tenuous linkages with and dependency on the state in the borderlands and on their ability to forge new connections with other communities on the margins or beyond the imperial boundaries.

Unrest or rebellions in the borderlands usually broke out when the state suffered setbacks in its domestic or foreign policies or when it attempted to impose new forms of surplus extraction. For instance, when Huarco successfully resisted Inca efforts to incorporate it into the imperial state in the late 1470s, other groups rebelled when its forces were not immediately defeated. The state was forced not only to continue its struggle with Huarco, which ultimately lasted three years, but also to suppress the unrest or revolts that appeared among other peoples. The state reproached these groups for the resistance they displayed and urged them to remain loyal friends or else they would be visited by a cruel war. At the same time, it enlarged the garrison located in the foothills on the edge of Huarco (Cieza de León 1967:194–197).

The best known frontier rebellion was the one that occurred in northern Ecuador during Wayna Qhapaq's reign. While the imperial armies were completing the conquest of Chachapoyas to the south, the peoples on the northern frontier of the state – the Quitos, the Pastos, the Carangues, the Cayambis, and the Huancavilcas – revolted, killing the governors, the spies, and the tax collectors that had been left there to oversee their activities. The revolt probably began around 1510. It is not clear whether the revolt was precipitated by unrest in other parts of the empire, like Chachapoyas, or whether the state precipitated the uprising by attempting to transform what the native peoples viewed as gift exchange and what the state construed as tribute payments into regular *mit'a* labor obligations.

In either event, the rebel tribes built fortresses and awaited the arrival of the imperial army, which included recruits from all quarters of the empire. When it entered the border area, the army's goal was to conquer the Pastos. As the Incas and their allies approached, the Pastos men retreated. Old people, women, and children, guarded by a few warriors, remained to meet the imperial army. They were easily defeated, and, as the army began to celebrate its easy victory, the soldiers became careless. Guards were not posted, as the soldiers drank and partied late into the night. Suddenly, under the cover of darkness, the Pastos warriors counterattacked, and the invading army, composed largely of Colla from the Lake Titicaca Basin, was slaughtered. The survivors escaped and made their way back to the encampments of their allies. Since an easy victory had eluded them, the Inca armies were forced to reenter the Pastos territory for the second time. On this occasion, the soldiers burned their fields and villages and killed rich and poor, men and women, young and old. After the Pastos were finally subdued, the emperor appointed a governor and saw that colonists were settled in the area, before turning his attention to the other groups that had participated in the revolt (Cobo 1956 vol. 2:91–93; Sarmiento de Gamboa 1960:261–263).

The Inca army encountered stiff resistance when it attacked the other rebel groups, and casualties were heavy on both sides. As the war raged on, the imperial army initiated another scorched-earth policy: destroying the rebels's crops and villages and devastating a large area. Some of the rebels escaped to the fortified strongholds of the Carangues, where they were received as allies. The emperor himself led the army against one of the Carangue fortresses. The battle that ensued was fierce, and, during one of the rebels's counterattacks, the emperor was toppled from his litter and almost killed. He and his kin were humiliated by this turn of events. As the emperor walked back to the encampment, he let his kin and the troops know just how angry he was at the disrespect and lack of support he had received. This marked the beginning of a mutiny and a series of battles that would be waged over a period of several years.

Shortly after their defeat at the hands of the Carangues, several of the Inca nobles planned a mutiny. Their complaints were that the emperor was contemptuous of them, that he failed to provide them with adequate provisions, and that they were suffering from exposure. The mutineers, together with the troops they led, resolved to travel to Tumipampa, the provincial capital in southern Ecuador (Wayna Qhapaq's birthplace), to seize the *wak'as* that watched over and ensured the good fortunes of the army. When they arrived at the shrine, the emperor demanded to know their intentions. They told the emperor that they were going to take the *wak'a* back to Cuzco; this would restore its dignity, as well as their own. Wayna Qhapaq then called upon the priests and priestesses of the state cult to intervene and take back the *wak'a* they had already appropriated. Ultimately, the emperor and his mutinous kin talked and resolved their differences. That night, the emperor sponsored an elaborate series of parties that lasted many days, in which loot, gifts, and *aclla* women were given to the soldiers.

Once the old army was placated and reinforced by new recruits, it undertook another assault on the Carangue fortresses. Once again, the soldiers carried out a scorched-earth policy, and eventually they torched the fortresses themselves, killing or capturing everyone who was inside. Some of the Carangues escaped and fled toward a lake where they attempted to hide in the reeds from the army pursuing them. A massacre ensued as the soldiers murdered thousands of men and adolescent boys (Cieza de León 1947:390). Only a few successfully eluded the invading army.

One of the survivors was a Carangue named Pinto who escaped into the rugged, forest-covered mountains to the east. Here he met bands of roving Cañari rebels and exiles, who had not been pacified earlier by Wayna Qhapaq and who had successfully resisted incorporation into the empire. While the Inca state was establishing garrisons and colonists in the area it had just conquered, Pinto and the Cañari rebels who had joined him were fomenting discontent for the state along the frontier. Given the decade-long revolt that was just coming to an end, the state was clearly not concerned at this point in time with bandits or groups plundering the countryside, but focused on the real possibility that the rebels might make alliances with restless elements in the borderlands. Troops were dispatched to locate the rebel band and to eliminate the threat it posed. The army eventually found the rebel strongholds and starved them into submission. Wayna Qhapaq offered Pinto gifts if he would recognize and submit to Inca rule; the rebel leader refused and was executed (Cabello Valboa 1951:382–383; Cobo 1956 vol. 2:91–93; Sarmiento de Gamboa 1960:261–263).

The Inca state's relation with the Chiriguana, who inhabited the mountain slopes east of Sucre, Bolivia, may help to explain its concern over the threat posed by Pinto and the renegade Cañaris (Larson 1988:13–50; Means 1917; Nordenskiöld 1917; Nowell 1946).[2] The Inca army first invaded the lands of the Chiriguana during the reign of Topa 'Inka; it broke off the invasion of the country because of a lack of provisions and stiff resistance, what chroniclers described as "the savagery of its inhabitants" (Garcilaso de la Vega 1960 vol. 1:270; Sarmiento de Gamboa 1960:263). After fortresses were built and garrisons were established along the frontier to protect its gains, the state turned its attention to potentially more productive expeditions and conquests in other regions. The Chiriguana once again attracted the attention of the Inca state in the early 1520s, while it was suppressing the frontier revolt in northern Ecuador and after it had expropriated extensive agricultural fields in the Cochabamba Valley, roughly one hundred twenty miles north-west of Sucre (Wachtel 1982). Wayna Qhapaq repaired the forts built during his father's reign and used Chiriguana troops in his campaigns against the Carangues (Garcilaso de la Vega 1960 vol. 1:271–273; Montesinos 1930:104–105; Sarmiento de Gamboa 1960: 263–264). Philip Means (1917) concluded from this that, while some Chiriguana seem to have been subject to the *mit'a* labor obligations of the state, a larger number, who resided outside the frontier, began to raid and plunder the Charcas borderlands east of Sucre.

It is possible to discern two broad, loosely organized confederations on the eastern edge of the empire adjacent to Charcas. One consisted of the Chiriguana and their Guaraní-speaking allies, some of whom lived as far away as the Paraguay River, roughly four hundred miles to the east. Their relations with the Inca state varied – depending on the time, the place, and the existing balance of forces – from sullen acquiescence to open hostility. Their relations with Chanes and their allies, who were apparently on good terms with the Inca state, were also antagonistic and frequently erupted into raids for plunder and captives. When the Chiriguana raided along the imperial frontier, they took captives, metal utensils, and gold and silver jewelry, which quickly found its way as far east as the Paraguay River. However, groups like the Caracara or the Candires, who were nominally under Inca control, also exchanged metal objects or precious metal with the lowland people – a practice that was frowned upon by the state, which attempted to control or restrict the distribution of metals (Moore 1958:40, 55–56, 116). The Chanes and their allies obtained metals through a group called the Payzunos in exchange for bows, arrows, and, by the early 1540s (if not before), slaves.

The Chiriguana resurfaced as a thorn in the side of the empire, especially after the state's military resources had been diverted to deal with the border insurrection in the northern provinces. The construction of the fortresses a generation earlier had indicated to the Chiriguana that the state intended to remain permanently in the borderlands, to secure the frontier, and to bring its inhabitants under the imperial rule. However, the state's policies for dealing with border populations were always narrowly developed: negotiation, intimidation, and the use of force covered the range of available options. When the troops were removed from the southern provinces, the state's capacity for controlling the movement of goods and people across the frontier was diminished. When the Chiriguana began to raid and plunder the borderlands under the Inca control, the state could not respond merely by requesting that they desist; to do so would have alienated other frontier peoples, like the Chanes, who apparently had cordial ties with the Incas that counterbalanced their antagonistic relations with the Chiriguana.

The state's attempt to make the Chiriguana an economically self-sufficient, culturally distinctive enclave, like subject populations in the core area of the empire, was unsuccessful. The inhabitants of the state-administered areas continually constructed and reproduced close relations with Guaraní-speaking communities in the hinterland, beyond the frontier. This had a number of implications. It meant that different political-economic relations prevailed in the administered and non-administered sections of the Chiriguana social formation. The state appropriated surplus labor and possibly expropriated land from the inhabitants of the administered areas, while their kin, who resided outside the imperial boundaries and retained their independence, had the ability to continue traditional use-rights and customary practices. It suggests that the Chiriguana, residing in the back country, probably received some of the goods that were distributed by the state to their kin on the other side of the border. This also meant they could raid communities in one area and exchange their spoils in another.

Class and state formation in frontier areas created contradictions and opportunities not only for the empire, but for the indigenous peoples of those areas. These new conditions led to the constitution of new alliances, the merging of formerly independent communities into new groups, and even the appearance of border states where none had existed before, as people recognized their shared position in the emerging system of production and examined the implications of such infringements on their traditional use-rights and practices. This does not mean that all frontier communities automatically opposed the state either passively or actively; in a number of them, both the peasants and their leaders benefited materially, though differentially, from their new dependent relationship with the empire. Even though the frontier policies of the Incas were narrow, they succeeded, in many instances, in transforming customary use-rights, in separating traditional leaders from the kin or subjects, in linking the fortunes of subject groups with those of the state, and in recasting old enmities so that communities remained pitted against one another and their neighbors.

4.2. Rebellions and Civil Wars

Revolts against the state usually occurred at moments when imperial power was weakened by other domestic or external problems, or when the level of discontent was increased suddenly by the imposition of new, harsher administrative measures and demands. Open rebellions erupted in several instances, fanned by the death of the emperor or even rumors of his demise. These coincided with succession disputes and the ensuing civil wars.

One of the more vividly remembered rebellions was fomented by the Colla, one of the Ayamara-speaking kingdoms in the Lake Titicaca basin, during the reign of Topa 'Inka; it took the state nearly twelve years to suppress their uprising. The Colla no longer wanted to be part of the imperial state, and they fought against it with thousands of warriors. The Incas were unable to defeat the Colla without the support of other subject populations in the empire. When Topa 'Inka requested their assistance, many remained silent and were not immediately forthcoming with aid. This infuriated the Inca leader, and he threatened to burn all the possessions of their *wak'as* unless they helped him. Eventually, at least some of them provided the aid he demanded (Avila 1966:130–135; Spalding 1984:103; Stern 1982:15).[3]

The Incas's relationship with the Colla and Lupaqa, another Aymara kingdom in the Titicaca Basin, began several generations earlier during the reign of Wiraqocha 'Inka. The core lands of the Colla were generally situated north of the lake, while those of the Lupaqa overlooked its western edge. The Inca leader allied his forces with the Lupaqa who, after raiding and plundering villages around Lake Titicaca, attacked and defeated the Canas, who resided north of the Colla. This laid the foundations for a struggle for political dominance in the basin between the Colla and Lupaqa, both of whom sought aid from the Incas. When the Colla leader discovered that the Incas had formed an alliance with the Lupaqa, his forces attacked their enemy before the Incas arrived to participate in the battle. They were defeated, and their villages looted. The Incas arrived after the battle and participated in the victory celebrations; however, they did not receive a share of the plunder (Cieza de León 1967:173–180). Thus, the Colla and Lupaqa were united under a single ruler (Sarmiento de Gamboa 1960:241–242).

After Pachakuti had ascended to the throne around 1438, the Inca ruler once again turned his attention to the Colla and led a column of soldiers toward the lake. His forces devastated communities at Ayaviri and Copacopa; when a Copacopa plot to assassinate the emperor failed and the identity of the organizers was revealed, more than twenty thousand men, women, and children were massacred (Pachakuti Yamqui 1927:187). The Inca ruler replaced the inhabitants of Ayaviri with *mitimae* colonists and continued his march to the south, receiving the submission of the inhabitants of Asillo and Azangaro. The Incas and the Colla forces clashed, and the Colla leader was captured. The whole province was brought under imperial control, when the state left garrisons, officials, and colonists to watch over its interests. The Colla leader was taken to Cuzco, where he was publicly insulted and trampled by the emperor before being decapitated (Cieza de León 1967:173–175; Sarmiento de Gamboa 1960:241–242).

The Colla revolted against Inca domination in the 1480s. A Colla soldier who deserted from Topa 'Inka's campaign into the forests of Antisuyo told the Colla lords and chieftains that the emperor had been killed (Cobo 1956 vol. 2:83; Sarmiento de Gamboa 1960:255). Since they were already chafing under Inca domination, the Colla leaders plotted a rebellion to rise as a single group against the imperial state. They killed the state officials posted in the province, constructed strongholds at various places, and readied their forces. The rebellion involved many battles; one siege conducted by Topa 'Inka on one of the fortresses lasted three years, before the Colla leaders escaped disguised as women. After nearly twelve years of struggle, the rebellion collapsed under the combined weight of the Inca armies and their allies. The rebel leaders and their *wak'as* were publicly humiliated by the emperor after they were captured. The *wak'as* were thrown into the lake, and the rebels were brought to Cuzco where they were further humiliated before they were skinned. At the end of the rebellion, herds, pasture, and agricultural fields were expropriated by the state. Soldiers were garrisoned among the Colla, who were required by the terms of the settlement to supply them with provisions and women. *Mitimae* colonists were moved into the region, and many Colla were resettled in villages outside the basin away from their kin. Limitations were also imposed on the number of Colla that could be in the capital city at any given moment – no more than one thousand men and women (Cieza de León 1967:179–185; Cobo 1956 vol. 2:83; Sarmiento de Gamboa 1960: 255–256).

The Colla uprising resembled some of the border wars the Inca state confronted in the sense that the peasants, herders, fishermen, and artisans who made up the underclass of Colla society joined their traditional leaders and neighbors in an open rebellion against imperial domination. In these instances, the underclasses or non-chiefly estates recognized the legitimacy and authority of the local *kurakas*, and the leaders acknowledged their customary responsibilities toward their subjects or kin. This distinguished the Colla revolt and the border wars from peasant revolts, like the one that occurred at about the same time in the Inca Valley, where the interests of the inhabitants of the farming hamlets opposed those of an indigenous ruling class that had allied itself with the imperial state, a ruling class they apparently toppled as soon as the threat of Inca intervention in the local affairs of the valley vanished in the mid-1530s.

If peasants's most distinctive characteristics are their attachment to land and conservative political attitudes resulting from a desire protect their use-rights to the means of production, then, in some instances, Andean peasant communities saw the Inca state, rather than their traditional leaders, as the main source of their oppression. However, it is equally important to note that not all Andean peasant communities opposed imperial policies that expropriated their land and appropriated their labor; some cooperated actively with the state and received land and labor in return for their service to the empire (Avila 1966:131–135).

While peasant resistance, local revolts, and border wars typically involved the inhabitants of a region and cross-class or cross-estate alliances, the civil wars that occurred in the imperial state built on cleavages within the Inca ruling class. These cleavages frequently followed lines drawn by the composition of the various royal corporations, and on the alliances that these competing factions were able to establish or maintain with elements of the provincial ruling classes or elites that had been incorporated into the dominant class of the empire. Such alliances were tenuous and frequently reflected the treatment of particular underclasses, defined by the intersection of class and ethnicity, by the state. Under these circumstances, the capacity of the local *kurakas* to aid the Inca faction they supported depended on their ability to retain the support of their own subjects or kin.

Two civil wars achieved particular prominence in Inca historical accounts. The earlier one occurred during the formation of the imperial state, when the faction led by Pachakuti 'Inka Yupanki struggled with the followers of his father and half brother, Wiraqocha 'Inka and 'Inka Urqon. The more recent one took place about a century later; it involved the successional

dispute between Washkar and 'Ataw Wallpa that was precipitated by the death of Wayna Qhapaq in 1527. It raged for several
years and was still in progress when the Spaniards arrived in
1532.

When Wayna Qhapaq died, all of his potential heirs had equal
claims to the royal tassel. They were supported by their kin.
One was Ninan Kuyuchi, who was actually designated to be his
father's successor; however, he died shortly after the old emperor. The second was Washkar, whose kin and principal supporters among the Incas were concentrated in the *panaqa* of Topa
'Inka. The third was 'Ataw Wallpa, who had the support of his
mother's kin in Pachakuti's *panaqa* and of the professional soldiers in the north led by two very experienced generals, Challkuchima and Kizkiz. There were other potential heirs as well.
Some joined forces with their more powerful brothers; others
went into hiding; and still others were probably assassinated.
Washkar imprisoned one of them, a younger brother named
Paullu 'Inka, on the grounds that he had an adulterous relationship with one of his wives or concubines. Paullu's real crime
may have been that he supported 'Ataw Wallpa. Several brothers,
who plotted to assassinate Washkar and replace him with one of
their own number, were executed when their plan was exposed
(Brundage 1963:267–272; Cabello Valboa 1951:394–398; Cieza de
León 1967:230–233).

'Ataw Wallpa and Washkar rapidly consolidated their positions and emerged as the leading candidates for the imperial
tassel. The relations between the two rivals deteriorated almost
as rapidly as their rise to prominence. Washkar was angered
because the *coya*, the dead emperor's principal wife and sister,
and the priests from Pachakuti's corporation who accompanied
the Wayna Qhapaq's mummy back to Cuzco had left his insignias, soldiers, and wives in the care of 'Ataw Wallpa in Ecuador.
He killed the priests, which angered the *coya* and their kin in the
Iñaqa corporation. Washkar then offended the other royal corporations when he threatened to seize their lands, and they
quickly allied themselves with 'Ataw Wallpa's faction, which
already had strong support from Pachakuti's descendants. The
coya reluctantly consented to Washkar's marriage to her
daughter, and 'Ataw Wallpa sent a secret emissary to the two
women, seeking their support. When Washkar discovered the
envoy's mission, he accused the two women of treachery, and,

after humiliating the envoy, sent him back to the north (Brundage 1963:272–275; Cabello Valboa 1951:408, 414–416). According to Sarmiento de Gamboa (1960:265–267), 'Ataw Wallpa also sent envoys to Washkar, proclaiming his subordinate status; however, these messengers were killed. After that, 'Ataw Wallpa refused to recognize his brother's claim to the royal tassel.

The northern part of the empire was quickly thrown into crisis as well. The danger increased after the old *kuraka* of the Cañaris, who had followed Wayna Qhapaq and 'Ataw Wallpa, died, since the loyalty of his successor was not assured. An emissary from Washkar named Atoc arrived in the area to undermine 'Ataw Wallpa's support and visited the Cañaris and the *mitimae* colonists, telling them that the ruler in Cuzco sought their friendship. The new Cañari leader proclaimed his loyalty to Washkar and, together with Atoc, attacked and captured 'Ataw Wallpa in Tumipampa. They intended to turn him over to Washkar, but 'Ataw Wallpa escaped and successfully rejoined his troops before they had the opportunity to do so (Cabello Valboa 1951:417–436; Cieza de León 1967:238–241).

As 'Ataw Wallpa was regrouping and Atoc was in Tumipampa seizing Wayna Qhapaq's wives and insignias, the Huancavilcas revolted, and a border war involving the Pacamoros tribes east of Cusibamba broke out in northern Peru (Sarmiento de Gamboa 1960:266). 'Ataw Wallpa sent troops to suppress the Huancavilcas's uprising and to stir up old animosities on the north coast to undermine any support Washkar's faction might have in the region. At the same time, some of Washkar's recruits, under the leadership of Wanka Auqui, attacked the Pacamoros and were defeated (Cabello Valboa 1951:427–435, 465–472; Sarmiento de Gamboa 1960:266–267).

In Tumipampa, Atoc organized the Cañaris, the *mitimaes* who had professed their loyalty to Washkar, and the fresh troops that had just arrived from Cuzco. They were attacked and defeated by 'Ataw Wallpa's two battle-seasoned veterans, Challkuchima and Kizkiz, who led forces composed of the full-time soldiers as well as loyal *mitimaes* and subject populations from Quito. Atoc was executed; Tumipampa was leveled; the Cañari villages and fields were burned; and their adult men and pregnant women were massacred (Brundage 1963:282–284; Cabello Valboa 1951:436–445; Cieza de León 1967:239–244; Sarmiento de Gamboa 1960:266–267).

Washkar's retreating forces, now under the command of Wanka Auqui, were pursued southward. They were reinforced by a large number of reluctant Chachapoyas who were recruited under duress. Kizkiz attacked and defeated them at Cajamarca, inflicting particularly heavy losses on the Chachapoyas. 'Ataw Wallpa's armies continued their march southward and arrived at Huamachuco, where the Inca leader himself decapitated the spokesman of Catiquilla, an oracle that supported his brother's ascent to the throne, and burned the *wak'a* and its shrine. By this time, 'Ataw Wallpa had reasserted his control over the tribes and polities in the northern part of empire that had opposed his rule (Sarmiento de Gamboa 1960:266).

Kizkiz and Challkuchima pursued Wanka Auqui and the remnants of his forces to the Pampa de Junín, where they clashed again. Wanka Auqui and the other survivors escaped to the provincial capital at Jauja, where they were reinforced by troops from the region – the Chancas, Soras, Ayamarcas, and Yauyos. The two armies battled outside of Jauja, and the generals were again victorious, which created deep-seated resentment among the local inhabitants. Wanka Auqui retreated to Yanamarca, where he and his forces were defeated. They retreated once more toward Cuzco, and 'Ataw Wallpa's generals pushed forward. Washkar reinforced his retreating northern army at Cotabamba, just outside Cuzco. He attacked his enemies and inflicted a surprising defeat on them; however, he did not follow up the victory by pursuing the retreating soldiers. That night, 'Ataw Wallpa's generals counterattacked and massacred Washkar's troops. Challkuchima pulled Washkar from his litter, and his troops pursued the defeated forces toward Cuzco. He sent the empty litter back to the capital to encourage the rumor that Washkar had been killed (Sarmiento de Gamboa 1960:266–271).

As mentioned before, in retaliation for the support Topa 'Inka's corporation gave Washkar, the generals destroyed his mummy bundle and the shrine where it was housed. They also executed the spokesman of the shrine as well as the members of the *panaqa*. Washkar's children, pregnant wives, and servants were also executed. Washkar himself was imprisoned.

In the meantime, 'Ataw Wallpa received notice of a small group of bearded strangers, led by Francisco Pizarro, who came from beyond the imperial frontiers. For about a year, the foreigners had been raiding and looting villages along the Ecuadorian coast and undermining his political control. In January 1532 they crossed the Gulf of Guayaquil and found that Tumbes, a town where they had left two Spaniards three years earlier, had been burned during the civil war and their countrymen sacrificed. In April they marched from the coast, together with a substantial native contingent, into the sierra in search of 'Ataw Wallpa. Pizarro planned to kidnap the Inca leader, as Cortés had done earlier in Mexico. They met in Cajamarca, one of the provincial capitals in the northern highlands, in mid-November 1532 (Hemming 1970:23–45; Kubler 1945).

'Ataw Wallpa was curious to meet the Spaniards, who had arrived in the city the day before and laid an ambush in the plaza. The Inca leader and his entourage arrived. After firing a cannon into the crowd, Pizarro's cavalry attacked the attendants and stampeded them into the wall at the end of the square. Those that escaped were hunted down and slain. 'Ataw Wallpa was pulled from his litter and held hostage. The Inca leader quickly noticed the Spaniards' obsession with gold and silver, and, fearing that the Spaniards were going to kill him, he sought to extricate himself from the situation by offering his captors large amounts of gold and silver as a ransom. Pizarro promised to free him as soon as the ransom was paid. Visitors came regularly to Cajamarca to confer with 'Ataw Wallpa and to bring him news of important events (Hemming 1970:47–48).

In December 1532 the Spaniards sent out exploring parties from Cajamarca. 'Ataw Wallpa told the Spaniards where they could acquire the precious metals. Following his advice, Hernando Pizarro, the brother of the Spanish leader, led one party in search of Pachacamac, the shrine of the famous coastal oracle that supported Washkar during the civil war that, according to 'Ataw Wallpa, possessed enormous wealth. The imprisoned Inca wreaked his vengeance on Pachacamac when the Spaniards sacked and looted the shrine in February 1533. A second expedition, led by Hernando de Soto and Pedro del Barco, set out about the same time for Cuzco; its intent was to remove gold and silver from Coricancha, the main shrine of the imperial cult (Zárate 1947:477).

After a few days, the party heading for Cuzco encountered Challkuchima, who was bringing important prisoners – Washkar and his closest relatives and supporters – northward. Washkar spoke with the Spaniards, telling them of his dispute with 'Ataw Wallpa and requesting their aid in resolving it. He promised them more precious metals and jewels if they would enlist and support his cause. The Spaniards ignored his plea and continued on their journey. However, messengers from Challkuchima brought news of the meeting to Cajamarca. The Spaniards wanted Challkuchima to bring Washkar north, but the general was reluctant to leave Jauja, fearing that the inhabitants of the region, badly defeated by his soldiers only a year or so before, might ally themselves with Washkar's faction or rebel against the state. When 'Ataw Wallpa learned that Pizarro was anxious to meet with Washkar, his immediate concern was that the Spaniards might free Washkar, and he did not want his rival free to organize resistance. He sent a message to Challkuchima ordering him to execute Washkar, the queen mother, his *coya*, and the other prisoners being brought to Cajamarca (Zárate 1947:477). The executions took place in Andamarca, outside of Jauja, in January or February 1533, since the Pachacamac expedition, which met up with Challkuchima's troops in Jauja in early March, made no mention of Washkar's presence in the camp.

This eliminated the threat posed by Washkar; however, a number of his supporters survived the massacres. Before he was finally executed in July 1533, 'Ataw Wallpa continued to eliminate potential rivals and contenders for the throne. He had two of his half-brothers killed after they departed from Cajamarca. Subsequently, Topa Wallpa, another brother and contender, came to Cajamarca and, fearing that 'Ataw Wallpa would have him killed, placed himself under Pizarro's protection (Hemming 1970:53–54, 78).

The Spaniards were reinforced in mid-April when Diego de Almagro arrived with a contingent of one hundred fifty-three men (Hemming 1970:76–77; Prescott 1968). Pizarro and Almagro agreed to combine forces to conquer Peru, but the reinforcements resented that they had not received shares of the ransom that poured into Cajamarca. The Spaniards also debated 'Ataw Wallpa's future. Some, notably Hernando de Soto, argued that he was an asset who could help them; others feared he posed a threat and that he had ordered the Andean peoples to mobilize and resist the foreigners. A decision was finally reached, and the Inca leader was garroted on 26 July 1533. Topa Wallpa, who had placed himself under Pizarro's protection, was crowned as soon as 'Ataw Wallpa was buried (Hemming 1970:86).

The Spaniards – along with Challkuchima and Topa Wallpa, their puppet emperor – left Cajamarca for Cuzco in early August. Two months later, on 12 October, they arrived in Jauja, after passing through country whose inhabitants had been loyal to Washkar's faction. Challkuchima's troops at Jauja were preparing to resist the Spaniards's advance. As the foreigners approached Jauja, they saw soldiers setting fire to the storehouses in this provincial capital. The Spaniards attacked on horseback and slaughtered the soldiers who had retreated across the river in an attempt to rejoin the main forces. Two days later, the Spaniards sent a squadron of horsemen to pursue the main force that was moving down the Mantaro Valley to join Kizkiz's army near Cuzco. The Spaniards killed soldiers as well as the women and servants who traveled with them (Hemming 1970:94–95).

Shortly after the Spaniards arrived in Jauja, Topa Wallpa, their puppet emperor, died. They were greatly distressed and did not have a clear picture of how to proceed or whom to put forth as his successor. They called a meeting to discuss the matter, since potential heirs and rumors abounded. In Quito, 'Ataw Wallpa's commanders were considering crowning a brother of the dead leader; Rumiñawi, one of 'Ataw Wallpa's generals, was allegedly planning to seize power for himself. More rumors had Kizkiz planning the coronation of Paullu 'Inka, one of 'Ataw Wallpa's supporters, near Cuzco. The leader of the Wankas presented himself as a candidate, arguing that the Incas themselves had installed him as a king. Challkuchima suggested 'Ataw Wallpa's young son as a successor; the Washkar faction suggested one of Topa Wallpa's brothers, presumably Manqo 'Inka, who was in Cuzco or its environs (Hemming 1970:96).

They did not immediately resolve the issue of succession. Instead, they moved southward from Jauja toward the imperial capital, following the same route as the army formerly led by Challkuchima. Since the inhabitants living along the section of the highland road in central Peru had either supported Washkar's factions or at least not openly resisted it during the early phase of the civil war, the soldiers from Quito were not greeted with enthusiasm. Along the way, the two forces fought major but ultimately indecisive battles at Vilcashuaman, Vilcaconga, and finally a pass overlooking Cuzco itself. While the battles slowed the Spaniards's progress, they did not prevent them from entering the capital on 15 November 1533 (Hemming 1970:107–117; Prescott 1968).

Outside of Cuzco, the Spaniards met Manqo 'Inka, who presented himself as the son of Wayna Qhapaq, a fugitive from 'Ataw Wallpa's soldiers who were trying to kill him. Pizarro saw in Manqo 'Inka the puppet ruler he had been seeking. Manqo 'Inka saw the Spaniards as allies who would help him end Kizkiz's attempt to hunt down and execute the remaining members of Washkar's faction. The Spaniards entered Cuzco as liberators, and, after looting the city and dividing the plunder, the next items on their agenda were to place Manqo 'Inka on the throne and secure his recognition and to eliminate the threat posed by Kizkiz. Manqo 'Inka assembled an army and, together with Spanish horsemen, attacked Kizkiz's soldiers. After several battles, Kizkiz's forces were shattered, and they began a long retreat to the north. Manqo 'Inka was crowned after the expedition against Kizkiz returned to Cuzco in late December 1533 (Hemming 1970:118–119, 126).

Kizkiz's retreating soldiers, however, posed a threat to the small Spanish garrison left at Jauja, so in late January 1534 Pizarro sent a small number of reinforcements. Kizkiz planned to attack Jauja from two directions and set fire to the city, but the plan went awry. Several thousand local inhabitants, supported by eighteen horsemen and a dozen Spanish foot soldiers, defeated Kizkiz's forces. The Wankas had rebelled against Inca rule. Pizarro's reinforcements arrived three weeks after the battle and, together with a contingent led by one of Manqo's brothers, they pursued Kizkiz's soldiers to a fortified position near Bonbon, which they were unable to capture. Both Pizarro and Manqo 'Inka sent additional reinforcements, and, after a series of battles, Kizkiz's forces broke off contact and retreated to the north to join Rumiñawi. At this point, while Manqo 'Inka and his Spanish allies had reasserted control over the central portion of the empire, Rumiñawi and his army were still a force to be contended with in Cajamarca, Tumipampa, and Quito (Hemming 1970:139–141).

The events that were about the unfold in the north were beyond the control of either Francisco Pizarro or Manqo 'Inka. The small garrison at the city of San Miguel, which the Spaniards had established several years earlier on the coast at Piura, was being inundated by several hundred soldiers of fortune who were seeking to gain a share of the vast wealth that was being recovered in the Andes. In late February 1534 Pedro de Alvarado, an adventurer from Central America with no formal connection to the expedition led by Pizarro and Almagro, landed with a force of several hundred men at Puerto Viejo in coastal Ecuador. When Sebastián de Benalcázar, whom Pizarro had put in charge of San Miguel, heard about Alvarado's expedition, he mounted his force and set out for Quito. Thus, two independent parties invaded the northern frontier of the empire, where they would encounter not only the forces led by Rumiñawi, but also some groups around Quito, who sought to reassert their autonomy, and others, like the Cañaris, who sought revenge for the devastation they suffered earlier by 'Ataw Wallpa's armies (Hemming 1970:151–168).

When Diego de Almagro joined Benalcázar in Quito in late 1534, Pizarro was able to reassert some control over events in Ecuador. However, Manqo 'Inka, who was persuaded by Pizarro to return from Jauja to Cuzco to organize his court, was unable to reestablish any effective imperial authority in the north. Manqo also had to confront several real problems in Cuzco. Many of the subject populations resettled by his predecessors around the imperial capital displayed mixed or dubious loyalties toward the new ruler. Many of the Incas also displayed ambivalent feelings about the new ruler, and opposition was crystallizing within the royal corporations and around his brother, Paullu, whose mother was the daughter of a Huaylas chieftain. Besides the dissension that was emerging among the Incas and the *mitimae* communities around Cuzco, tensions were also increasing among the Spaniards, and between them and the indigenous peoples (Hemming 1970:169–188).

By 1535, Manqo 'Inka was beginning to realize that the Spaniards were dangerous, that they constituted the present and future threat to his rule. As a result, he began devising plans to expel them from the country and to consolidate his authority. He sent Paullu, his main rival for power, with Almagro's expedition to Chile; this removed him, if only temporarily, from the political intrigues that were taking place within the indigenous communities around the imperial capital. After Almagro and Paullu left and Pizarro had departed for the north, Manqo 'Inka made plans to eliminate his rivals and to expel the Spaniards,

whom he had come to view as an invading force rather than a
mere challenge to his power. He secretly assembled an army at
Yucay in the Urubamba Valley, and in April 1536 he slipped out
of the city to join his troops. They captured and executed
isolated groups of Spaniards and then attacked the Spanish
garrison in Cuzco; the Spaniards counterattacked and the siege
lasted only a few days. Manqo 'Inka had not received the
support he anticipated from the inhabitants of the northern
provinces, who were either ambivalent to his calls for help or
belonged to groups that were originally part of or loyal to 'Ataw
Wallpa's faction (Kubler 1944, 1947).

In his memoirs, written in 1571, Pedro Pizarro assessed the
importance of the civil war for the Spaniards' cause:

> Had Wayna Qhapaq been alive when we Spaniards entered this land
> it would have been impossible to win it. . . . Also, if the land had not
> been divided by the war between Washkar and 'Ataw Wallpa we
> could not have entered or conquered it (Pizarro 1963:181).

The hegemony of the imperial state that existed at the end of
Wayna Qhapaq's reign collapsed in less than a decade. It was
rapidly replaced by a devastating civil war between factions of
the imperial ruling class. A series of insurrections broke out
along the frontiers as recently encapsulated peoples attempted
to reassert their autonomy and repel the invasion by foreigners
whose numbers and influence grew steadily after 1532. By 1536
segments of the old ruling class had transformed the civil war
into a protracted armed struggle, the goal of which was to
dislodge the invading forces and eliminate their hold on the
native peoples. At the same time, the apparent unity of outsiders
crumbled as internal disputes erupted and plunged them head-
long into their own civil war.

Chapter 5

The Clash of Empires and the Formation of Colonial Society

Colonialism implies the rule of one people by another. The dominant image is that of a clash between two vastly different "worlds" – two peoples separated by history, language, culture. The result subjugates a colonized race or people, defined as degraded and inferior, to the economic, political, and cultural forces of an expansionist, imperial people. . . . The misleading element in this image is the way it homogenizes colonized peoples, placing them into a single social category, and thereby overlooks one of their most important struggles – the building of solidarity and unity against the forces of fragmentation. (Steve Stern, "The Struggle for Solidarity")

The invasion of the Inca state in 1531 was an important phase in the formation of a Spanish empire. The foundations for Pizarro's expedition, as well as the backdrop for the events it unleashed, occurred in Europe before and after Charles I assumed the Aragonese-Catalonian throne following the death of Ferdinand, his maternal grandfather, in 1516. Since Ferdinand's daughter and his mother – Isabella – had been declared incompetent, Charles also claimed the crown of Castile and its American possessions. A decade earlier, he had inherited the Low Countries from his father and laid claim to the Duchy of Burgundy, which had reverted to the king of France. Three years later, he inherited the Habsburg estates of Austria, Tyrol, and southern Germany from Maximilian, his paternal grandfather, and had himself proclaimed emperor of Germany. Charles himself was a Burgundian, who spoke no Spanish, spent little time in his Spanish possessions, and used Spanish money to finance the royal court in Brussels and his wars of conquest elsewhere in

Europe. His policies, as well as his complete reliance on Burgundian advisors, quickly aroused the opposition of both the landed aristocracy and bourgeois elements in the cities (Lynch 1965:35–58).

The antecedents for Castilian commercial expansion, colonization, and conquest in the Americas and North Africa can be found in the political-economic developments and struggles that occurred earlier, during the fifteenth century, on the Iberian peninsula. These included the decline of the Mediterranean-oriented commercial economies of Catalonia and Aragon and the emergence of Genoa as an important center of mercantile activity; the growth of large ranch-based wool production in Castile and export to textile factories in Flanders; the expansion of shipbuilding and related industries on the northern Atlantic coast in connection with the wool trade; the marriage of Isabella and Ferdinand, which linked the interests of the Aragonese and Castilian dynasties under conditions favorable to the latter, and opposed them to the concerns of France and Portugal; the 1482–1492 civil war in Granada, the last Moorish state on the peninsula, which facilitated the final phase of the Reconquest under Castilian direction; and Castile's demand for new sources of slave labor, raw materials, and finished goods (Elliott 1970: 13–76; Gibson 1966:1–23; Vivens Vives 1969:175–277).

The first expeditions to the Americas were commercial ventures. For instance, Columbus's first two voyages were financed with the backing of royal officials. Even though the Castilian crown provided no direct monetary support, it did grant him the post of governor general of the territory and one-tenth of the merchandise it produced (Elliott 1970:59–62; Sauer 1966:17, 71, 106). However, his investors quickly lost confidence when the admiral failed to produce the quantities of gold he promised earlier; the two thousand native Americans he sold in the slave markets of Europe and the Canary Islands did not satisfy their expectations for profit. The Crown also lost confidence in him; he was replaced as governor of the Indies in 1499 because he was unable to quell civil unrest in Hispaniola and reorganize its failing economy. By the end of the century, other expeditions were already being organized, financed, and sent out to search for gold.

The locus of these activities gradually expanded to include the pearl coast of Venezuela and Panama. However, even as late as

1518 Spanish settlement was confined to towns in the Greater Antilles and scattered hamlets on the mainland, where the colonists had established themselves mostly as farmers, artisans, shopkeepers, and unskilled workers who rubbed shoulders on a daily basis with petty officials, soldiers of fortune, poor sailors, failed prospectors and miners, native Americans, slave hunters, and slaves brought against their will from various ports in the Americas, Europe, and Africa. This changed in 1518, when slave-raiding expeditions along the coasts of Yucatan and Mexico returned to the islands with reports of wealthy native civilizations.

The governor of Cuba commissioned Hernán Cortés, a prominent resident of the island and a financial investor in the expedition, to establish contact with the Mexican civilizations. After landing in coastal Veracruz, he led a force of more than five hundred colonists and soldiers – almost all of whom were residents of the Indies – into the interior toward the heartlands of the native civilizations. Along the way, they established alliances with native populations that were already enemies of the Aztec state and its ruling class. By the time the expedition reached the Aztec capital in the fall of 1519, it had been reinforced by thousands of native allies. The Spaniards captured the Aztec emperor and turned him into a puppet ruler while they looted the city. The population of Tenochtitlan rebelled and drove the invaders out of the city in June 1520. Cortés and his allies responded and laid siege to the city for more than a year, depriving its residents of food and water. The inhabitants surrendered in 1521. As the news of his discoveries and conquests spread throughout the Indies and reached Spain, more Spaniards arrived in Mexico.

From the beginning of the expedition, Cortés struggled to dissociate himself from the governor's sponsorship and to establish an independent relationship with the new emperor, Charles (Elliott 1971). In 1519 he sent Montezuma's gifts, part of the plunder, and envoys to Charles's court in order to gain support for his cause; the emperor, for his part, wanted to extract as much wealth as possible from the Cortés venture. By 1522 Cortés had partially succeeded. The emperor appointed him captain general and governor of New Spain; he also sent four bureaucrats, who arrived in Mexico two years later, to share power with the governor.

The members of the expedition were not paid for nearly two years, and they demanded *encomiendas* as compensation for their service in the conquest of Mexico. The *encomienda* was a set of practices that developed during the reconquest of the Iberian peninsula and was reconstituted in the Antilles; it granted the recipients permission to use labor extracted from specified native districts for their own purposes. The *encomiendas* were awarded by the governor for a limited period of time (Lockhart 1969; Simpson 1966). The institution was contested. The recipients of *encomiendas* continually struggled to have them granted in perpetuity to themselves and their dependents; the emperor opposed this practice on the grounds that it would create a relatively uncontrollable colonial aristocracy. Ultimately, he agreed with Cortés's argument that this form of compensation was the only way of guaranteeing the continuous flow of treasure from New Spain to the imperial coffers.

Even before Cortés marched inland toward the Mexican plateau and Vasco Núñez de Balboa saw the Pacific Ocean for the first time, rumors about another wealthy civilization, located somewhere to the south, were already circulating among the Spanish inhabitants of Panama. By 1514 the residents of Panama, the city Balboa established on the Pacific shores of the isthmus, were building ships and beginning to explore the coast and offshore islands in search of this rich land, which they called Birú (Murphy 1941). In the early 1520s three residents of Panama who were anxious to join the search for Birú were Francisco Pizarro, Diego de Almagro, and Fernando de Luque. By 1524 they had raised enough money to build one boat and to repair and refurbish another. They then purchased a license of departure from the governor of Panama, which effectively gave him a share in their venture as well. Pizarro sailed eastward in mid-November with an expedition of one hundred twelve Spaniards and at least seventeen Indians and Blacks. Almagro followed four months later with a crew of seventy, fifty of whom were Spaniards, while Luque remained in Panama to watch over their interests. The two expeditions skirted the coast of Colombia, stealing food from its inhabitants and plundering villages. The natives retaliated and inflicted heavy casualties on several occasions. The survivors, twenty out of the one hundred twenty-nine in Pizarro's contingent, returned to Panama in late July or early August 1525.

In 1526 the three adventurers made preparations for a second expedition. They raised more money and bought back the governor's share from the first venture. The boats were replaced or repaired, supplies were purchased, and a new crew was enlisted. Pizarro set sail in November; the new expedition had two boats, three large canoes, and a crew of several hundred, which included both Indians and Black slaves. In March 1527 one of the boats captured a seagoing balsa off the Ecuadorian coast, south of the Esmeraldas River. It carried fine textiles and other objects for trade, and its crew wore fine clothes and jewelry made from precious metals and stones (Sáamanos 1910). This afforded the Spaniards a preview of the vast wealth of the Inca state; they learned the balsa had come from Tumbes. However, the prevailing winds made it difficult for the expedition to proceed southward, so the boats anchored for several weeks in the vicinity of Tecumes at the mouth of the Esmeraldas River. During this period, the expedition was attacked repeatedly by the local inhabitants, and one of the Black slaves jumped overboard and swam ashore, where he was incorporated into one of the local communities and participated in the stubborn resistance that the Spaniards encountered on their subsequent incursions into this region in the early 1530s (Murphy 1941:16, 25; Ruiz Naharro 1927:195).

When the winds improved, the boat carrying Pizarro and his contingent sailed southward along the Peruvian coast past Tumbes and the Santa River. The Spaniards returned to Tumbes, where several of them chose to remain, and a few Indians were taken on board before they set sail for Panama. However, the new governor of Panama was displeased with Pizarro's actions. Pizarro had deliberately ignored the governor's instructions to return to Panama before sailing along the Peruvian coast. Given the governor's antagonism after Pizarro's return, it soon became apparent to the three partners that one of them should travel to Spain to obtain the direct support of King Charles.

Pizarro and his entourage arrived at Toledo, the site of the imperial court, in the summer of 1528. While Pizarro's account attracted Charles's attention almost immediately, it took more than a year for an agreement to be reached. It was signed by the emperor's mother on 26 July 1529. It granted titles to the three partners: Almagro was ennobled and made commandant of Tumbes; Luque was appointed, subject to papal approval, bishop of Tumbes; Pizarro was also ennobled, appointed governor and captain-general of Peru, and given extensive territorial concessions, administrative powers, and the ability to grant *encomiendas*. The agreement also specified the conditions under which the conquest should be carried out: the expedition should include at least one hundred fifty men from Spain and one hundred men from Panama; Pizarro and his recruits must leave Spain by 26 January 1530, and they should leave Panama within six months of their arrival in that colony (Means 1964:24–26).

At the same time, Almagro and Luque busied themselves in Panama, financing and organizing a third expedition. They obtained boats and enlisted men from as far away as Nicaragua. Needless to say, they were less than enthusiastic about the terms of the imperial agreement and the unequal treatment they received. The inequities between the titles, salaries, and powers they received and those assigned to Pizarro generated ill will, quarrels, and recriminations that stalked Pizarro from the moment he set foot in Panama until he was assassinated eleven years later.

Pizarro left Panama in January 1531 with three ships and about one hundred eighty men. They attacked Coaque in northern Ecuador and sent a considerable amount of gold and silver back to Panama, and then settled down to await reinforcements. Supplies, about twenty men, a dozen horses, and three royal treasury officials finally arrived. The main force, many of them weakened from wounds or ravaged by disease, then moved over land along the coast of Ecuador toward Puná Island, where they were savagely attacked by the indigenous population. After more than three months, the beleaguered Spaniards on Puná were reinforced, when Hernando de Soto landed a party of about a hundred men from Nicaragua and Panama. In February 1532 they returned to mainland and headed toward Tumbes, the provincial capital the Spaniards had visited more than four years earlier. After staying there for several months, they moved again, establishing the city of San Miguel in a well-watered portion of the Piura Valley, located near a good port at the mouth of the river. About forty Spaniards, mostly those in poor health, became the citizens of San Miguel and received *encomiendas* in the area. The remainder set out to meet the Inca leader, 'Ataw Wallpa, whom they learned was in the mountains to the east (Lockhart 1972:7–9).

Pizarro's model for the conquest of the Inca state was based on the actions and experiences of Cortés a decade earlier in Mexico. His forces made alliances with groups that were happy to be relieved of the burdens imposed by the imperial state, and with competing factions in the Inca ruling class. They kidnaped 'Ataw Wallpa and held him for ransom. Gold, silver, and precious jewels seemed to flow into Cajamarca in quantities that vastly surpassed any previously encountered in the Indies. Their abundance staggered even the wildest expectations of the most imaginative Spaniard. When the ransom was divided and distributed among the men who had participated in the kidnaping, which excluded the force led by Almagro and strained relationships, even those who received the smallest shares suddenly became wealthy men whose assets were almost entirely liquid.

Many of the men wished to return to Spain with their newly acquired wealth, and there was little to hold them in Peru. Thus, Pizarro was faced with the problem of convincing them to remain in the Andes, since their departure would seriously weaken or curtail altogether further efforts to extract labor or products from the indigenous peoples. Like Cortés, he distributed *encomiendas* to retain his forces and their loyalty. These grants to exercise authority over the people assigned to them were awarded not only to his companions-in-arms, but to the followers of Almagro and Pedro de Alvarado, and to some members of the native ruling class – like Paullu Topa, a potential heir to the Inca throne – who were useful to the Spaniards's cause (Kubler 1947:192–193).

King Charles was enormously pleased when his share of the plunder – the royal fifth, which actually amounted to about forty percent of the value seized -- reached Seville. He used it to finance his wars and dreams of imperial expansion in Europe. As a result, a significant portion of the treasure that reached Castile flowed steadily toward Charles's court and the industrial and financial centers of northern Europe. In addition, the arrival of so much treasure acted like a magnet that attracted immigrants to an enormously wealthy civilization located in a remote and little-known land.

5.1. The Plunder Economy: War, Resistance, and Immigration

War and resistance bring death. (Karen Spalding, *Huarochirí*)

Karen Spalding (1984:115–134) has called the first three decades of Spanish settlement in the Andes the period of the plunder economy: the goal of the invaders was to steal treasure. They looted *wak'as* and imperial storehouses located in the provincial capitals for status goods – jewelry, fine cloth, and objects made from precious metals – as well as for basic subsistence items. While it is difficult, if not impossible, to estimate how much was actually taken, it is clear that both the invaders and their native allies continued to plunder local shrines and installations of the Inca state well into the 1550s; in some instances, the theft of food may have been a motivation as important as either greed or revenge.

However, plunder was not the only goal of the leaders of the first expeditions. They also sought to establish realms in which they had both authority and the ability to increase their wealth by extracting labor and tribute from the native communities they had subordinated. They attempted to accomplish this through _encomienda_ grants to partisans and allies. By 1536 Pizarro had granted about five hundred *encomiendas* ; thus, fewer than one-fourth of the two thousand Spaniards and other foreigners who had arrived in Peru had received grants (Lockhart 1968:12). Those who had been awarded them had no wish to transform the organization of the local communities, since their capacity to extract labor and tribute depended on maintaining the existing structures and establishing good working relationships with the *kurakas*, the traditional leaders who symbolized the collective identity and interests of these communities (Stern 1981). In the early years, the native communities provided labor, personal service, and payments in kind that sustained the *encomenderos* and their retainers. Later, they would have to provide monetary payments and goods for the *encomenderos* to sell (Rowe 1957: 159–161).

Conditions were far from tranquil and stable during this period. The Spaniards were able to establish and maintain their toehold in the Andes by virtue of the civil war and the regional rebellions of the late 1520s and early 1530s. They capitalized on the instability of the empire by kidnaping one of the rivals for the Inca throne, and then prolonged the successional dispute in the imperial ruling class when they killed him. By 1535 the Spaniards maintained the illusion of supporting the Inca state and its ruler; at the same time, they attempted to influence his decisions, control his actions, and suppress his opponents. Groups like the Cañaris or the Wankas – whose members had suffered under Inca rule – were in open rebellion against the imperial state and had allied themselves with the Spaniards; other communities independently sought to reassert their autonomy.

In 1535, as the Spaniards prepared to invade Chile and Chachapoyas and to deal with Alvarado's incursion into Quito, the Inca ruler, Manqo 'Inka, slipped out of Cuzco to organize an attack on the Spaniards remaining in the core area of the state. As the Spanish forces dispersed and moved toward the peripheries, the Inca leader and his forces began to kill travelers and isolated settlers. Soon they laid sieges against the Spaniards remaining in Cuzco, Lima, and Trujillo. The siege of Cuzco began in March 1536 and lasted for thirteen months; it was particularly fierce, and large parts of the city were burned during the attacks. When Almagro's expedition returned to Cuzco toward the end of March 1537 and reinforced its beleaguered inhabitants, Manqo 'Inka and his forces withdrew to the wilderness of Vilcapampa and established their capital at Vitcos. For the next three decades, they waged guerrilla warfare on the Spaniards; their attacks were frequent and particularly intense in Charcas and Collao during the late 1530s and 1540s (Hemming 1970; Kubler 1944, 1947).

By the end of the year the tensions between Pizarro and Almagro finally boiled over and erupted into open conflict. In December 1537 Pizarro sent his brother, Hernando, to punish Almagro for his crimes against the state. The two factions met and fought a particularly bloody battle at Las Salinas outside of Cuzco in early April 1538, where Almagro and his forces were aided by Paullu Topa and six thousand Indians who supported his claim to the Inca throne. Almagro and the other leaders of his party were captured and executed three months later; Paullu Topa fled from the battle and was able to switch his allegiance to Pizarro's faction, since the governor could not afford to have him join Manqo 'Inka's forces. Hernando Pizarro was able to establish control over the Spaniards in Cuzco, who, for the most

part, supported Almagro because of his assistance in the last
days of the siege; Pizarro's brother succeeded partly through
diplomacy and partly by sending the more unruly of Almagro's
supporters on expeditions. Francisco Pizarro persisted in his
attacks on Almagro's teenage son and his remaining supporters;
after more than three years, a band of them assassinated the
governor and some of his supporters in the palace.

News of events in Peru slowly trickled back to King Charles,
who was already growing increasingly annoyed because he had
received no gold or silver from the colony since his portion of
'Ataw Wallpa's ransom arrived in January 1534. This dereliction
of duty was noticed, and in early 1539 Pizarro sent his brother to
take the royal fifth to the king. Hernando Pizarro reached
Charles's court a year later. The king accepted the plunder and
imprisoned him because his brother had ignored royal decrees.
In order to reestablish his authority in Peru Charles sent
Cristóbal Vaca de Castro to Peru to investigate and report on the
situation and to succeed Pizarro as governor, when he learned
that the latter had been killed.

Vaca de Castro learned about Pizarro's murder in Colombia in
April 1541. As he moved southward toward Lima, the new
governor organized forces loyal to the crown to combat the
remnants of Almagro's faction that opposed his governorship
and, hence, the king himself. In 1542 Almagro's son and his
supporters allied themselves with Manqo 'Inka and moved to
Vilcas, where they attempted to negotiate with Vaca de Castro.
However, the discussions broke down and the two sides clashed
at Chupas, outside Huamanga. When the fighting was over,
two hundred forty men had been killed on the battlefield and
another thirty of the rebels were captured and subsequently
executed for opposing the crown.

In a further attempt to reassert his authority in the colonies,
King Charles promulgated the New Laws, which were introduced in Peru in 1542 and 1543. These provisions attempted to
curb the power of the *encomenderos* and thus prevent the formation of a hereditary, colonial nobility that could either thwart or
challenge the power of the crown. They prohibited the governor
from granting new *encomiendas*, prevented the *ecomenderos* from
willing these grants to their heirs, and required church and royal
officials to relinquish their *encomiendas*. When the new viceroy
attempted to enforce these provisions of the New Laws in 1544,

the *encomenderos* – led by Gonzalo Pizarro, another of Francisco's brothers – rebelled. This struggle waxed and waned for four years. From the inception of the revolt until the viceroy's assassination in January 1546, anyone supporting Pizarro's cause was publicly flogged and even the governor, Vaca de Castro, was imprisoned (Gibson 1966:58–59; Lockhart 1968:15–16).

Once more, it was necessary for King Charles to send an emissary to reestablish order in Peru. This time, his envoy was Pedro de la Gasca, who bore the title of President of the Audiencia of Lima and carried with him extensive powers, which included blank letters bearing the king's signature (Means 1964:93). In July 1546 he revoked the New Laws and offered amnesty to rebels who would acknowledge his authority. Pizarro and his followers refused to relinquish the power they had seized after the viceroy's death. In December La Gasca accused Pizarro of treason; fifteen months later, forces loyal to Gasca attacked Pizarro and his comrades near the southern end of Lake Titicaca. The rebels were victorious, forcing La Gasca to borrow money from Lima merchants so he could raise another army. In early April 1548 the rebels and the royalists fought a decisive battle at Anta. When the rebel forces deserted, Pizarro was captured and executed a few days later. Many *encomenderos* died during this phase of the civil war. During this period, Paullu Topa greeted La Gasca as he entered Cuzco at the same time he was continuing to provide very real support to Pizarro. After the battle, La Gasca redistributed some of the vacant *encomiendas* to individuals who had demonstrated their loyalty to the crown during the struggle, while others reverted to the crown or were forced to pay pensions (Hemming 1970:270–272).

After quelling the *encomenderos*'s revolt, La Gasca organized the finances of the colony and collected an enormous sum of money for the Crown before returning to Spain in January 1550. An uneasy truce prevailed between the *encomenderos* and the state for the next few years, as neither the judges of the *audiencia* nor the new viceroy who had arrived in September 1551 were able to rule effectively. The truce was broken when the viceroy published a new set of laws in June 1552, which eliminated the *mit'a* labor tax and reduced the tribute payments owed by the native communities to the *encomenderos*, who were predictably outraged (Rowe 1957:170–179). By November 1553 the *encomenderos* in the south – around Cuzco, Arequipa, and Huamanga –

were sufficiently organized and rebelled under the leadership of
Francisco Hernández Girón, a respected citizen of Cuzco who
held one of the richest *encomiendas* in Peru. They rebelled because they wanted to be able to force the native communities to
mine for silver and grow coca, which they sold for cash. Their
rebellion was crushed after eleven months; its leaders were
executed and their *encomiendas* confiscated. The *encomienda*
granted to Hernández Girón was given to Sayri Topa, who had
perhaps succeeded Manqo 'Inka as emperor but not guerrilla
leader after the latter was assassinated in 1545 (Hemming 1970:
278–279, 293–295, 366–369).

The neo-Inca state, the civil wars between factions of ruling-
class Spaniards, and their struggles with King Charles and his
representatives were not the only threats to Peru during the age
of the plunder economy. The inhabitants also had to contend
with runaway slaves, banditry, sabotage, and lawsuits.

Slaves participated in all of the early expeditions to Peru.
Some were native Americans born and captured in the circum-
Caribbean area; others, perhaps the majority, were the
American-born descendants of slaves brought from Africa; and
still others were captured and brought from the west coast of
Africa. In 1535 four hundred slaves were shipped from Panama
to Peru, and in the same year one hundred fifty Blacks accompanied Almagro to Chile. Slaves participated in all phases of the
civil war among the Spaniards, and the rebel leader, Hernández
Girón, offered to free all slaves who joined his forces during the
1553–1554 rebellion. By the mid-1550s, there were about three
thousand slaves, mostly male, in Peru, and their potential
power was a matter of concern for the eight thousand Spanish
residents of the area (Bowser 1974:4–11; Lockhart 1968:145–146).
As early as 1535, the Spaniards saw slaves as both a source of
labor and a threat to their security. The colony promulgated
strict laws to regulate the activities of slaves. Slaves who vio-
lated the curfew laws in Lima were severely punished; first
offenders received a hundred lashes, second offenders were
emasculated, and third offenders were exiled, thus depriving
their owners of access to their labor. Slaveowners were liable for
any damages caused by slaves, and by the 1550s they were
using freedmen – individuals who had purchased their freedom
or been emancipated – to patrol the countryside for runaways
and to prevent the formation of *cimarron* communities – bands of

escaped slaves and their companions (Bowser 1974:147–151).

There were already *cimarron* communities in Peru by the 1540s. In 1545, about two hundred escaped slaves established a community in a marshy area of the Huaura Valley north of Lima; armed with European weapons, they raided the surrounding countryside, attacked travelers, and allegedly planned to overthrow the Spaniards and take the *encomiendas* for themselves. They were eventually attacked by the Spaniards, and all of them were killed in the battle that ensued. A smaller band – about twenty slaves and their companions – formed in the Piura Valley around 1540 and operated for more than a decade. Another band, composed of both runaways and Spaniards, hassled farmers and travelers in the vicinity of Lima around 1549. *Cimarron* communities continued to emerge and to be suppressed well into the seventeenth century. A particularly troublesome group, composed of Black slaves and native *mitayos* who had run away from nearby gold mines, formed in Vilcabamba in 1602; they posed enough of a threat that the governor sent Cañaris, who were loyal to the state, to track them down. This group evaded the posse, however, when attention was turned to a band of plantation Blacks who set fire to the buildings of a nearby estate, killing the native workers who remained loyal to the owner, and almost capturing the owner himself. The actions of these bands sparked a local uprising that lasted for several days. After it was suppressed, the Spaniards found that the uprising had been planned and that the participants had been secretly stockpiling food and supplies for more than two years. In 1604 there was a second uprising in Vilcabamba; this one also involved an alliance between Blacks and Indians (Bowser 1974:176–177; Lockhart 1968:188–189).

Sabotage seems to have increased in frequency and intensity, particularly in the waning years of the plunder economy era. While the demands of the *encomenderos* for native labor and tribute remained high and relatively constant throughout the period, the size of the native communities forced to contribute to their well-being declined, especially after the havoc caused by the widespread epidemics that appeared in the mid-1520s, 1546, and 1558–1559. Their numbers were even further diminished as members ran away, giving up their traditional claims to land, or failed to return from *mit'a* labor obligations in distant areas (Spalding 1970:645–646, 1984:165–177). This effectively increased the levels of surplus extracted from the members of those who remained in their natal communities. The natives knew they were being exploited, and they frequently fought back with those readily available weapons that required almost no organization at all: theft, carelessness, neglect, or arson. The Spaniards's concern with sabotage and subversion suggests that these crimes were not uncommon and the damages were often extensive. For instance, an *encomendero* in the Huamanga area during the 1560s complained that the native shepherds assigned to watch over his flocks lost or stole seven thousand sheep (Stern 1982:49).

By the 1550s, the native communities were beginning to flood the viceregal courts in Lima, Quito, and La Plata with petitions and suits to regain lands they had lost. Many of the disputes were between the native communities; in some instances, the communities sued *kuraka* and their allies over land rights (Larson 1988:40; Rostworowski de Diez Canseco 1988a:53–61; Stern 1982:115). While these disputes occasionally dragged on for decades, "the natives' juridical activity constituted far more than an occasional nuisance" for the Spaniards (Stern 1982:128); they quickly developed into a major strategy for protecting individual and community interests. By helping the natives avoid or reduce their *mit'a* labor and tribute obligations, they began to disrupt production and create labor shortages.

James Lockhart (1968:133–149) has suggested that between twenty-five and fifty percent of the eight thousand Spaniards in Peru during the mid-1550s were rootless, idle vagrants, who had no access to the labor or tribute of the native communities. Some lived off the generosity and hospitality of wealthy *encomenderos* – retainers who were expected to follow the lead of their hosts – while others received money when they enlisted in the armies that waged the various campaigns of the civil war. Some were rogues, confidence men, and gamblers who preyed mainly on their countrymen; others were vagabonds and fugitives who had fled to the "Indian country" of Collao in the 1540s, where they began to constitute an enormous problem. Many of them became armed bandits who roamed the countryside, stealing food, looting villages, and robbing travelers. After each phase of the civil war, some of the transients were siphoned off by the *entradas*, or expeditions, that searched for treasure in wilderness areas; others, who had acquired modest amounts of silver, returned to Spain where they lived off incomes derived from investments. A few became commercial farmers and ranchers during the 1550s – entrepreneurs who supplied agricultural produce and livestock to the eight hundred Spaniards and fifteen thousand transient Indian miners who dug for silver in the mines in Upper Peru (Larson 1988:43–50).

By the 1550s, only a small portion of the Spanish population in Peru had access to native labor and tribute through the *encomienda* system. The remainder of the Spaniards, those who were neither transients nor *encomenderos*, eked out livelihoods as farmers, peddlers, shopkeepers, artisans, merchants, and professionals (Lockhart 1968:49–134). They stood between the *encomenderos* and the native communities that served them. Increasingly, they found that their interests opposed and were eroded by actions of the *encomenderos*, who still sought to have their privileges made hereditary, and by the Indians who were still able to draw on the productive power of their own communities for the goods and services they offered for sale in the marketplaces at prices far below those of the Spaniards (Spalding 1973, 1984:148–151). This conflict became apparent in the late 1550s, when the *encomenderos* offered Philip II, who had ascended to the imperial throne in 1557 and was in desperate need of money, a large bribe to bestow and confirm their feudal authority. Some of the *kurakas* responded by offering the crown 100,000 ducats more than the *encomenderos*'s highest offer. The Spaniards, who opposed the *encomenderos*, also sought to enlist Philip's aid, even though they were hopelessly divided over how to deal with the problem.

The new king was confronted with crises in both Europe and Peru. His father's attempt to create a European empire had failed and left the Crown of Castile bankrupt and even more dependent on the nobility than it had been earlier. Philip could not raise taxes without the nobility's permission, nor could he intervene in the internal affairs of his realms outside Spain without risking the revolt of his nobles and townspeople (Elliott 1970:181–211, 231–235; Rodríguez-Salgado 1988). His only solution to the European crisis was to increase the amount of treasure he extracted from the American colonies. Of course, when he ordered the royal treasury officials in Peru to send even more silver, the Crown was brought into open conflict with the governors and viceroys who were attempting to establish royal authority in the colony. In the late 1550s the viceroy of Peru, the Marqués de Cañete, was using the crown's silver as an inducement to promote settlement in the new towns he had founded and to support a viceregal guard. At the same time, silver production was beginning to decline, given the mining technology available, and by the 1560s the treasury of Peru regularly had an annual deficit. Thus, Philip's demands added to the economic crisis and the political unrest already beginning to surface in Peru (Spalding 1984:141–146).

In the 1560s, Spanish colonial authorities discovered the existence of several independent movements that gave voice to the anger and frustration of their participants and that threatened both peace and stability. While they never erupted, they indicated just how profoundly troubled the colony was. The movements organized among the Spanish and mestizo communities of Cuzco and Lima had their parallels among the native communities of the highlands. Besides the rebels of the neo-Inca state, who posed a continual threat, a new movement emerged in the mid 1560s among communities that the Spaniards assumed had accepted their domination. It was a millenarian movement, called *taki onqoy*, which advocated resistance to Spanish settlers and customs and argued that the Andean peoples must achieve solidarity by transcending their differences, both the traditional ones and the new ones resulting from the class divisions that crystallized after the Spaniards arrived. Both men and women supported the movement; they replaced *kurakas* who were discredited by virtue of their association with the Spaniards. They believed that, when solidarity was achieved, the *wak'as* would wage war on the Spaniards and eliminate them. The Spaniards became alarmed when they learned that native uprisings were imminent and discovered arms caches at several places in the mountains (Spalding 1984:146–147; Stern 1982:51–79; Wachtel 1971, 1973:255–275).

5.2. The Crisis of the 1560s

If people live by plunder for centuries, there must, after all, always be something there to plunder; in other words the objects of plunder must be continually reproduced. (Karl Marx, *Capital: A Critique of Political Economy*)

> Plunder cannot become the basis of a sociopolitical system that permits a ruling group to extract surplus from those it rules over a period of time. (Karen Spalding, *Huarochirí*)

The crisis that erupted in Andean society during the late 1520s was political. It involved the rapid disintegration of an imperial state that had consolidated power and was attempting to further centralize its control by elaborating state-based institutions and practices and by incorporating local elites into the ruling class to ensure the continued extraction of surplus labor from subject populations. The collapse was precipitated by a civil war between factions of the ruling class and by local revolts, in which at least some communities attempted to reassert their traditional autonomy. Given the balance of forces and chaotic conditions that developed by the mid-1530s, no faction of the traditional ruling class was able to seize effective control of the state apparatus and assert its dominance. As a result, the power of the Inca state was weakened significantly and, more important, decentralized. Its capacity to expropriate land and appropriate surplus labor were diminished and, in some regions, eliminated altogether, since control of the means and processes of production remained in the hands of the local communities and their traditional leaders. However, the process of surplus extraction, as well as the forms deployed during the imperial years, persisted at the local and regional levels. In effect, Andean society was separated into small, mutually hostile political units, as formerly autonomous regions or those that were constituted during the imperial regime reestablished or claimed their self-sufficiency.

The disruption created by the civil wars and revolts had begun before the Spaniards arrived and continued after they inserted themselves as both spectators and performers in the destabilization and dismantling of the imperial state and the decentralization of political power those processes entailed. They did not, however, arise, phoenix-like, from the ashes to assert immediate hegemony over the Andean peoples. In fact, the frequency of rebellions, civil wars, acts of sedition, and banditry during the period of the plunder economy suggest something quite different. Political power was usually weak, often transitory, and occasionally absent altogether; it was shared and contested, rather than the Spaniards's exclusive possession.

Neither the Spaniards, who ransacked shrines and state installations for treasure and received *encomiendas* to support
themselves, nor members of the native ruling class, some of
whom were also awarded *encomiendas*, had any wish to transform the existing production relations as long as the plunder
remained plentiful – although they did extend the forms of
surplus extraction to include tribute payments in kind and
money as well as in labor service. The *encomenderos* did not
disrupt the traditional production relations, but instead established working relations with local *kurakas*. They became part of
an economic system that supported the few by exploiting the
many, but left the means, organization, and processes of production under the control of the *kurakas* and the subject communities. Their incomes depended on the availability of
treasure, which was plentiful when they arrived, and on their
ability to protect their privileges. As late as 1565, the tribute
extracted by one *encomendero* accounted for seventy percent of
his money income, after the products were converted into
commodities and sold, and fully supported his other activities
(Spalding 1984:134). However, the weaknesses and fragility of
this economic system became apparent during the crisis of the
1560s. The catalysts of the crisis were the depletion of plunder
and the demands for new forms of native labor that were
structured differently in various regions because of the economic growth occurring around Lima and Potosí (Stern
1982:189–193; 1985).

Carlos Sempat Assadourian (1979, 1983) has argued that the
production of silver bullion emerged as the dominant sector of
the Andean economy toward the middle of the sixteenth century; this coincided with the depletion of plunder and the
discovery of high-grade ore in 1545 at Potosí (Bakewell 1984;
Brading and Cross 1972). Gold and silver – first the plunder that
was melted down and cast as ingots and then, increasingly,
metals extracted from various mining ventures – linked the
Andean colonies with Spain and Europe. However, only between sixty and sixty-five percent of the silver bullion produced
in Peru reached Europe; the remainder was spent in the Americas, where it fueled the development of distinctive regional
economies that were connected by commerce and structured by
their commercial ties to Lima and Potosí. These growth poles –
with their vast urban concentrations, demand for diverse prod-

ucts, inflated prices, and strategic commodities – exerted enormous influence, even on distant regions. The demands of Lima and Potosí, as well as the goods and services they provided, forged strong links with several formerly autonomous, self-sufficient regions. The inhabitants of Ecuador, Peru, Bolivia, Chile, Argentina, and Paraguay were increasingly bound to Lima and Potosí and their lives affected by what was happening in those two cities, as their traditional economic systems and production regimes were transformed.

Silver mining was the motor of this new economic system. As Steve Stern (1985:138–139) observed, it created a new pan-Andean economic space, characterized by uneven regional development and interregional markets that were linked together by the logic of the merchant capitalist. It reorganized material life around the production of commodities for these markets and diminished the control that native communities exerted over their own means of production and labor power by minimizing the resources they were able to devote to their subsistence production and reproduction, and by forcing them to provide cheap labor and other resources for commodity-producing enterprises that satisfied the seemingly insatiable demands of the growth poles.

Let us briefly consider how this new economic system worked. Soon after silver was discovered at Potosí, the population of the mining town swelled to include more than seven thousand miners, most of whom were *yanakunas*, retainers who leased rights to mine particular veins in return for a share of the ore, or *encomienda* Indians, who used a portion of the silver they produced to pay the tribute they owed to their *encomenderos*. Both groups kept the silver refined beyond the amounts required for those payments, and some of them amassed small fortunes, even after paying the typically inflated prices for food and other necessities that prevailed in Potosí. The Indians also controlled the smelting process. To acquire pure silver, the Spaniards had to sell the ore they received as tribute or shares to Indian smelters, who refined the ore and then resold the metal to them. The Spaniards also gained more pure silver by providing goods that were in high demand around the mines; for example, the sale of coca leaf accounted for about half the value of all the commodities purchased at Potosí. Altogether, more than ninety percent of the goods sold in Potosí were produced in the Andes (Bakewell 1984:14–19, 33–60; Stern 1988a:850–851, 1988b:887–888).

For example, the coca leaf and other goods consumed at Potosí were mass-produced in regions like Pocona, the economies of which were transformed as production for the market replaced subsistence cultivation. During the 1550s the members of *encomienda* communities were required to pay fixed rents in specified products; thus, the control they exercised over what they grew diminished, and their self-sufficiency was weakened as they were forced to rely on commercial transactions to purchase the subsistence goods they were no longer able to produce for themselves. The high prices coca brought at Potosí allowed the *encomenderos*, who were indirectly engaged in its production, and merchants and traders, who trafficked in it, to accumulate enormous profits that were not taxed by the colonial state (Larson 1988:46–49). Regional economies quickly became specialized; the inhabitants of Córdoba grew cotton, while the *encomenderos* in Tucumán, Arequipa, Huánuco, and Piura bred mules, which they sold to transport coca leaf, silver bullion, and other goods throughout the Andean area (Sempat Assadourian 1983:19–23, 46, 213).

Lima was the other growth pole of the Andean economic space that began to flourish in the 1550s. It quickly provided the main linkage with Europe and the other colonies in the Americas, the sole port of entry and departure for the outside world. By virtue of its role as the political and legal hub of the colony, Lima attempted to regulate contact and commerce with the outside. The bullion shipped to Spain and commodities imported from Europe were supposed to pass through the capital city. As the city's population grew, markets appeared for food and other subsistence goods that could no longer be produced locally in quantities sufficient to satisfy its demands. Produce grown for the market replaced grain production in the immediate vicinity of the city, as grain farming was displaced outward to coastal valleys located north and south of the capital. The grain and other commodities they produced were transported by boat as coastal shipping and commerce became increasingly important sources of income (Lockhart 1968:77–95, 114–134; Sempat Assadourian 1983:163–170).

The crisis of the 1560s also had political and economic dimensions. A central element involved who would control the labor power of the indigenous communities in the new economic system that was beginning to form in the Andes. The maintenance of the plunder economy required that the native communities continue to produce goods and services that could be converted into commodities by the *encomenderos*, and that the social and demographic reproduction of the communities was insured so they could meet the demands of the *encomienda* system. However, the civil unrest of the plunder era, the *encomenderos*'s high levels of demand for native labor, and the disruption caused by epidemics and individuals who abandoned their natal communities for a variety of reasons weakened the productive capacities of those communities (Spalding 1984:134). Also, the *encomenderos* and the *kurakas* were the only classes that had legally defined regular access to the labor power and products of the native population. Furthermore, even though the productive capacities of the native communities were diminished and being channeled in new directions, they still retained firm control over the means and organization of production, and exerted some control over their own labor power and time. The result of this particular concatenation was that the native communities, who owed fixed amounts of tribute and labor to the *encomenderos* who converted the products of their labor into commodities, were often able to compete rather successfully (in spite of the decline in their productive capacities) with both the *encomendero* and non-*encomendero* segments of the colonial population in the context of the emerging market economy.

The political dimension of the crisis involved the growing numbers of immigrants, many of whom were armed and had no source of income, and questions regarding the distribution of the surplus expropriated from the native communities. How much surplus could be extracted, who would receive it, what was the Crown's share, and how was the apparatus required to maintain social order to be financed were hotly contested issues. The Crown's representatives resolved differences within the *encomendero* class and reestablished social order by redistributing *encomiendas* to individuals who supported their efforts. However, when La Gasca and his successors used royal funds to create and support an incipient colonial bureaucracy – notaries and city officials – they found themselves in conflict with the Crown's demands for revenues.

A third precipitant of the crisis involved the decline in silver production during the 1560s, as the readily accessible and high-grade ores located near the surface of Potosí were depleted, and the miners were forced to dig deep shafts to gain access to veins that ultimately yielded lower-grade ores. The effect was a per capita decline in silver production. This slowed down the development of the interregional economy propelled by Potosí and Lima (Stern 1988a:850–851). It also coincided with the Crown's growing demands for additional revenues, which were already heavily dependent on the silver bullion that flowed from Potosí through Lima to Spain. When policies were implemented to secure these revenues, they weakened or undermined efforts by the royal governors to institute structures or practices that would facilitate the maintenance of order in a socially fragmented and very unruly colony (Spalding 1984:139–142).

The festering resentment manifested in the *taki onqoy* movement and its effects on everyday life – less cooperation and more passive resistance, hostility, and sabotage – and in the military plots to annihilate Spanish settlers brought the crisis into focus during the mid-1560s. While the Spaniards depended on maintaining good working relations with the *kurakas* to acquire the goods and services of the native communities, they had not established institutions or practices that guaranteed regular access to either if these relations deteriorated. They had to deal with the problem of social control, and, given the very real possibilities for insurrection and economic collapse, they had to resolve it quickly (Stern 1982:56–72).

Lope García de Castro, the acting viceroy from 1564 to 1569, instituted a series of reforms that were intended to mold the Spanish and Indian segments of the colonial population into a single organic entity that would be internally stable and that would promote economic development and simultaneously protect the interests of the ruling classes. First, he appointed *corregidores* in each province to control the actions of the *kurakas* and to curb the abuses of the *encomenderos*; they made the major administrative decisions, while the *kurakas* handled recurrent matters and became, in effect, their agents. Second, he began the resettlement of the members of spatially dispersed native communities into villages, or *reducciones*, that were grouped into parishes, each of which had its own priest and *corregidor*-appointed civil official or governor, usually the *kuraka*, to prevent problems when taxes had to be collected (Rowe 1957:161–163). It took García de Castro and his successor, Francisco de Toledo, more than a decade to complete the implementation of the plan for strategic hamlets and the construction of an accompanying political infrastructure that owed its allegiance, at least nominally, to the colonial state, and that was supposed to spy and report on the thoughts and deeds of the village residents in order to maintain internal security (Spalding 1970). When the viceroys created a colonial bureaucracy composed of officials with broad powers, including tax collecting, they focused attention on the question of how and by whom these officials would be paid, and brought into the open the central contradictions that existed between different levels of the state apparatus.

5.3. The Formation of Colonial Society

> The fifth viceroy of Peru, Francisco de Toledo, was given the task of organizing the political structure of the kingdom so as to meet the demands from the Spanish population for a share of the labor and goods of the members of Andean society while generating sufficient income for the royal treasury in Peru to pay the costs of government and still remit something back to Spain. (Karen Spalding, *Huarochirí*)

Between 1569 and 1580, Toledo carried out reforms and implemented policies that led to the reorganization of everyday life in the colony. Toledo was one of many minor noblemen who linked their careers with the ambitions of King Philip. Philip's goal was to create a centralized state with the Crown as its center of gravity and a bureaucratic apparatus that was loyal to the Crown rather than to other factions of the ruling class. To achieve this aim, Philip had to subordinate the nobility, while simultaneously ensuring that its members continued to receive surplus labor and goods from the direct producers they exploited. He accomplished this by appropriating the judicial powers of the nobility for the Crown and by using them to reinforce the state's control over the direct producers. The resolution of these struggles in Spain provided Toledo with a blueprint for the course of action he would pursue after he arrived in Peru (Spalding 1984:157).

By the time Toledo arrived in Peru, royal officials had already appropriated the judicial powers of the *encomenderos*, and the state already played an important role in setting the levels of exploitation, defining the mechanisms of surplus extraction, and determining how it would be distributed. The state and its various civil and religious officials were preventing the *encomenderos* from having direct access to the native population, and were gradually replacing them as the major agents of surplus extraction. Toledo elaborated patronage powers of the state, which officials had begun to assume in the 1540s with the redistribution of *encomiendas*. Thus, by 1569 the colonial government was already assigning the surplus labor and products of native communities to individuals who had supported its actions. During his reign as viceroy, Toledo consolidated these powers and provided a legal foundation for them. In the 1570s the state and its representatives would become the sole agents of surplus extraction; they would also determine how the products and labor of the native communities were transferred to the Spanish segment of colonial society (Spalding 1984:157–158).

While the reforms Toledo continued or instituted were extensive, three practices had particularly important and far-reaching implications for our concerns: the forced resettlement of native communities, tribute payments, and forced labor service.

It took nearly a decade to complete the resettlement of Indian communities that traditionally lived in widely scattered small settlements or that became even further dispersed during the civil unrest that followed the collapse of the Inca state. The members of these communities resisted attempts to relocate them in villages, where they could be more easily counted, assessed tribute and labor taxes, and spied upon by the state's civil and religious representatives. A particularly insidious piece of legislation, which accompanied the resettlement program, required that the Indians must actually sleep in the villages at night; this provision made it increasingly difficult for them to work agricultural fields or to use pastures that were located more than three or four miles from the villages. In the 1580s the state defined the fields and pastures in which the Indians were unable to work as vacant lands, which reverted to the Crown. A decade later, the colonial authorities held the first of a series of periodic auctions in which these vacant lands were sold to the highest bidder. This provided the Crown and the colony with a new source of revenue (Spalding 1984:158, 180–181).

The basic tax levied on the Indian population by the state was tribute. Before 1570, the *encomenderos* collected tribute from the native communities in the form of silver or goods; this allowed them to vary their demands from one year to the next to reflect their own needs and the capacities of the communities to fulfill these assessment. Toledo changed this policy. He levied tribute, a fixed amount of silver or its equivalent, on all able-bodied men between the ages of 18 and 50, rather than on the community as a whole. He exempted members of the native elite from tribute payments. In addition, the state's representative, the *corregidor de indios*, took over the collection of tribute, which excluded the *encomenderos* from the process. They used a portion of the money they collected to pay salaries that were set by the vice-royalty; the remainder was delivered to *encomenderos* who held *encomiendas* in the province and to the royal treasury in Lima (Spalding 1984:161–162).

Toledo's tribute levy forced native men to sell goods or services in the market to acquire the silver they needed to pay the tax. It also permitted the state to sell the goods it received as payments in lieu of silver at annual auctions. As Karen Spalding (1984:162–164) observed, this subsidized merchants and non-food producers, most of whom were Spaniards, by providing them with access to the products of Indian society. It also gave them a buffer against food shortages caused by poor harvests. In addition, it provided a small measure of relief to the native peoples who were liable for tribute, because they had to pay the same fixed amount from one year to the next, regardless of the harvest size.

The *mit'a* was the second tax levied on each province by Toledo. It was a forced labor tax that was conceived as a way to lower production costs by requiring those individuals against whom the tax was assessed to work at particular tasks, which the state defined as essential, for a specified period of time at legally assigned wages. The *mitayos* served six-month terms, which did not include the amount of time or the costs they incurred as they traveled to the localities where they were to work. At any moment, one-sixth to one-seventh of the able-bodied men in a province were fulfilling their *mit'a* obligations, while their neighbors and kin assumed their responsibilities at home. In some instances, since the *mitayos* were supposedly receiving wages, their tribute assessments were increased.

The viceroy had appropriated the power to assign *mit'a* labor to individuals who were performing tasks deemed essential by the state. Most of the *mitayos* were assigned to work around the two growth poles of the colonial economy: Potosí and Lima. The *mit'a* provided the mine owners with a steady supply of cheap, unskilled labor. This was particularly important for both the mine owners and the colonial state at a time when the quality of the ores was declining and it was becoming increasingly more difficult and expensive to mine them. It allowed the owners to replace the skilled native miners, who had previously controlled the production and refining processes, with unskilled workers, who were required to work for a six-month period at a legally set wage that was both inadequate and frequently not paid. The state was attempting to ensure that its revenues from the mines remained stable or even increased. The state also underwrote production costs around Lima, the other growth pole of the colonial economy. Here *mitayos* from the hinterland were employed on coastal estates to produce foodstuffs that were sold in the capital, and to provide services, such as postal delivery, that the state subsidized for the ruling classes (Spalding 1984:164–166).

Toledo's *mit'a* labor tax had a massive effect on colonial society, most especially on the native population. It further subsidized the state and certain sectors of the ruling class. It assumed that the native communities in the provinces were stable and that they possessed sufficient resources to reproduce themselves both socially and demographically. However, neither was necessarily true. The *mit'a* system ultimately promoted migration, since foreign residents in a province were not subject to the labor tax. This meant, of course, that the migrants had left their natal communities, relinquishing their traditional claims and obligations, and giving up the security provided by intimate association with kin. In addition, the creation of provincial bureaucracies composed of various civil and religious officials opened up new avenues of social mobility within the native communities during the closing decades of the sixteenth century (Spalding 1970, 1984:165–166).

The policies implemented by Toledo resolved the political and economic crisis of the 1560s. The tribute and *mit'a* levies permitted the state to appropriate a considerable portion of the surplus labor and product of the native communities. The state and its representatives became the agency through which surplus from the Indian communities flowed to the Spanish segment of the colonial population and to the Crown. Since the state held the powers to appoint provincial officials and to assign native labor to individuals engaged in what it deemed essential production, access to the state bureaucracy and to the surplus it controlled became the basis for both privilege and wealth, the major determinant of socioeconomic position and social mobility in the colonial society that congealed during the Toledan era. This meant that politics and access to the political realm had important, if not dominant, roles in shaping the form and character of the colonial society from the 1570s until the 1660s, when the viceregal economy once more faltered and began to decline, bringing with it an even more comprehensive redistribution of the labor and wealth of the native communities and the accompanying social dislocations that resulted from this restructuring of the colonial political economy (Spalding 1970:663–664; 1984:166–167).

Toledo had not intended to restructure the social relations and culture of the native communities; they were defined legally as a distinct republic, whose internal relationships and customs were to be respected and maintained by the colonial courts and authorities (Spalding 1984:158). However, his decrees ultimately had the opposite effect. By treating the various communities as interchangeable components of a *república de indios*, they obscured and eventually extinguished the significance of the traditional distinctions that existed between communities. At the same time, new distinctions were constructed between the homogenized Indian communities that were subject to tribute and *mit'a* exactions by the state, and the various *mestizo* and Spanish classes that existed outside and were exempt from one or both of the levies.

The exploitation and extortion instituted by the Toledan decrees were a rich medium that allowed resentment to fester and occasionally erupt, spilling its contents over the surface of everyday life in the colony. However, the social and cultural transformations underwritten by the decrees had shifted the terms of the conflict between the oppressor and the oppressed. The master-slave relation came to be framed increasingly in terms of conflicting worldviews or ideologies, and the masters wanted not only the slaves's wealth and labor, but their souls. As early as the 1560s, when the *taki onqoy* movement spread over Huamanga and threatened to grow into an even wider crisis, colonial authorities recognized the explosive power and danger posed by heretical religious practices centered in the native communities. Parish priests were deployed to spread the doctrine during the closing decades of the sixteenth century. On the surface, they seemed to have succeeded; however, the idolatry trials that took place between 1600 and 1621 showed just how superficial their efforts had been. As a result, almost continuous campaigns were waged against native beliefs and ceremonies until the 1670s. In their minds, the colonists linked heresy with the fear of invasion and with the knowledge that they were vastly outnumbered by the people they exploited. Their fears were heightened during the 1660s as the economy began to stagnate, as pirates and foreign warships appeared with increasing frequency in the coastal waters, and as a plot to destroy Lima was exposed: native artisans planned to burn the city and seek aid from the English who were at war with Spain (Spalding 1984:265–270).

The regime that consolidated and centralized political and juridical power in the 1570s controlled the extraction of labor and tribute from the native communities and its redistribution to the dominant classes of colonial society. Its policies furthered the development of diverse regional economies that were connected through a network of interregional markets. The interaction of the subsistence and commercial spheres inextricably linked the histories of the native communities and the immigrants in this increasingly monetarized market economy. Class relations were reconstituted in the process. Rural communities were impoverished, both through emigration and increased taxes, and their members were given a new Indian identity that both defined and described their place in the new system of production relations.

Conclusions

Human life does not exist outside history. (Joan Robinson, "History versus Equilibrium")

History can create optical illusions. If state formation is analyzed as a process rather than an event or a brief period, the picture changes. (Christine Gailey, *Kinship to Kingship*)

This book views class and state formation from the perspective of peripheral or encapsulated peoples rather than from those of groups that succeeded in establishing their hegemony. Class and state formation are not the inevitable end products of some evolutionary trajectory, but rather historical processes that cannot be reduced either to simple economic determinism or to the capacities of great men who persuasively mobilize the masses or deviously manipulate patron-client relationships to achieve their ends. Several related themes thread their way through the book's fabric. Some strands are concerned with the processes and structures that underlie everyday life. Others are more concerned with the particularities of everyday life in the Andean world.

The Inca empire and the Andean states that preceded it were based on coercion and violence and on their capacities to construct and sustain political systems that allowed the group defined as the conquerors to expropriate land and extract surplus labor from the subjugated communities. Even though this relationship was not at the forefront of every interaction, as Karen Spalding (1984:294) observed, it structured everyday life. The Inca ruling class erected a political system that was supposed to ensure the continuous flow of labor from the subject peoples to the ruling class. To accomplish this, the Inca elite preserved the authority of local leaders while subordinating the communities they represented; it incorporated the *kurakas* into

157

the state apparatus and, hence, into an imperial ruling class, whose composition was continually being transformed as it was being constituted. Thus, the processes of state formation that occurred in Andean America challenge theories that fail to consider the role of violence and coercion and that do not examine whether and how the authority of local leaders was modified as subordinated communities were incorporated into imperial states.

The Inca state and its predecessors manifested various forms of what Samir Amin (1980) and others have called the tributary mode of production. The Inca empire was "Asiatic" in the sense (1) that it had consolidated and centralized political power and had the ability to intervene in the production and reproduction of a number of local communities; (2) that the communities were predominantly organized through kinship, and (3) that production was organized at the level of the local communities and involved items, use-values, that were used or consumed by the producers to ensure the reproduction of the community. Nonsubsistence, artisanal work occurred largely during periods when labor time was not completely used up by food production (Taylor 1979:174–185). When the Inca state enveloped local communities in the course of imperial expansion, it challenged them for control over their labor power and means of production – portions of their lands and herds. It employed the traditional leaders of the communities, who were recast as local representatives of the state, to gain access to their surplus labor and to intervene in the local processes of production and reproduction by demanding labor power above and beyond that required for local consumption. It appropriated this labor power, as a means of production, through political and/or ideological means, rather that through economic compulsion (Amin 1980:69; Taylor 1979:182).

Imperial Inca society manifested the articulation of several modes of production. The linkages were exceedingly complex because some of the communities incorporated into the empire were already class-stratified, tribute-based states; others were non-stratified or kin-stratified groups whose production relations were built on various forms of the communal mode of production. The capacity, and apparently even the desire, of the imperial state to encapsulate or penetrate the production and reproduction processes of communities with diverse production relations varied. In some instances, the state was able to exert considerable control over the production and reproduction relations of the communities it enveloped; in other instances, its control over these processes was marginal or transitory. This diversity of articulations, reflecting differences in the state's penetration and transformation of local relations of production and reproduction, was historically constituted. The result was that the empire resembled an enormously complicated patchwork of relations. While the imperial rulers may have aspired to the "crystalline" integration of the peoples they subordinated, as Frank Salomon (1986:217) has suggested, the diversity of the relationships between the state and its subjects worked against the realization of an empire composed of an expanding number of more or less identical parts. Thus, the Andean evidence is at odds with theoretical formulations that characterize diversity not in terms of articulated modes of production, but in terms of fixed position in a developmental trajectory that inevitably leads toward statehood: chiefdoms evolve into states. As we have seen, chieftainships do not automatically develop into states; instead, the institutions and practices of state-based societies represent a means by which diverse modes of production are linked.

The diverse forms of articulation provided the underpinnings for a set of contradictions that could intersect in complex ways, and for their expression in the class structure of the imperial state, in the relations of the state with groups living on the periphery beyond its effective control, and in the various conflicts they engendered. The contradictions involved the opposing interests of the various ideologically constituted, corporate landholding groups in Inca society; the conflicts created by the continually changing composition of the imperial ruling class resulting from the incorporation of various local leaders who had forged political and marital alliances with the Inca ruling elite; the continuation of exploitative relations or their development when communities were incorporated into the empire; the loss of control over their means of production and the labor of their members that communities faced when they were threatened with encapsulation and subjugation; and the rivalries that continued between different subordinated communities for control over land and other means of production. The contradictions meant that, while the Incas were able to penetrate and transform local relations of production, their capacity to do so rested on fragile foundations that were continually threatened by conditions that could lead to their disintegration and collapse. The realities of state formation in the Andes also call into question theories of the state that emphasize their integrative capacities and ability to maintain social order, and that fail to give serious consideration to the structural contradictions and potentially volatile conditions engendered by state institutions and practices.

The ideology of *pax incaica* provided little more than an illusion of tranquility, a thin veneer at best, to the core reality of a conflict-ridden society. For all but a few years of the century when it claimed hegemonic powers, the Inca state and the imperial ruling class were forced to engage in armed struggle to suppress the open conflict generated by the contradictions that structured everyday life. They also employed means other than force and coercion to achieve and maintain conditions that would ensure the flow of labor that guaranteed their continued existence. They installed provincial officials whose jobs were to uncover the extent of potential unrest among subject populations; they instituted a repressive legal code that was designed to discourage resistance or confrontation with the state; and they initiated a series of practices that linked the production and reproduction of local communities with their own interests. The extent and duration of the civil unrest that wracked the empire, as well as the existence of such repressive laws, indicate that neither the ruling class nor the state apparatus it was erecting was able to contain successfully the effects of the underlying contradictions.

Some groups, particularly those that benefited materially from their position in the system of production being erected by the state, supported imperial hegemony. At the same time, other communities, also enveloped and subordinated by the state, contested its claims. The subordination of local communities was always complicated, since attempts to dominate or persuade could evoke a variety of responses, ranging from collaboration and compliance in one part of the spectrum through acquiescence and dissatisfaction to resistance and open rebellion in another. Furthermore, these were not mutually exclusive responses. Communities that seemed to comply with the demands of the state during the day were often the same ones that undermined its exactions at night. Communities that acquiesced to the state when certain conditions prevailed were the same ones that rebelled openly when new circumstances developed.

From the perspective of communities incorporated into the state, an important fact of everyday life in fifteenth- and sixteenth-century Andean society was that the imperial ruling class was composed largely, if not entirely, of outsiders, since many of the pre-Incaic local elites also claimed foreign origins. In this respect, the Incas and the rulers of Chincha, as well as the Spaniards who succeeded them, were identical. States benefited outsiders, regardless of whether they were truly foreigners, as the Incas or the Spaniards must have seemed to peoples living in northern Ecuador, or merely local leaders who claimed separate origins from their subjects and extorted surplus from them. They rewarded the denial of kinship. From the communities's viewpoint, what really distinguished one foreign state and ruling class from another were the amounts and kinds of surplus they demanded, how they attempted to disguise their extortion and exploitation by dressing them up in the garb of traditional relations based on the cooperation and reciprocity characteristic of close kin and neighbors, and the alien institutions and practices they attempted to impose as they meddled with the local relations of production.

Since the class structures erected in these communities were based on relations of exploitation and thus were expressions of exploitation, antagonism was an intrinsic, rather than historically contingent, aspect of interclass relations in imperial Inca society. This also meant that individuals belonging to different classes had interests, formed by virtue of their class positions, that conflicted. The class structures that constrained, enabled, and empowered human actors in these communities were themselves "the ever present *condition* (material cause) and continually reproduced *outcome* of human agency" (Bhaskar 1979:43). They were the product of intentional activity. However, the ability of individuals to pursue and realize particular goals, based on beliefs and desires shaped by their participation in a given class position, varied because of the structural capacities of their class. Class, of course, was not the only basis of stratification in the Inca state, since ethnicity and gender crosscut class structures and developed in different ways. In some situations, the balance of forces was so tipped in favor of the exploiting classes that the extraction labor and goods must have appeared almost as a routine process, since the communities's capacity to resist had been effectively, if only momentarily, contained (Callinicos 1988:52, 89–90, 101).

The class structures that shaped everyday life in the communities encapsulated by the Inca state were not fixed, invariant entities mechanically reproduced from one season or year to the next. They were instead socially and historically constituted, responsive in part to the flow of events created by underlying mechanisms and, within limits, to attempts by the members of the various constituent classes to discover their interests and explore the extent of their powers (Callinicos 1988:132). As a result, they were liable to change. Furthermore, the courses of action pursued by the members of particular classes were not completely constrained by the existing class structures; these individuals were usually able to choose from an array of possible alternatives. Thus, in some instances, especially those where discrepancies in the balance of forces were minimized, the members of exploited classes were able to pursue courses of action that provided real opportunities for change. In tribute-based societies, like the Inca state, where centralized political power rested on flimsy foundations, such changes could weaken, but not eliminate, the existing contradictions. They could lead to the disintegration of the state apparatus that concentrated and centralized power, and they could fragment and occasionally erode the capacities of the exploiting class to extract surplus.

The fragmentation of political power meant that local lords struggled to maintain the exploitative relations that ensured their existence; this put them at odds with the direct producers, whose labor and goods they appropriated, and with other lords in the vicinity. This process does not automatically result in the appearance and dominance of new modes of production. It can, however, lead to the development of new forms of the tributary and communal modes of production, new articulations between them, and new struggles. Situations like the one just described prompted Robert Brenner's (1986:32) observation that state formation was "the pre-capitalist analogue to the capitalist drive to *accumulate capital*," and his suggestion that much of the dynamic of tributary states results from conflict.

The colonial system that took shape during the era of the plunder economy, roughly from the 1530s to the 1570s, was also based on a form of the tributary mode of production, in which political power was significantly less concentrated and centralized than it had been during the Inca regime. Like the Incas, the Spaniards were also outsiders who, by virtue of the *encomiendas* they received, claimed the right to appropriate surplus labor and tribute from local communities. The Spanish colonies in the Andes were formed at a time when Europe was still dominated by feudalism. As a result, political power was decentralized and political integration was weak. In Spain, the monarch struggled with local nobles for control over the wealth extracted from direct producers. In a sense, the *encomenderos* attempted to constitute themselves as a quasi-autonomous colonial nobility, as feudal lords dependent on the Crown for their social position and only mildly responsive during the early years to its demands for treasure. Their ability to control the extraction of native labor was challenged almost immediately by later immigrants from Europe, who lacked *encomiendas*, and by the local communities themselves, which retained control over subsistence production and sought to assert control over the production processes that developed as a result of silver production (Spalding 1984:294–296).

The Andean colonies were only marginally. dependent on linkages with Europe during the plunder economy era. Import substitution stimulated the development of a market-centered cash economy and encouraged the formation of artisanal and merchant classes that were not directly engaged in subsistence production, the development of cash crops, and the flow of goods between the towns and the surrounding countryside. The colonies were self-sufficient within a few years, and the value of their exports exceeded the costs of the luxury goods imported. The development of regionally specialized economies in the 1550s was linked with the growth of interregional commerce, both of which were spurred by silver production at the Potosí mines.

Thus, the fragmented local and regional political economies that developed and reasserted their self-sufficiency after the power and integrative capacities of the Inca state began to wane in the late 1520s acquired new identities in the 1550s. These identities were not determined by the patterns of production that prevailed earlier in particular regions. They were based instead on the commodities that communities began to produce as they were integrated into an emerging pan-Andean economic system – one that was driven by the production of precious metals and held together by a network of interregional markets where regionally produced goods were bought and sold. The political-economic processes on which these identities rested entailed new articulations of the tributary and communal modes of production and preserved a pattern of uneven development that was different from the configurations that existed during the period of Inca rule and immediately after its collapse. One consequence was that peoples who had belonged to different tribes or polities during the Inca regime were increasingly identified as Indians, the members of an emergent underclass defined in quasi-racial terms. This situation created conditions for the appearance of new social conflicts and opportunities for alliances that were no longer completely isomorphic to the older kin and ethnic collectivities that were gradually being eroded.

After the aborted uprising of the mid-1560s, the Andean colonies were drawn more tightly into Spain's orbit. A decade after King Philip succeeded in concentrating political and juridical power in the hands of the Crown and the bureaucracy he created, his representative, Francisco de Toledo, initiated parallel reforms in the viceroyalty of Peru. With the support of the Crown and the later immigrants to the colony, Toledo consolidated political and juridical power in the hands of a newly constituted state apparatus that ensured a steady flow of precious metals to the Crown and guaranteed the members of the colony's privileged classes regular access to labor drawn from the indigenous communities. The linkages constructed between the Andean colonies and Spain in the 1570s involved the colonial bureaucracy, treasury officials, and merchant houses that dominated the international trade in foreign luxury goods (Spalding 1984:296).

The colonial state erected by Toledo bore a strong resemblance to the Inca state constructed a century and a quarter earlier by the Pachakuti and Topa 'Inka. Both were tribute-based states that concentrated and centralized political and judicial power. Both extracted surplus from the indigenous communities and expropriated some of their means of production to support a multiethnic leisured class. What distinguished this colonial society from its imperial predecessor was that it promoted a territorial division of labor. It fostered the diversification and interdependency of regional political economies, not their homogenization and self-sufficiency, and ensured their integration into the wider colonial system through an increasingly monetarized market exchange. The interaction of the subsistence and commercial spheres, as Steve Stern (1982:185–186) remarked, integrated the native communities into the commercial economy and made their members increasingly dependent on money, large amounts of which were appropriated by the colonial state and the newly constituted dominant classes. Emigration and the increasing impoverishment of the Indian tributaries in the countryside were predictable consequences of the class and state structures that were consolidated by the 1570s, as was the certainty that new forms of resistance would emerge and new identities would be constructed.

In the preceding pages, I have attempted to explain class and state formation from the perspective of communities and classes whose voices are too often muzzled. They were the peoples who lived on the margins of Andean states and were impressed into them, and whose opposition to their exactions has not figured prominently in accounts of the rise of Andean civilization. Ignoring their participation in that process denies the importance of the role they played. It perpetuates and promotes the views of the powerful, the self-proclaimed bearers of culture and sources of inspiration for historical movement. Such a view distorts and trivializes history. Recognizing the presence of these groups and acknowledging the role they played challenges the validity of accounts that disregard them. It also raises questions about whose interests are served by claims that oppressive social relations and violence are the immutable, natural outcome of human history.

Notes

Introduction

1. Ake Wedin (1966) has begun to investigate various writers's portrayals of Inca civilization. Unfortunately, there is still no study that equals Peter Hulme's (1986) *Colonial Encounters*, Benjamin Keen's (1971) *The Aztec Image in Western Thought*, or Edward Said's (1979) *Orientalism* in scope. No study thus far adequately traces the development and impact of divergent views about Inca society; analyzes the linkages between the changing social and historical milieux in which individuals or groups wrote about Inca civilization and the representations they constructed; or relates theoretical conflicts involving accounts of the Incas and their subjects to underlying socioeconomic, political, and ideological struggles. Sabine MacCormack (1985), Anthony Pagden (1982), and Michael Ryan (1981) have explored how representations of Inca civilization were assimilated into and eventually transformed various sixteenth- and seventeenth-century debates about the nature of human society and good government.

2. There was sufficient testimony available in the late sixteenth century to permit several chroniclers, notably Pedro Sarmiento de Gamboa and Miguel Cabello Valboa, to assign calendrical dates to the reigns of the Inca kings who oversaw the construction of the imperial state (Rowe 1945). Cabello Valboa (1951) asserted that this process began in the 1430s. A recently assayed set of radiocarbon measurements, bracketing the incorporation of the Huancas into the empire, places imperial expansion into the Mantaro Valley of central Peru in the mid-fifteenth century and attests to the brevity of Inca rule in that area (Earle *et al.* 1987:79–82).

3. The amount of the ransom is based on Hemming's (1970:74) estimate that eleven tons of gold objects were melted down, yielding 13,420 lbs. of pure gold and that the silver objects yielded 26,000 lbs. of pure silver. If one denies the legality of primitive accumulation, and considers only the ransom as loan with a 10 percent interest rate compounded annually, generous by IMF standards, then Castile and other countries with ties to the Habsburg Empire currently owe the Andean peoples principal and interest amounting to something in the

neighborhood of $830,000,000,000,000,000,000,000,000 US, or 83×10^{25}. An annual interest rate of 5 percent on the ransom's principal would yield a payment in the vicinity of 86×10^{15}. Rather than focusing on which interest rate would more accurately reflect the changing conditions that prevailed during the 466 years that have passed since the ransom was paid, it is more important to note that the ransom constituted only a miniscule fraction of one percent of the total revenues extorted from the Andean peoples during the sixteenth and seventeenth centuries.

4. The anthropological literature on the origin of the state, or state formation, is enormous. Peter Rigby (1987) initiates a discussion that contrasts the implications of theories that embody an explicitly evolutionary model with those that focus on the origin and development of political power as the dynamic element.

Chapter 1: The Historical Landscape

1. The calendrical dates employed in this section are approximate; they are "best-guess estimates" based radiocarbon age determinations of securely dated archaeological materials that can be assigned, either directly or by cross-dating, to particular periods in the relative chronological framework proposed by John Rowe (1960a). In this scheme, six periods are recognized after the introduction of pottery in ancient Peru; from earliest to most recent, they are the Initial Period, Early Horizon, Early Intermediate Period, Middle Horizon, Late Intermediate Period, and Late Horizon. The periods are defined on the basis of changes in the sequence of pottery styles in the Ica Valley. Each period is further divided into subperiods, or epochs, on the basis of additional changes observed in the pottery styles of Ica.

Chapter 4: Quiescence, Resistance, and Rebellion

1. This claim must be tempered to some extent by the fact that warfare probably had a distinctly seasonal character. It follows John Rowe's (1945) chronology of events based on the comparison and correlation of various documentary sources. From 1438 to roughly 1462, the Incas were either at war with the Chancas or allied with them as they conquered northward and ultimately established a garrison at Cajamarca. During the 1460s, the Inca state subordinated southern Ecuador and waged a prolonged war with the Kingdom of Chimor that probably ended about 1470 (Rowe 1948:40). They subjugated the south coast of Peru in the early 1470s and then waged a three-year struggle with Huarco (Cañete) later in the decade (Menzel 1959). The great Colla rebellion that erupted in the 1480s took twelve years to suppress (Avila

1966:131). The civil strife following Topa 'Inka's death around 1493 lasted several years. Wayna Qhapaq's forces did not secure the area around Quito until about 1500 (Salomon 1986:146). This implies that the state's incursions further north occurred during the first quarter of the sixteenth century and were still taking place when the Chiriguana attacked the Bolivian frontier in the mid-1520s and at the time of Wayna Qhapaq's death in 1527 (Means 1918; Nordenskiöld 1917; Nowell 1946). The civil war and rebellions that accompanied the successional dispute between Washkar and 'Ataw Wallpa erupted almost immediately thereafter and continued until 1538, when the Spaniards defeated the last of the Inca armies in Bolivia. At that point, Andean resistance to the Spaniards became localized. However, in 1537, a civil war broke out among the Spaniards, which lasted until 1554. The Spaniards subsequently sent a series of military expeditions against Vitcos, the major pocket of Inca resistance, which was finally defeated in 1572.

2. There are two accounts of the social conditions and relations that existed east of the Inca Empire during the first quarter of the sixteenth century. Aleixo Garcia, a Portuguese, was the first European to explore the Paraguay River and cross the Chaco. According to Erland Nordenskiöld (1917:103–106), who based his account on the earlier work of Rui Díaz de Guzman (1910), Garcia left Santos on the coast of Brazil in the early 1520s to explore the interior. He and his companions, two to four other Portuguese and some friendly coastal Indians, set out over land. They crossed the Paraná River and eventually came to Paraguay River. They were well received by the Guaraní-speaking inhabitants of the villages and persuaded several thousand to accompany them on their explorations to the west. They fought their way across the Gran Chaco, the plain that lies between the river and the Andes Mountains. After many days, they reached the mountains between Mizque and Tomina. They attacked and plundered villages under Inca control and killed everyone they found. When the Charcas counterattacked, they retired to the lowlands, laden with the cloth, metal utensils, and gold, silver, and copper objects they had stolen. Garcia was killed, but more Indians followed him to the territories where he had been, and settled on the frontier near Tarija.

Alvar Nuñez Cabeza de Vaca (1946:555–556, 572–573, 579–580, 582–583) provides an overview of the conditions and complex social relations that prevailed east of Charcas in the early 1540s. The Chiriguana were Guarani-speaking peoples who maintained cordial relations with communities that spoke closely related dialects and lived on both sides of the Paraguay River, four hundred miles to the east. They had antagonistic relations with the Caracaras and Candires (groups that were under Inca control or that lived in the borderlands of Charcas), with the Chanes who resided along the imperial frontier to the south, and with the Chimenos, Tarapecocies, and Sacocies – tribes that inhabited areas to the south or east. The Guarani had attacked the villages of the Chanes, Tarapecocies, Sacocies, and Orejones for war captives, metal objects, and other kinds of plunder; some refugees from these raids had banded together and resided in a multiethnic settlement called Puerto de los Reyes on the Paraguay River. The Tarapecocies claimed that a group called the Payzunos who lived to the west gave them precious metals that its members had obtained from the Chanes, Chimenos, Caracaras, and Candires in exchange for bows, arrows, and slaves.

3. The inhabitants of Huarochirí preserved their own account of the Colla revolt. The Colla peoples revolted because they no longer wanted to be Incas. The war raged for nearly a dozen years, and, when the Topa 'Inka requested the help of his subjects, Pariacaca, the most important of the local *wak'as*, sent his son, Macahuisa, to assist the Incas. Macahuisa killed most of the rebels and herded the few survivors, all important men, back to Cuzco, where he received both the service and increased offerings of the Incas. The tone of the account makes it clear that the Incas could not have suppressed the revolt without the intervention of the *huarochirianos*.

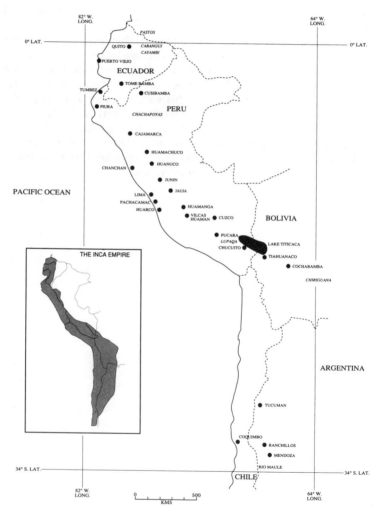

Map of the Central Andes

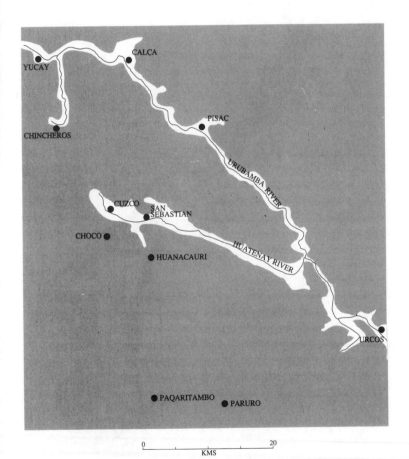

Map of Cuzco and its Environs

Map of the Inca State

Glossary

aclla chosen women, sequestered from their natal communities, who resided in provincial capitals and made beer and wove for the state.

altiplano high flat or gently rolling, alpine grasslands; more specifically, the grasslands of the Lake Titicaca basin in southern Peru and northern Bolivia.

'apo the administrator or prefect of one of the four quarters of the empire, the largest territorial divisions of the state; usually a close Inca kinsman of the emperor.

ayllu from the word meaning "to group"; a corporate landholding group, often a bilateral kindred.

ceques a series of imaginary lines radiating outward in all directions from the Temple of the Sun in Cuzco; a number of shrines were located on each ceque; these were the sites of rituals, essential for agricultural production, that were performed on particular days.

chinchaysuyu the northern quarter, or territorial division, of the empire.

chunga an administrative and work unit composed of about ten households.

corregidor a Spanish colonial appointed in each province to control the actions of the *kurakas*, to curb the abuses of the *encomenderos*, and to make major local-level administrative decisions.

coya the principal wife of the Inca ruler; his sister in some instances.

encomienda a grant made by the Spanish king or governor that gave its recipients (*encomenderos*) permission to use labor extracted from specified native districts for their own purpose.

entrada a Spanish expedition whose members sought fortune in wilderness areas.

huno an administrative unit composed of roughly ten thousand households.

khipukamayoq a record keeper who used khipus – multi-colored, knotted strings attached to a main cord – to record inventories, census data, etc., in some instances, and as a mnemonic aid for remembering oral historical traditions, in other cases.

kuraka a traditional leader subject to the customary expectation of the community.

mindalá transient frontier merchant from communities in and beyond the northern borderlands of the state.

mit'a taking one's turn to perform a labor obligation consisting of a specified number of days of work.

mitimae an individual performing a mit'a labor obligation; also called mitmakuna, literally mit'a people.

mitmakuna see mitimae.

mitayo see mitimae.

paqarina a place of origin, often a cave, that was frequently the site of a shrine.

pachaca an administrative and work unit composed of about one hundred households.

panaqa one of the royal Inca landholding corporations, each of which was founded by an emperor to support his wives, their descendants and a cult honoring his body and memory after he died.

pucara a hilltop fortress or stronghold.

qhapaq powerful and wealthy men who were able to call upon large numbers of kin or people for assistance.

reducción a strategic hamlet or village where indigenous peoples were resettled in the 1560s to promote internal security in the colonial state.

runakhipukamayoq literally, record keepers or census takers.

taki onqoy a millenarian movement in the 1560s that advocated solidarity among Andean peoples and resistance to Spanish settlers and their customs.

tawantinsuyu literally, the land of the four quarters, which was the Incas's name for their imperial state.

tokoyrikoq an inspector who stood outside the administrative hierarchy and connected the Inca and non-Inca layers of the administration to ensure that the labor demands of the state and its ruling class were met. They visited districts, investigated the activities of governors and *kurakas*, and reported their findings to the emperor and his counselors.

tokrikoq a governor who resided in one of the provincial capitals established throughout the empire; a member of an Inca *panaqa*.

wak'a a sacred place or thing; often the site of a shrine; occasionally an archaeological site.

waranga an administrative and work unit composed of roughly one thousand households.

yana servile retainers removed from their natal communities; also called *yanakuna*, literally, retainer people.

zinchi war chief, strong man.

Bibliography

Abélès, Marc
  1981   'Sacred kingship' and the formation of the state. In *The study of the state*, edited by Henri J. M. Claessen and Peter Skalník, pp. 1–13. Mouton Publishers, The Hague, Paris, and New York.

Abercrombie, Nicholas, Stephen Hill, and Bryan S. Turner
  1980   *The dominant ideology thesis*. George Allen and Unwin,. Ltd., London.

Acosta, José de
  1954   *Historia natural y moral de las Indias* [1590]. Biblioteca de Autores Españoles, tomo 73, pp. 1–247. Ediciones Atlas, Madrid.

Adorno, Rolena
  1986   *Guaman Poma; writing and resistance in colonial Peru*. University of Texas Press, Austin.

Albers, Patricia and Jeanne Kay
  1987   Sharing the land: a study in American Indian territoriality. In *A cultural geography of North American Indians*, edited by Thomas E. Ross and Tyrel G. Moore, pp. 47–91. Westview Press, Boulder.

Albornoz, Christóbal de
  1967   Instrucción para descubrir todas las guacas del Pirú y sus camayos y haziendas [1580]. *Journal de la Société des Américanistes*, tome LVI, no. 1, pp. 17–39. Paris.

Althusser, Louis and Etienne Balibar
  1970   *Reading Capital* [1968], translated by Ben Brewster. New Left Books, London.

Alva, Walter
  1988   Discovering the New World's richest unlooted tomb. *National Geographic*, vol. 174, no. 4, pp. 510–550. Washington.

Amin, Samir
  1976   *Unequal development; an essay on the social formations of peripheral capitalism* [1973]. Monthly Review Press, New York and London.
  1978   *The Arab nation; nationalism and class struggles* [1976]. Zed Publications, London.

1980   *Class and nation, historically and in the current crisis* [1979].
        Monthly Review Press, New York and London.
Anonymous
1906   Discurso de la sucesión y gobierno de los Yngas [c. 1570]. In
        Juicio de límites entre el Perú y Bolivia, edited by Víctor M.
        Maúrtua, tomo 8, pp. 149–165. Imprenta de los Hijos de M.
        G. Hernández, Madrid.
1962   Discurso de la sucesión y gobierno de los Incas [no earlier
        than 1571]. In *El Cuzco y el gobierno de los Incas*, edited by Julio
        A. Lina. Librería é Imprenta D. Miranda, Lima.
Asad, Talal
1980   Ideology, class and the origin of the Islamic state. *Economy and
        Society*, vol. 9, no. 4, pp. 450–473. Henley-on-Thames.
Avila, Francisco de
1966   *Dioses y hombres de Huarochirí; narración quechua recogida por
        Francisco de Avila* [1598?], translated by José María Arguedas.
        Instituto de Estudios Peruanos, Lima.
Bakewell, Peter
1984   *Miners of the red mountain; Indian labor in Potosí, 1545–1650.*
        University of New Mexico Press, Albuquerque.
Benditt, John
1988   Earliest Americans. *Scientific American*, vol. 258, no. 6,
        pp.28–30. New York.
Benfer, Robert A.
1984   The challenges and rewards of sedentism: the preceramic
        village of Paloma, Peru. In *Paleopathology at the origins of
        agriculture*, edited by Mark N. Cohen and George J. Armela-
        gos, pp. 531–558. Academic Press, Orlando.
1986   Holocene coastal adaptations: changing demography and
        health at the fog oasis of Paloma, Peru, 5,000–7,800 B.P. In
        Andean archaeology; papers in memory of Clifford Evans, edited by
        Ramiro M. Matos, Solveig A. Turpin, and Herbert H. Eling,
        Jr. Institute of Archaeology, University of California, Los
        Angeles, Monograph XXVII, pp. 45–64. Los Angeles.
Berezkin, Yuri Y.
1978a   The social structure of the Mochica through the prism of
        mythology (ancient Peru) [in Russian]. *Vestnik Drevnei Istorii*,
        vol. 3, no. 145, pp. 38–59. Moscow.
1978b   Chronologie des étapes moyenne et tardive de la culture
        mochica (Pérou) [in Russian]. *Sovyetskaya Archaelogia*, no. 2,
        1978, pp. 78–96. Moscow.
Betanzos, Juan de
1924   Suma y narración de los Incas, señores que fueron de estas
        provincias del Perú. . . [1551]. In *Colección de libros y documen-
        tos referentes a la historia del Perú*, edited by Horacio H.

Urteaga, 2nd ser., tomo 8, pp. 75–208. Imprenta y Librería Sanmarti y Ca., Lima.

Bettelheim, Charles
1972 Theoretical comments. In *Unequal exchange; a study of the imperialism of trade* [1969], by Arghiri Emmanuel, pp. 271–322. Monthly Review Press, New York and London.
1975 *The transition to socialism* [1968], translated by Brian Pearce. Harvester Press, Ltd., Hassocks.

Bhaskar, Roy
1979 *The possibility of naturalism; a philosophical critique of the contemporary human sciences.* Humanities Press, Atlantic Highlands.

Bowser, Frederick P.
1974 *The African slave in colonial Peru, 1524–1560.* Stanford University Press, Stanford.

Brading, David A. and Harry E. Cross
1972 Colonial silver mining: Mexico and Peru. *The Hispanic American Historical Review*, vol. LII, no. 4, pp. 545–579. Durham.

Bram, Joseph
1941 *An analysis of Inca militarism.* American Ethnological Society Monograph 4. New York.

Bray, Warick
1986 Finding the earliest Americans. *Nature*, vol. 321, no. 6072, p. 726. London.

Brenner, Robert
1986 The social basis of economic development. In *Analytical Marxism*, edited by Jon Elster, pp. 23–53. Cambridge University Press, Cambridge.

Browman, David L.
1976 Demographic correlations of the Wari conquest of Junin. *American Antiquity*, vol. 41, no. 4, pp. 465–477. Washington.
1978 Toward the development of the Tiwanaku state. In *Advances in Andean archaeology*, edited by David L. Browman, pp. 327–349. Mouton Publishers, The Hague, Paris, and New York.
1981 New light on Andean Tiwanaku. *American Scientist*, vol. 69, no. 4, pp. 408–419. New Haven.

Brundage, Burr C.
1963 *Empire of the Incas.* University of Oklahoma Press, Norman.

Burger, Richard L.
1987 The U-shaped pyramid complex at Cardal, Peru. *National Geographic Research*, vol. 3, no. 3, pp. 365–375. Washington.

Cabello Valboa, Miguel
1951 *Miscelánea antártica; una historia del Perú antiguo* [1586]. Instituto de Etnología, Facultad de Letras, Universidad Nacional Mayor de San Marcos, Lima.

178   *Bibliography*

Cabeza de Vaca, Alvar Nuñez
1946   *Comentarios de Alvar Nuñez Cabeza de Vaca, adelantado y gobernador del Río de la Plata* [1555]. Biblioteca de Autores Españoles, tomo 22, pp. 549–599. Ediciones Atlas, Madrid.
Calancha, Antonio de
1638   *Crónica moralizada del órden de San Agustín en el Perú, con sucesores egenplares en esta monarquía.* Pedro Lacavallería, Barcelona.
Callinicos, Alex
1988   *Making history; agency, structure and change in social theory.* Cornell University Press, Ithaca.
Carrión Cachot, Rebecca
1948   La cultura Chavín: dos nuevas colonias: Kuntur Wasi y Ancón. *Revista del Museo Nacional de Antropología y Arqueología*, vol. II, no. 1, pp. 99–172. Lima.
Castro, Cristóbal de and Diego Ortega Morejón
1936   *Relación y declaración del modo que este valle de Chincha y sus comarcanos se governavan. . .* [1558]. Studien zur Kulturkünde, Band 3. Quellan zur Kulturgeschichte des präkolumbischen Amerika, edited by Herman Trimborn, pp. 236–246. Strecker under Schröder Verlag, Stuttgart.
Cieza de León, Pedro
1947   *La crónica del Perú* [1553]. Biblioteca de Autores Españoles, tomo XXVI, pp. 349–458. Ediciones Atlas, Madrid.
1967   *El señorío de los Incas* [1553]. Instituto de Estudios Peruanos, Lima.
Cobo, Bernabé
1956   *Historia del nuevo mundo* [1653], 2 vols. Biblioteca de Autores Españoles, tomos 91 and 92. Ediciones Atlas, Madrid.
Cook, Anita G.
1983   Aspects of ideology in Huari and Tiwanaku iconography: the central deity and sacrificer. In *Investigations of the Andean past; papers from the First Annual Northeast Conference on Andean Archaeology and Ethnohistory*, edited by Daniel H. Sandweiss, pp. 161–185. Latin American Studies Program, Cornell University, Ithaca.
Daggett, Richard
1987   Toward the development of the state on the north central coast of Peru. In *The origins and development of the Andean state*, edited by Jonathan Haas, Sheila Pozorski, and Thomas Pozorski, pp. 70–82. Cambridge, University Press, Cambridge.
Dávila Brizeño, Diego
1965   Descripción y relación de la provincia de los Yauyos toda, anan Yauyos, y lorin Yauyos. . . [1586]. In *Relaciones geográficas de las Indias*, edited by Don Marcos Jímenez de la Espada.

Biblioteca de Autores Españoles, tomo 183, pp. 155–165. Ediciones Atlas, Madrid.

Derrida, Jacques
1983   The time of a thesis: punctuations. In *Philosophy in France today*, edited by Alan Montefiore, pp. 34–50. Cambridge University Press, Cambridge.

Diakonoff, Igor M.
1972   Socio-economic classes in Babylonia and the Babylonian conception of social stratification. In *Gesellschaftsklassen im Alten Zweistromland und in den angrenzenden Gebieten – XVIII*. Recontre assyriologique internationale, edited by D. O. Edzard. Bayerische Akademie der Wissenschaften, Philosophisch-Historische Klasse, Abhandlungen, Heft 75, pp. 41–49. Munich.

Diamond, Stanley
1951   *Dahomey: a proto-state in West Africa*. Ph.D. Dissertation in Anthropology, Columbia University. New York.
1974   *In search of the primitive; a critique of civilization*. Transaction Books, New Brunswick and London.

Díaz de Guzman, Ruiz
1910   Historia argentina del descubrimiento, población y conquista de las provincias del Río de la Plata [1612]. In *Colección de obras y documentos relativos a la historia antigua y moderna de las provincias del Río de la Plata*, edited by Pedro de Angelis, pp. 11–111. Librería Nacional de J. Lajouane and Cia., Buenos Aires.

Dillehay, Tom D.
1984   A late Ice-Age settlement in southern Chile. *Scientific American*, vol. 251, no. 4, pp. 106–117. New York.
1985   A regional perspective of preceramic times in the Central Andes. *Reviews in Anthropology*, vol. 12, no. 3, pp. 193–205.
1988   The peopling of the Americas: new sites and old problems. *Past; The Newsletter of the Prehistoric Society*, no. 4, pp. 7–9. Cambridge.

Dollfus, Olivier
1965   Les Andes centrales du Pérou et leurs piedmonts. *Travaux de l'Institut Francais d'Etudes Andines*, tome XII. Paris and Lima.
1978   Les Andes intertropicales: une mosaique changeante. *Annales: Economies, Sociétés, Civilisations*, tome 33, no. 5–6, pp. 895–303. Paris.

Donnan, Christopher B.
1964   An early house from Chilca, Peru. *American Antiquity*, vol. 32, no. 2, pp. 137–144. Salt Lake City.

Drews, Robert
1983   *Basileus: the evidence for kingship in Geometric Greece*. Yale

Classical Monographs 4. Yale University Press, New Haven and London.

Duviols, Pierre
1977   La dinastía de los Incas: monarquía o diarquía? Argumentos heurísticos a favor de una tesis estructuralista. *Journal de la Société des Américanistes*, tome LXVI, pp. 78–83. Paris.

Earle, Timothy, Terence D'Altroy, Christine Hastorf, Catherine Scott, Cathy Costin, Glenn Russell, and Elsie Sandefur
1987   *Archaeological field research in the Upper Mantaro, Peru, 1982–1983: Investigations of Inka expansion and exchange.* Institute of Archaeology, University of California, Los Angeles, Monograph XXVIII. Los Angeles.

Earls, John
1976   Evolución de la administración ecológica inca. *Revista del Museo Nacional*, tomo XLII, pp. 207–245. Lima.

Earls, John and Irene Silverblatt
1978   *La realidad física y social en la cosmología andina.* Acts du XLIIᵉ Congrès International des Américanistes, Paris, 2–9 September 1976, vol. IV, pp. 299–325. Paris.

Elliott, John H.
1970   *Imperial Spain, 1469–1716* [1963]. Penguin Books, Harmondsworth.
1971   Cortés, Velázquez and Charles V. In *Hernán Cortés: letters from Mexico*, translated and edited by Anthony R. Pagden, pp. xi–xxxvii. Grossman Publishers, New York.

Espinoza Soriano, Waldemar
1976   Las mujeres secundarias de Huayna Capac: dos casos de señorialismo feudal en el imperio Inca. *Revista del Museo Nacional*, tomo XLII, pp. 247–298. Lima.

Estete, Miguel de
1947   *La relación del viaje que hizo el Señor Capitan Hernando Pizarro. . .desde el pueblo de Caxamlaca á Parcama, y allí á Jauja* [1534]. Biblioteca de Autores Españoles, tomo XXVI, pp. 338–343. Ediciones Atlas, Madrid.

Falkenstein, Adam
1974   *The Sumerian temple city* [1954], translated by Maria de Jong Ellis. Sources and Monographs in the Ancient Near East, vol. 1, fasc. 1. Udena Publications, Los Angeles.

Feldman, Robert A.
1980   *Aspero, Peru: architecture, subsistence economy, and other artifacts of a preceramic maritime chiefdom.* Ph.D. Dissertation in Anthropology, Harvard University. Cambridge.
1985   Preceramic corporate architecture: evidence for the development of non-egalitarian social systems in Peru. In *Early ceremonial architecture in the Andes*, edited by Christopher B. Don-

nan, pp. 71–92. Dumbarton Oaks Research Library and Collection, Washington.

1987 Architectural evidence for the development of nonegalitarian social systems in coastal Peru. In *The origins and development of the Andean state*, edited by Jonathan Haas, Sheila Pozorski, and Thomas Pozorski, pp. 9–14. Cambridge University Press, Cambridge.

Foster, Benjamin
1981 A new look at the Sumerian temple state. *Journal of the Economic and Social History of the Orient*, vol. XXIV, no. 3, pp. 225–241. Leiden.

Foster-Carter, Aidan
1978 The modes of production controversy. *New Left Review*, no. 107, pp. 47–78. London.

Fox, Richard G.
1971 *Kin, clan, raja and rule; state-hinterland relations in preindustrial India*. University of California Press, Berkeley, Los Angeles, and London.

Franquemont, Edward M.
1986 The ancient pottery from Pucara, Peru. *Ñawpa Pacha* 24, pp. 1–30. Berkeley.

Gailey, Christine W.
1984 The kindness of strangers: transformations of kinship in precapitalist class and state formation. *Culture*, vol. V, no. 2, pp. 3–16. Montreal.

1987 *Kinship to kingship; gender hierarchy and state formation in the Tongan Islands*. University of Texas Press, Austin.

1991 The dialectics of culture in the work of Stanley Diamond. In *Dialectical anthropology; essays presented to Stanley Diamond*, edited by Christine W. Gailey, vol. 1, Civilization in crisis: anthropological perspectives. University Presses of Florida, Tallahassee (forthcoming).

Gailey, Christine W. and Thomas C. Patterson
1987 Power relations and state formation. In *Power relations and state formation*, edited by Thomas C. Patterson and Christine W. Gailey, pp. 1–26. Archeology Section, American Anthropological Association, Washington.

1988 State formation and uneven development. In *State and society: the emergence and development of social hierarchy and political centralization*, edited by Barbara Bender, John Gledhill, and Mogens Larsen, pp. 77–90. George Allen and Unwin, London.

Garcilaso de la Vega, Inca
1960 *Comentarios reales de los Incas* [1609], 3 vols. Biblioteca de Autores Españoles, tomos 133–135. Ediciones Atlas, Madrid.

Gearing, Fred
  1958   The structural poses of 18th century Cherokee villages. *American Anthropologist*, vol. 60, no. 6, pp. 1148–1157. Menasha.
  1961   The rise of the Cherokee state as an instance in a class: the "Mesopotamian" career to statehood. In *Symposium on Cherokee and Iroquois culture*, edited by William N. Fenton and John L. Gulick. Bureau of American Ethnology Bulletin 180, pp. 125–134. Washington.
  1962   *Priests and warriors: social structures for Cherokee politics in the 18th century.* American Anthropological Association Memoir 93. Menasha.

Gelb, Ignace J.
  1969   On the alleged temple and state economies in ancient Mesopotamia. In *Studi in onore di Edoardo Volterra*, tomo VI. Publicazioni della Facoltà di Giurisprudenza dell 'Università di Roma 45, pp. 137–154. A Guiffrè, Milan.
  1972   From freedom to slavery. In *Gesellschaftsklassen im Alten Zweistromland und in den angrenzenden Gebieten – XVIII.* Recontre assyriologique internationale, edited by D. O. Edzard. Bayerische Akademie der Wissenschaften, Philosophisch-Historische Klasse, Abhandlungen, Heft 75, pp. 81–92. Munich.

Geschiere, Peter
  1982   *Village communities and the state; changing relations among the Maka of southeastern Cameroon since the colonial conquest.* Kegan Paul International, Ltd., London, Boston, and Melbourne.

Gibson, Charles
  1966   *Spain in America.* Harper and Row, Publishers, New York, Evanston, and London.

Gledhill, John
  1978   Formative development in the North American Southwest. In *Social organization and settlement*, edited by David Green, Colin Haselgrove, and Matthew Spriggs. B.A.R. International Series (Supplementary) 47, pt. ii, pp. 241–290. Oxford.

Godelier, Maurice
  1977   The concept of social and economic formation: the Inca example. In *Perspectives in Marxist anthropology.* Cambridge Studies in Social Anthropology 18, pp. 63–69. Cambridge University Press, Cambridge.

Goncalez Holguin, Diego
  1952   *Vocabulario de la lengua general de todo el Peru llamada lengua quechua o del Inca* [1608]. Ediciones del Instituto de Historia, Universidad Nacional Mayor de San Marcos, Lima.

González, Alberto Rex
  1961   The La Aguada culture of northwestern Argentina. In *Essays in pre-Columbian art and archaeology*, by Samuel K. Lothrop and

others, pp. 389–420. Harvard University Press, Cambridge.

Guidon, N. and G. Delibrias
1986   Carbon-14 dates point to man in the Americas 32,000 years ago. *Nature*, vol. 351, no. 6072, pp. 769–771. London.

Haas, Jonathan
1987a   The exercise of power in early Andean state development. In *The origins and development of the Andean state*, edited by Jonathan Haas, Sheila Pozorski, and Thomas Pozorski, pp. 31–35. Cambridge University Press, Cambridge.
1987b   Introduction. In *The origins and development of the Andean state*, edited by Jonathan Haas, Sheila Pozorski, and Thomas Pozorski, pp. 1–4. Cambridge University Press, Cambridge.

Hemming, John
1970   *The conquest of the Incas*. Harcourt Brace Jovanovich, New York.

Hilton, Rodney
1985   Introduction. In *The Brenner debate; agrarian class structure and economic development in Pre-industrial Europe*, edited by T. H. Aston and C. H. E. Philpin, pp. 1–9. Cambridge University Press, Cambridge.

Hobsbawm, Eric and Terence Ranger, editors
1983   *The invention of tradition*. Cambridge University Press, Cambridge.

Huaman Poma de Ayala, Felipe
1936   *Nueva crónica y buen gobierno* [1615]. Travaux et Mémoires de l'Institut d'Ethnologie, tome XXIII. Institut d'Ethnologie, Université de Paris, Paris.

Hulme, Peter
1986   *Colonial encounters; Europe and the native Caribbean, 1492–1797*. Methuen & Co., Ltd., London and New York.

Hyslop, John
1985   *Inkawasi, the new Cuzco, Cañete, Lunahuaná, Peru*. British Archaeological Reports, International Series, no. S234. Oxford.

Isbell, William H.
1983   Shared ideology and parallel political development: Huari and Tiwanaku. In *Investigations of the Andean past; papers from the First Annual Northeast Conference on Andean Archaeology and Ethnohistory*, edited by Daniel H. Sandweiss, pp. 186–208. Latin American Studies Program, Cornell University, Ithaca.
1985   El origen del estado en el valle de Ayacucho. *Revista Andina*, no. 3, pp. 57–106. Cuzco.

Jacobson, Thorkild
1943   Primitive democracy in ancient Mesopotamia. *Journal of Near Eastern Studies*, vol. II, no. 3, pp. 159–172. Chicago.
1957   Early political development in Mesopotamia. *Zeitschrift für*

Assyriologie und voderasiatische Archaologie, Band 52, pp. 91–140. Berlin.

Janssen, J. J.
  1978   The early state in ancient Egypt. In *The early state*, edited by Henri J. M. Claessen and Peter Skalník, pp. 155–176. Mouton Publishers, The Hague, Paris, and New York.

Julien, Catherine
  1988   How Inca decimal administration worked. *Ethnohistory*, vol. 35, no. 3, pp. 257–279. Durham.

Katz, Friederich
  1966   *The ancient American civilizations*. Weidenfeld and Nicolson, London.

Keen, Benjamin
  1971   *The Aztec image in Western thought*. Rutgers University Press, New Brunswick.

Kirchkoff, Paul
  1949   The social and political organization of the Andean peoples. In *Handbook of South American Indians*, edited by Julian H. Steward; vol. 5, The comparative ethnology of South American Indians. Bureau of American Ethnology Bulletin 143, pp. 293–313. Washington.

Koepcke, Hans-Wilhelm
  1961   *Synokologische Studien an der Westseite der peruanischen Anden*. Bonner Geografische Abhandlungen, Heft 29. Ferdinand Dummlers Verlag, Bonn.

Kolata, Alan L.
  1986   The agricultural foundations of Tiwanaku: a view from the heartland. *American Antiquity*, vol. 51, no. 4, pp. 748–762. Washington.
  1987   Tiwanaku and its hinterland. *Archaeology*, vol. 40, no. 1, pp. 36–41. Brattleboro.

Krader, Lawrence
  1975   *The Asiatic mode of production; sources, development and critique in the writings of Karl Marx*. Van Gorcum, Assen.
  1976   *Dialectic of civil society*. Van Gorcum, Assen.

Kubler, George
  1944   A Peruvian chief of state: Manco Inca (1515–1545). *The Hispanic American Historical Review*, vol. XXIV, no. 2, pp. 253–276. Durham.
  1945   The behavior of Atahualpa, 1531–1533. *The Hispanic American Historical Review*, vol. XXV, no. 4, pp. 413–427. Durham.
  1947   The neo-Inca state (1537–1572). *The Hispanic American Historical Review*, vol. XXVII, no. 2, pp. 189–203. Durham.

Larson, Brooke
  1988   *Colonialism and agrarian transformation in Bolivia; Cochabamba,*

1550–1900. Princeton University Press, Princeton.
Las Casas, Bartolome de
1948   De las antiguas gentes del Perú [1555]. In *Los pequeños grandes libros de historia americana*, edited by Francisco A. Loayza, ser. I, tomo XVI, pp. 1–152. Editorial de Domingo Miranda, Lima.
Lathrap, Donald W., Angelika Gebart-Sayer, and Ann M. Mester
1985   The roots of the Shipibo art style: three waves on Imiríracocha on there were "Incas" before the Incas. *Journal of Latin American Lore*, vol. 11, no. 1, pp. 31–119. Los Angeles.
Leacock, Eleanor B.
1982   Relations of production in band society. In *Politics and history in band societies*, edited by Eleanor B. Leacock and Richard B. Lee, pp. 159–170. Cambridge University Press, Cambridge.
1983   Primitive communism. In *A dictionary of Marxist thought*, edited by Tom Bottomore, Laurence Harris, Victor G. Kiernan, and Ralph Miliband, pp. 394–395. Harvard University Press, Cambridge.
Lears, T. J. Jackson
1985   The concept of cultural hegemony: problems and possibilities. *The American Historical Review*, vol. 90, no. 3, pp. 567–593. New York.
Lehmann-Nitsche, Roberto
1928   Coricancha; el Templo del Sol en el Cuzco y las imágenes de su altar mayor. *Revista del Museo de La Plata*, tomo XXXI, pp. 1–260. Buenos Aires.
Lockhart, James
1968   *Spanish Peru, 1532–1560; a colonial society*. The University of Wisconsin Press, Madison.
1969   Encomienda and hacienda: the evolution of the great estate in the Spanish Indies. *The Hispanic American Historical Review*, vol. XLIX, no. 3, pp. 411–430. Durham.
1972   *The men of Cajamarca; a social and biographical study of the first conquerors of Peru*. Latin American Monographs, no. 27. University of Texas Press, Austin and London.
Lynch, John
1965   *Spain under the Habsburgs, vol. 1, Empire and absolutism, 1516–1598*. Oxford University Press, New York.
MacCormack, Sabine
1985   *A conflict of myths: Genesis, classical antiquity and the rise of the Incas*. Paper presented at the Wilson Center, Smithsonian Institution, Washington, DC.
MacNeish, Richard S., Thomas C. Patterson, and David L. Browman
1975   *The central Peruvian prehistoric interaction sphere*. Papers of the Robert S. Peabody Foundation for Archaeology, vol. VII. Andover.

Mann, Michael
   1986   *The sources of social power, vol. 1, A history of power from the beginning to A.D. 1760.* Cambridge University Press, Cambridge.
Markham, Clements
   1920   Introduction. In *Memorias antiguas historiales del Perú*, by Fernando Montesinos, translated and edited by Philip A. Means. The Hakluyt Society, 2nd ser., no. XLVIII, pp. 3–15. London.
Marx, Karl
   1965   *Pre-capitalist economic formations* [1859]. International Publishers, New York.
   1968   The Eighteenth Brumaire of Louis Bonaparte [1852]. In *Karl Marx and Frederick Engels; selected works in one volume*, pp. 97–180. International Publishers, New York.
   1977   *Capital; a critique of political economy, vol. 1* [1867], translated by Ben Fowkes. Vintage Books, New York.
Massey, Sarah A.
   1986   *Sociopolitical change in the upper Ica Valley, B.C. 400 to 400 A.D.: regional states on the south coast of Peru.* Ph.D. Dissertation in Anthropology, University of California at Los Angeles. University Microfilms, Ann Arbor.
Means, Philip A.
   1917   A note on the Guarani invasions of the Inca empire. *The Geographical Review*, vol. IV, no. 6, pp. 482–484. New York.
   1964   *Fall of the Inca Empire and the Spanish rule in Peru: 1530–1780* [1931]. Gordian Press, New York.
Menzel, Dorothy
   1959   The Inca occupation of the south coast of Peru. *Southwestern Journal of Anthropology*, vol. 15, no. 2, pp. 125–142. Albuquerque.
   1960a *Results of archaeological research done under the Fulbright Program in Peru in 1957, 1958, and 1959; studies of the south coast of Peru in Ica, Pisco, Chincha and Cañete Valleys.* Manuscript, Ica.
   1960b Archaism and revival on the south coast of Peru. In *Man and culture; selected papers of the Fifth International Congress of Anthropological and Ethnological Sciences*, Philadelphia, 1–9 September 1956, edited by Anthony F. C. Wallace, pp. 596–600. University of Pennsylvania Press, Philadelphia.
   1964   Style and time in the Middle Horizon. *Ñawpa Pacha* 2, pp. 1–105. Berkeley.
   1968   New data on the Huari Empire in Middle Horizon Epoch 2A. *Ñawpa Pacha* 6, pp. 57–114. Berkeley.
   1976   *Pottery style and society in ancient Peru; art as a mirror of history in the Ica Valley, 1350–1570.* University of California Press, Berkeley, Los Angeles, and London.
   1977   *The archaeology of ancient Peru and the work of Max Uhle.* Robert

H. Lowie Museum of Anthropology, University of California, Berkeley.

Menzel, Dorothy and John H. Rowe
1966   The role of Chincha in late pre-Spanish Peru. *Ñawpa Pacha* 4, pp. 63–76. Berkeley.

Menzel, Dorothy, John H. Rowe, and Lawrence E. Dawson
1964   *The Paracas pottery of Ica; a study in style and time.* University of California Publications in American Archaeology and Ethnology, vol. 50. University of California Press, Berkeley and Los Angeles.

Millon, René
1988   The last years of Teotihuacan dominance. In *The collapse of ancient states and civilizations*, edited by Norman Yoffe and George Cowgill, pp. 102–164. The University of Arizona Press, Tucson.

Molina, Cristóbal de
1943   Fabulas y ritos de los Incas [1573]. In *Las crónicas de los Molinas*, edited by Carlos A. Romero, Raul Porras Barrenechea, and Francisco A. Loayza. Los pequeños grandes libros de historia americana, ser. I, tomo IV, pp. 1–84. Librería e Imprenta D. Miranda, Lima.

Montaigne, Michel de
1958   *The complete essays of Montaigne* [1578–1588], translated by Donald M. Frame. Stanford University Press, Stanford.

Montesinos, Fernando
1930   *Memorias antiguas historiales y politicas del Perú* [1644]. Colección de libros y documentos referentes a la historia del Perú, edited by Horacio H. Urteaga, 2nd ser., tomo VI. Librería e Imprenta Gil, Lima.

Moore, John H.
1988   *Ethnos and ethnic process on the North American Plains.* Manuscript, Norman.

Moore, Sally F.
1958   *Power and property in Inca Peru.* Columbia University Press, New York.

Morris, Craig
1972   State settlements in Tawantinsuyu: a strategy of compulsory urbanism. In *Contemporary archaeology; a guide to theory and contributions*, edited by Mark P. Leone, pp. 393–401. Southern Illinois University Press, Carbondale.
1974   Reconstructing patterns of non-agricultural production in the Inca economy: archaeology and ethnohistory in institutional analysis. In *The reconstruction of complex societies*, edited by C. Moore, pp. 49–60. American School of Oriental Research, Philadelphia.

1982   The infrastructure of Inka control in the Peruvian central highlands. In *The Inca and Aztec states, 1400–1800; anthropology and history*, edited by George A. Collier, Renato I. Rosaldo, and John D. Wirth, pp. 153–171. Academic Press, New York.

1985   From principles of ecological complementarity to the organization and administration of Tawantinsuyu. In *Ecology and civilization; an interdisciplinary perspective on Andean ecological complementarity*, edited by Shozo Masuda, Izumi Shimada, and Craig Morris, pp. 477–490. University of Tokyo Press, Tokyo.

Morris, Craig and Donald E. Thompson

1985   *Huánuco Pampa: an Inca city and its hinterland*. Thames and Hudson, London and New York.

Moseley, Michael E.

1975   *The maritime foundations of Andean civilizations*. Cummings Publishing Company, Menlo Park.

1978   *Pre-agricultural coastal civilizations of Peru*. Carolina Biological Supply Company, Burlington.

1983   The good old days *were* better: agrarian collapse and tectonics. *American Anthropologist*, vol. 85, no. 4, pp. 773–799. Washington.

Moseley, Michael E. and Robert A. Feldman

1988   Fishing, farming, and the foundations of Andean civilization. In *The archaeology of prehistoric coastlines*, edited by Geoff Bailey and John Parkington, pp. 125–134. Cambridge University Press, Cambridge.

Muller, Viana

1977   The formation of the state and the oppression of women: a case study in England Wales. *Review of Radical Political Economy*, vol. 9, no. 3, pp. 7–21. New York.

1985   Origins of class and gender hierarchy of Northwest Europe. *Dialectical Anthropology*, vol. 10, nos. 1–2, pp. 93–106. Amsterdam.

1987   Kin reproduction and elite accumulation in the archaic states of Northwest Europe. In *Power relations and state formation*, edited by Thomas C. Patterson and Christine W. Gailey, pp. 81–97. Archeology, Section, American Anthropological Association, Washington.

1988   *Gender and kinship in ranked societies and chiefdoms in Northwest Europe: 1800 B.C. to A.D. 100*. Ph.D. Dissertation in Anthropology, New School for Social Research, New York.

Murphy, Robert C.

1941   The earliest Spanish advances southward from Panama along the west coast of South America. *The Hispanic American Historical Review*, vol. XXI, no. 1, pp. 2–28. Durham.

Murra, John V.
1961   Social structural and economic themes in Andean ethnohis-
        tory. *Anthropological Quarterly*, vol. 34, no. 2, pp. 47–59.
        Washington.
1966   New data on retainer and servile populations in Tawantin-
        suyu. In *Actas y memorias del XXXVI Congreso Internacional de
        Americanistas*, Sevilla, 1964, tomo II, pp. 35–45. Instituto "Gon-
        zalo Fernandez de Oviedo," Madrid.
1967   La visita de los Chupachu como fuente etnológica. In *Visita de
        la provincia de León de Huánuco en 1562*, edited by John V.
        Murra; *tomo I. Visita de los cuatro waranqa de los Chupachu*,
        pp. 381–496. Universidad Nacional de Hermilio Valdizán,
        Fácultad de Letras y Educación. Huánuco.
1968   An Aymara kingdom in 1567. *Ethnohistory*, vol. 15, no. 2,
        pp. 115–151. Seattle.
1972   El 'control vertical' de un máximo de pisos ecológicos en la
        economía de las sociedades andinas. In *Visita de la provincia de
        Huánuco en 1562, by Iñigo Ortiz de Zuñiga*, tomo II, pp. 427–
        468. Universidad Nacional Hermilio Valdizan, Huánuco.
1978   La guerre et lest rébellions dans l'expansion de l'état Inka.
        Annales: Economies, Sociétés, Civilisations, tome XXXIII, no.
        5–6, pp. 927–935. Paris.
1980   The economic organization of the Inka state. *Research in Econo-
        mic Anthropology, Supplement 1*. JAI Press, Greenwich.
1982   The *mit'a* obligations of ethnic groups to the Inka state. In *The
        Inca and Aztec states, 1400–1800; anthropology and history*, edited
        by George A. Collier, Renato I. Rosaldo, and John D. Wirth,
        pp. 237–262. Academic Press , New York.
1984   Andean societies before 1532. In *The Cambridge history of Latin
        America*; vol. I, Colonial Latin America, edited by Leslie Bethell,
        pp. 59–90. Cambridge University Press, Cambridge.
Murra, John V. and Craig Morris
1976   Dynastic oral tradition, administrative records and archaeo-
        logy in the Andes. *World Archaeology*, vol. 7, no. 3, pp. 269–279.
        Henley-on-Thames.
Murúa, Martín de
1946   *Historia del orígen y genealogía real de los reyes Incas del Perú*
        [1590], edited by Constantino Bayle. Biblioteca "Missionalia
        Hispanica", vol. II. Consejo Superior de Investigaciones Cienti-
        ficas, Instituto Santo Toribio de Mogrovejo, Madrid.
Netherly, Patricia J.
1977   *Local level lords on the north coast of Peru*. Ph.D. Dissertation in
        Anthropology, Cornell University. Ithaca, University Micro-
        films, Ann Arbor.
Nordenskiöld, Erland von

1917   The Guarani invasion of the Inca empire in the sixteenth
        century: an historical Indian migration. *The Geographical
        Review*, vol. IV, no. 1, pp. 103–121. New York.
Nowell, Charles E.
1946   Aleixo García and the white king. *The Hispanic American
        Historical Review*, vol. 26, no. 4, pp. 450–466. Durham.
Olsen, Keld
1986   *Inkariget—en arkaisk civilisation*. Institut for Etnologi og Antro-
        pologi Specialeraekke, no. 10. Københavns Universitet, Copen-
        hagen.
Ossio, Juan M.
1977   Guaman Poma y la historiográfia indianista de los siglos XVI
        y XVII. *Historia y Cultura*, no. 10, pp. 181–206. Lima.
Pachakuti Yamqui, Juan de Santa Cruz.
1927   *Relación de antigüedades deste reyno del Pirú* [early 17th century].
        In Colección de libros y documentos referentes a la historia
        del Perú, 2a ser., tomo IX, pp. 125–235. Imprenta y Librería
        Sanmarti y Ca., Lima.
Pagden, Anthony
1982   *The fall of natural man; the American Indian and the origins of
        comparative ethnology*. Cambridge University Press, Cambridge.
Patterson, Thomas C.
1966   *Pattern and process in the Early Intermediate Period pottery of the
        central coast of Peru*. University of California Publications in
        Anthropology, vol. 3. University of California Press, Berkeley
        and Los Angeles.
1971   Population and economy in central Peru. *Archaeology*, vol. 24,
        no. 4, pp. 316–321. Brattleboro.
1973   *America's past; a New World archaeology*. Scott-Foresman and
        Company, Glenview and London.
1974   Pachacamac revisited; some comments on methods of inter-
        preting archaeological evidence. In *Perspectives in palaeoanthro-
        pology*, edited by Asok K. Ghosh, pp. 65–72. Firma K L
        Mukhopadhyay, Calcutta.
1983a   *The theory and practice of archaeology; a workbook*. Prentice-Hall,
        Englewood Cliffs.
1983b   The historical development of a coastal Andean social forma-
        tion in central Peru: 6000 to 500 B.C. In *Investigations of the
        Andean past; papers from the First Annual Northeast Conference on
        Andean Archaeology and Ethnohistory*, edited by Daniel H. Sand-
        weiss, pp. 21–37. Latin American Studies Program, Cornell
        University, Ithaca.
1984   *The Ancón Shellmounds and social relations on the central coast of
        Peru during the second millenium B.C.* Paper presented at the
        annual meeting of the Institute for Andean Studies, January,

1984, Berkeley. Manuscript, Philadelphia.
1985a Pachacamac – an Andean oracle under Inca rule. In *Recent studies in Andean prehistory and protohistory*; Papers from the Second Annual Northeast Conference on Andean Archaeology and Ethnohistory, edited by D. Peter Kvietok and Daniel H. Sandweiss, pp. 159–176. Latin American Studies Program, Cornell University, Ithaca.
1985b The Huaca La Florida, Rimac Valley, Peru. In *Early ceremonial architecture in the Andes*, edited by Christopher B. Donnan, pp. 59–69. Dumbarton Oaks Research Library and Collection, Washington.
1985c Exploitation and class formation in the Inca state. *Culture*, vol. V. no. 1, pp. 35–42. Montreal.
1986 Ideology, class formation, and resistance in the Inca state. *Critique of Anthropology*, vol. VI. no. 1, pp. 75–85. Amsterdam.
1987a Tribes, chiefdoms, and kingdoms in the Inca Empire, In *Power relations and state formation*, edited by Thomas C. Patterson and Christine W. Gailey, pp. 117–127. Archeology Unit, American Anthropological Association, Washington.
1987b *Class struggle, state formation, and archaism in ancient Peru.* Paper presented at the Southern Marxist Scholars Conference, March 13–15, 1987, Durham. Manuscript, Philadelphia.
1987c Merchant capital and the formation of the Inca state. *Dialectical Anthropology*, vol. 12, no. 2, pp. 217–227. Dordrecht.
1987d La creación de cultura en las formaciones sociales pre-estatales y no-estatales. *Gens; Boletín de la Sociedad Venezolana de Arqueólogos*, vol. 3, no. 1, pp. 15–25. Caracas.
1990 Pre-state societies and cultural styles in ancient Peru and Mesopotamia: a comparison. In *Upon this foundation: The Ubaid reconsidered*, edited by Elizabeth Henrickson and Ingolf Thuesen. Carsten Niebuhr Institute Publications, no. 10 pp. 293–324. Copenhagen (forthcoming).
1991 Andean cosmologies and the Inca state. In *Dialectical anthropology; essays presented to Stanley Diamond*, edited by Christine W. Gailey, *vol. 1, Civilization in crisis: anthropological perspectives*. University Presses of Florida, Tallahassee (forthcoming).
Patterson, Thomas C. and Edward P. Lanning.
1968 Los medios ambientes glacial tardío y postglacial de Sudamerica. *Boletín de la Sociedad Geográfica de Lima*, tomo LXXXVI, pp. 1–19. Lima.
Patterson, Thomas C., John P. McCarthy, and Robert A. Dunn.
1982 Polities in the Lurín Valley, Peru during the Early Intermediate Period. *Ñawpa Pacha* 20, pp. 61–82. Berkeley.
Paulsen, Allison C.
1983 Huaca del Loro revisited: the Nasca-Huarpa connection. In

Investigations of the Andean past; papers from the First Annual Northeast Conference on Andean Archaeology and Ethnohistory, edited by Daniel H. Sandweiss, pp. 98–112. Latin American Studies Center, Cornell University, Ithaca.

Pauw, Cornelius de
1768   *Recherches philosophiques sur les Américains*, 2 vols. G. J. Decker, Berlin.

Pease, Franklin
1982   The formation of Tawantinsuyu: mechanisms of colonization and relationship with ethnic groups. In *The Inca and Aztec states; anthropology and history*, edited by George A. Collier, Renato I. Rosaldo, and John D. Wirth, pp. 173–198. Stanford University Press, Stanford.

Peters, Ann H.
1986   *Pachinga: habitation and necropolis in the lower Pisco Valley*. Paper presented at the annual meeting of the Society for American Archaeology, April, 1986, New Orleans, Louisiana. Manuscript, Ithaca.

Pizarro, Pedro
1963   *Relación del descubrimiento y conquista de los reinos del Perú* [1571]. Biblioteca de Autores Españoles, tomo 168, pp. 161–244. Ediciones Atlas, Madrid.

Poggi, Gianfranco
1983   *Calvinism and the capitalist spirit; Max Weber's Protestant Ethic*. The University of Massachusetts Press, Amherst.

Polo de Ondegardo, Juan
1916a   *Los errores y supersticiones de los indios, sacados del tratado y aueriguación que hizo el licenciado Polo* [1559]. In Collección de libros y documentos referentes a la historia del Perú, edited by Horacio H. Urteaga, ser. 1, tomo III, pp. 1–43. Imprenta y Librería Sanmartí y Ca., Lima.
1916b   *Relación de los fundamentos acerca del notable daño que resulta de no guardar a los indios sus fueros* [1571]. In Colección de libros y documentos referentes a la historia del Perú, edited by Horacio H. Urteaga, ser. 1, tomo III, pp. 45–188. Imprenta y Librería Sanmartí y Ca., Lima.
1916c   *Relación del linaje de los Incas y como extendieron ellos sus conquistas* [1567]. In Colección de libros y documentos referentes a la historia del Perú, edited by Horacio H. Urteaga, ser. 1, tomo IV, pp. 45–94. Imprenta y Librería Sanmarti y Ca., Lima.
1940   Informe del Licenciado Juan Polo de Ondegardo al Licenciado Briviesca de Muñatones sobre la perpetuidad de las encomiendas en el Perú [1561]. *Revista Histórica*, tomo XIII, pp. 125–196. Lima.

Ponce Sanginés, Carlos

1961   *Informe de labores*. Centro de Investigaciones Arqueológicas en Tiwanaku Publicación no. 1. La Paz.

Pozorski, Sheila
1987   Theocracy vs. militarism: the significance of the Casma Valley in understanding early state formation. In *The origins and development of the Andean state*, edited by Jonathan Haas, Sheila Pozorski, and Thomas Pozorski, pp. 15–30. Cambridge University Press, Cambridge.

Pozorski, Sheila and Thomas Pozorski
1987   *Early settlement and subsistence in the Casma Valley, Peru*. University of Iowa Press, Iowa City.

Prescott, William H.
1968   *History of the conquest of Peru* [1847], 2 vols. consolidated. AMS Press, New York.

Price, Barbara J.
1977   Shifts in production and organization: a cluster interaction model. *Current Anthropolgy*, vol. 18, no. 2, pp. 209–234, Chicago.

Proulx, Donald
1966   *Cultural relationships between the Ica and Nazca Valleys, Peru during the Early Intermediate Period*. Paper presented at the annual meeting of the Society for American Archaeology, April, 1966, Reno, Nevada. Manuscript, Amherst.

Quilter, Jeffrey
1980   *Paloma: mortuary practices and social organization of a preceramic Peruvian Village*. Ph.D. Dissertation in Anthropology, University of California at Santa Barbara. University Microfilms, Ann Arbor.

1985   Architecture and chronology at El Paraíso, Peru. *Journal of Field Archaeology*, vol. 12, no. 4, pp. 279–297. Boston.

Quilter, Jeffrey and Terry Stocker
1983   Subsistence economies and the origins of Andean complex societies. *American Anthropologist*, vol. 85, no. 3, pp. 545–562. Washington.

Ravines, Rogger and William H. Isbell
1976   Garagay: un sitio ceremonial temprano en el Valle de Lima. *Revista del Museo Nacional*, tomo XLI, pp. 253–275. Lima.

Renfrew, Colin
1977   Space, time and polity. In *The evolution of social systems*, edited by Jonathan Friedman and Michael J. Rowlands, pp. 89–112. Gerald Duckworth and Co., Ltd., London.

1986   Introduction: peer polity interaction and socio-political change. In *Peer polity interaction and socio-political change*, edited by Colin Renfrew and John Cherry, pp. 1–18. Cambridge University Press, Cambridge.

Rey, Pierre-Philippe
1982   *Class alliances* [1973], translated by James F. Becker. Inter-
         national Journal of Sociology, vol. XII, no. 2, pp. ii-xiv, 1–120.
         Armonk.
Rigby, Peter
1985   *Persistent pastoralists; nomadic societies in transition.* Zed Press,
         London.
1987   Class formation among East African pastoralists: Maasai of
         Tanzania and Kenya. In *Power relations and state formation,*
         edited by Thomas C. Patterson and Christine W. Gailey,
         pp. 57–80. Archeology Section, American Anthropological
         Association, Washington.
Robinson, Joan
1980   History versus equilibrium [1974]. In *Collected economic papers,*
         Joan Robinson, vol. 5, pp. 48–58. The MIT Press, Cambridge.
Rodríguez-Salgado, M. J.
1988   *The changing face of empire; Charles V, Philip II and Habsburg
         authority, 1551–1559.* Cambridge University Press, Cambridge.
Rostworowski de Diez Canseco, María
1953   *Pachacutec Inca Yupanqui.* Editorial Torres Aguirre, Lima.
1960   Succession, coöption to kingship, and royal incest among the
         Incas. *Southwestern Journal of Anthropology,* vol. 16, no. 4,
         pp. 417–427. Albuquerque.
1961   *Curacas y sucesiones, costa norte.* Imprenta Minerva, Lima.
1962   Nuevos datos sobre tenencia de tierras reales en el Incario.
         Revista del Museo Nacional, tomo XXXI, pp. 130–159. Lima.
1963   Dos manuscritos inéditos con datos sobre Manco II, tierras
         personales de los Incas y mitimaes. *Nueva Coronica,* no. 1, pp.
         223–239. Lima.
1964   Nuevos aportes para el estudio de medición de tierras en el
         Virreynato e Incario. *Revista del Archivo Nacional del Perú,* tomo
         XXVIII, entregas I y II, pp. 1–31. Lima.
1966   Las tierras reales y su mano de obra en el Tahuantinsuyu.
         *Actas y Memorias del XXXVI Congreso Internacional de America-
         nistas, Madrid 1964,* tomo 2, pp. 31–34. Sevilla.
1970   Mercaderes del valle de Chincha en la época prehispánica: un
         documento y unose comentarios. *Revista Española de Antropo-
         logía Americana,* tomo V, pp. 135–177. Madrid.
1972a   Breve informe sobre el señorío de Ychma o Ychima. *Boletín
         Seminario de Arqueología,* no. 13, pp. 37–51. Lima.
1972b   Las etnías del valle de Chillón. *Revista del Museo Nacional,*
         tomo XXXVIII, pp. 250–314. Lima.
1975   Pescadores, artesanos y mercaderes costeños en el Perú prehis-
         panico, *Revista del Museo Nacional,* tomo XLI, pp. 311–351. Lima.
1977   Plantaciones prehispanicas de coca en el vertiente del Paci-

fico. In *Etnía y sociedad*, pp. 155–195. Instituto de Estudios Peruanos, Lima.

1980 Guarco y Lunahuaná, dos señoríos prehispánicos, costa sur-central del Perú. *Revista del Museo Nacional*, tomo XLIV, pp. 153–153–214. Lima.

1988a *Conflicts over coca fields in XVIth-century Perú.* Memoirs of the Museum of Anthropology, University of Michigan, no. 21. Ann. Arbor.

1988b Historia del Tawantinsuyu. *Historia Andina 13.* Instituto de Estudios Peruanos, Lima.

Rousseau, Jérôme
1978a On estates and castes. *Dialectical Anthropology*, vol. 3, no. 1, pp. 85–95. Amsterdam.

1978b Class et ethnicité. *Anthropologie et Sociétés*, vol. 2, no. 1, pp. 61–69. Quebec.

Rowe, John H.
1945 Absolute chronology in the Andean area. *American Antiquity*, vol. X, no. 3, pp. 265–284. Menasha.

1946 Inca culture at the time of the Spanish conquest. In *Handbook of South American Indians*, edited by Julian H. Steward; vol. 2, The Andean civilizations. Bureau of American Ethnology Bulletin 143, pp. 183–330. Washington.

1948 The kingdom of Chimor. *Acta Americana*, tomo VI, no. 1–2, pp. 26–59. Mexico.

1957 The Incas under Spanish colonial institutions. *The Hispanic American Historical Review*, vol. XXXVII, no. 2, pp. 155–199. Durham.

1958 The age grades of the Inca census. In *Miscellanea Paul Rivet, octogenario dictata.* XXXI Congreso Internacional de Americanistas, tomo II, pp. 499–522. Universidad Nacional Autónoma de México, México.

1960a Cultural unity and diversification in Peruvian archaeology. In *Man and culture; selected papers of the Fifth International Congress of Anthropological and Ethnological Sciences*, Philadelphia, Sept. 1–9, 1956, edited by Anthony F. C. Wallace, pp. 627–631. University of Pennsylvania Press, Philadelphia.

1960b The origins of Inca creator worship. In *Culture in history; essays in honor of Paul Radin*, edited by Stanley Diamond, pp. 408–429. Published for Brandeis University by Columbia University Press, New York.

1962 La arqueología de Ica. *Revista de la Facultad de Letras, Universidad Nacional "Luís Gonzaga" de Ica*, año I, no. 1, pp. 113–131. Ica.

1967 What kind of settlement was Inca Cuzco? *Ñawpa Pacha 5*, pp. 59–76. Berkeley.

1979a   An account of the shrines of ancient Cuzco. Ñawpa Pacha 17,
        pp. 1–80. Berkeley.
1979b   Standardization of Inca tapestry tunics. In The Junius B. Bird
        pre-Columbian textile conference, edited by Ann P. Rowe, Eli-
        zabeth P. Benson, and Anne-Louise Schaffer, pp. 239–264.
        The Textile Museum and Dumbarton Oaks, Trustees for
        Harvard University, Washington.
1982   Inca policies and institutions relating to the cultural unifica-
        tion of the empire. In The Inca and Aztec states; anthropology and
        history, edited by George A. Collier, Renato I. Rosaldo, and
        John D. Wirth, pp. 93–118. Stanford University Press,
        Stanford.

Ruiz Naharro, Pedro
1927   Relación de los hechos de los españoles en el Perú desde su descubri-
        miento hasta la muerte del marques Francisco Pizarro. Colección
        de libros y documentos referentes a la historia del Perú,
        edited by Horacio H. Urteaga, tomo VI, pp. 187–213. Imprenta y
        Librería Sanmarti y Ca., Lima

Ryan, Michael
1981   Assimilating new worlds in the sixteenth and seventeenth
        centuries. Comparative Studies in Society and History, vol. 23,
        no. 4, pp. 519–538. Cambridge.

Sáamanos, Juan de
1910   Relación de los primeros descubrimientos de Francisco
        Pizarro y Diego de Almagro [1527]. In The antiquities of Manabi,
        Ecuador, final report. Contributions to South American ar-
        chaeology; the George G. Heye Expedition, by Marshall H.
        Saville, vol. II, pp. 278–281. Irving Press, New York.

Said, Edward W.
1979   Orientalism. Vintage Books, New York.

Ste. Croix, Geoffrey E. M. de
1981   The class struggle in the ancient Greek world from the Archaic Age
        to the Arab Conquest. Cornell University Press, Ithaca and
        London.
1984   Class in Marx's conception of history, ancient and modern.
        New Left Review, no. 146, pp. 94–111. London.

Salazar-Burger, Lucy and Richard L. Burger
1983   La araña en la iconografía del Horizonte Temprano en la costa
        norte del Perú. Beitrage zur Allgemeinen und Vergleichenden
        Archaologie, Band 4, pp. 213–253. Bonn.

Salomon, Frank
1978a   Pochteca and mindalá: a comparison of long-distance traders
        in Ecuador and Mesoamerica, Journal of the Steward Anthropo-
        logical Society, vol. 9, no. 2, pp. 231–246. Urbana.
1978b   Systemes politiques verticaux aux marches de l'Empire Inca.

Annales; Economies, Sociétés, Civilisations, tome XXXIII, no. 5–6, pp. 967–989. Paris.

1982   Chronicles of the impossible: notes on three Peruvian indigenous historians. In *From oral to written expression: native Andean chronicles of the early Colonial Period,* edited by Rolena Adorno. Foreign and Comparative Studies, Latin American Series, no. 4, pp. 9–40. Maxwell School of Citizenship and Public Affairs, Syracuse University, Syracuse.

1986   *Native lords of Quito in the age of the Incas; the political economy of north Andean chiefdoms.* Cambridge University Press, Cambridge.

Samaniego, Lorenzo, Enrique Vergara, and Henning Bischof

1985   New evidence on Cerro Sechin, Casma Valley, Peru. In *Early ceremonial architecture in the Andes,* edited by Christopher B. Donnan, pp. 165–190. Dumbarton Oaks Research Library and Collection, Washington.

Sancho de la Hoz, Pedro

1938   *Relación para S. M. de lo sucedido en la conquista y pacificación de estas provincias de la Nueva Castilla y de la calidad de la tierra . . .* [1534]. Biblioteca Peruana, primera parte, no. 2, pp. 117–185. Desclée, De Brouwer, Paris.

Santillan, Fernando de

1927   *Relación del orígen, descendencia, y política y gobierno de los Incas* [1563–1564]. Colección de libros y documentos referentes a la historia del Perú, edited by Horacio Urteaga, ser. 2, tomo IX, pp. 1–124. Imprenta y Librería Sanmarti y Ca., Lima.

Sarmiento de Gamboa, Pedro

1960   *Historia de los Incas* [1572]. Biblioteca de Autores Españoles, tomo 135, pp. 189–279. Ediciones Atlas, Madrid.

Sauer, Carl O.

1966   *The early Spanish Main.* University of California Press, Berkeley and Los Angeles.

Schaedel, Richard P.

1978   Early state of the Incas. In *The early state,* edited by Henry J. M. Claessen and Peter Skalník, pp. 289–320. Mouton Publishers, The Hague, Paris, and New York.

1985a   The transition from chiefdom to state in northern Peru. In *Development and decline; the evolution of sociopolitical organization,* edited by Henri J. M. Claessen, Pieter van de Velde, and M. Estellie Smith, pp. 156–169. Bergen and Garvey Publishers, South Hadley.

1985b   Coast-highland interrelationships and ethnic groups in northern Peru (500 B.C.–A.D. 1980). In *Andean ecology and civilization: an interdisciplinary perspective on Andean ecological complementarity,* edited by Shozo Masuda, Izumi Shimada, and Craig Morris, pp. 443–474. University of Tokyo Press, Tokyo.

Schweigger, Erwin.
   1964   El litoral peruano, 2nd ed. Gráfica Morsom, S.A., Lima.
Scott, James C.
   1985   Weapons of the weak; everyday forms of peasant resistance. Yale
           University Press, New Haven and London.
Semenov, Yuri I.
   1980   The theory of socio-economic formations and world history.
           In Soviet and Western anthropology, edited by Ernest Gellner,
           pp. 29–58. Gerald Duckworth and Co., London.
Sempat Assadourian, Carlos
   1979   La producción de la mercancía dinero en la formación del
           mercado interno colonial: el caso del espacio peruano, siglo
           XVI. In Ensayos sobre el desarrollo económico de México y América
           Latina (1500–1975), edited by Enrique Florescano, pp. 223–292.
           Fondo de la Cultura Económica, Mexico.
   1983   El sistema de la economía colonial; el mercado interior, regiones y
           espacio económico. Editorial Nueva Imagen, Mexico.
Shady, Ruth and Arturo Ruiz
   1979   Evidence for interregional relationships during the Middle
           Horizon on the north-central coast of Peru. American Anti-
           quity, vol. 44, no. 4, pp. 676–684. Washington.
Sherbondy, Janet
   1977   Les réseaux d'irrigation dans la géographie politique de
           Cuzco. Journal de la Société des Américanistes, tome LXVI,
           pp. 45–66. Paris.
   1982   The canal systems of Hanan Cuzco. Ph.D. Dissertation in An-
           thropology, University of Illinois, Urbana. University Micro-
           films, Ann Arbor.
Sider, Gerald M.
   1976   Lumbee Indian cultural nationalism and ethnogenesis. Dialec-
           tical Anthropology, vol. 1, no. 2, pp. 161–172. Amsterdam.
Simpson, Leslie B.
   1966   The encomienda in New Spain; the beginning of Spanish Mexico.
           University of California Press, Berkeley and Los Angeles.
Silverblatt, Irene
   1976   Principios de organización femenina en el Tawantinsuyu.
           Revista del Museo Nacional, tomo XLII, pp. 299–340. Lima.
   1978   Andean women in Inca society. Feminist Studies, vol. 4, no. 3,
           pp. 37–61. College Park.
   1987   Moon, sun, and witches; gender ideologies and class in Inca and
           colonial Peru. Princeton University Press, Princeton.
   1988a   Imperial dilemmas, the politics of kinship, and Inca recon-
           structions of history. Comparative Studies in Society and History,
           vol. 30, no. 1, pp. 83–102. New York.
   1988b   Women in states. Annual Review of anthropology, vol. 17,

pp. 427–460. Annual Reviews, Inc., Palo Alto.

Siskind, Janet
1978   Kinship and mode of production. *American Anthropologist*, vol. 80, no. 4, pp. 860–872. Washington.

Southall, Aidan
1988   The segmentary state in Africa and Asia. *Comparative Studies in Society and History*, vol. 30, no. 1, pp. 52–82. Cambridge.

Spalding, Karen
1970   Social climbers: changing patterns of mobility among the Indians of colonial Peru. *The Hispanic American Historical Review*, vol. L, no. 4, pp. 645–664. Durham.
1973   *Kurakas* and commerce: a chapter in the evolution of Andean society. *The Hispanic American Historical Review*, vol. LIII, no. 4, pp. 581–599. Durham.
1984   *Huarochirí; an Andean society under Inca and Spanish rule.* Stanford University Press, Stanford.

Spengler, Oswald
1918–   The decline of the West, translated by C.F. Atkinson, 2 vols.
1922   Alfred Knopf, New York.

Springborg, Patricia
1987   The contractual state: reflections on orientalism and despotism. *History of Political Thought*, vol. VIII, no. 3, pp. 395–433. Devon.

Stern, Steve J.
1981   The rise and fall of Indian-White alliances: a regional view of "conquest" history. *The Hispanic American Historical Review*, vol. 61, no. 3, pp. 461–491. Durham.
1982   *Peru's Indian peoples and the challenge of Spanish conquest.* The University of Wisconsin Press, Madison.
1983   The struggle for solidarity; class, culture, and community in highland Indian America. *Radical History Review*, no. 27, pp. 21–45. New York.
1985   New directions in Andean economic history; a critical dialogue with Carlos Sempat Assadourian. *Latin American Perspectives*, issue 44, vol. 12, no. 1, pp. 133–148. Los Angeles.
1988a   Feudalism, capitalism, and the world-system in the perspective of Latin America and the Caribbean. *American Historical Review*, vol. 98, no. 4, pp. 829–872. Washington.
1988b   *Reply*: "Ever more solitary." *American Historical Review*, vol. 98, no. 4, pp. 886–897. Washington.

Steward, Julian H.
1950   Area research: theory and practice. *Social Science Research Council Bulletin* 63. New York.

Strong, William Duncan and John M. Corbett
1943   A ceramic sequence at Pachacamac. In *Archeological studies in*

Peru, 1941–1942. Columbia Studies in Archeology and Ethnology, vol. 1, no. 2, pp. 27–121. Columbia University Press, New York.

Sullivan, Lawrence E.
1985   Above, below, and far away: Andean cosmogony and ethical order. In *Cosmogony and ethical order; new studies in comparative ethics,* edited by Robin W. Lovin and Frank E. Reynolds, pp. 98–129. The University of Chicago Press, Chicago and London.

Tattersall, Ian
1985   The human skeletons from Huaca Prieta, with a note on exostoses of the external auditory meatus. In *The preceramic excavations of the Huaca Prieta, Chicama Valley, Peru,* by Junius B. Bird, John Hyslop, and Milica D. Skinner. Anthropological Papers of the American Museum of Natural History, vol. 62, no. 1, pp. 60–64. New York.

Taylor, John
1979   *From modernization to modes of production; a critique of the sociologies of development.* Humanities Press, Atlantic Highlands.

Thapar, Romila
1981   The state as empire. In *The study of the state,* edited by Henry J. M. Claessen and Peter Skalník, pp. 409–426. Mouton Publishers, The Hague, Paris, and New York.

Thomson, George D.
1961   *The first philosophers; studies in ancient Greek philosophy.* Lawrence and Wishart, London.

Tosi, Joseph A., Jr.
1960   *Zonas de vida natural en el Perú; memoria explicativa sobre el mapa ecológico del Perú.* Instituto Interamericano de Ciencias Agrícolas de la OEA, Zona Andina, Lima.

Toynbee, Arnold
1933–   *A study of history,* 10 vols. Oxford University Press,
1954   Oxford.

Uhle, Max
1903   *Pachacamac; report of the William L. Pepper, M.D., L.L.D. Peruvian expedition of 1896.* Department of Anthropology, University of Pennsylvania, Philadelphia.

van Bakel, Martin A., Renée R. Hagesteijn, and Pieter van de Velde
1986   Introduction. In *Private politics; a multi-disciplinary approach to 'big-man' systems,* edited by Martin van Bakel, Renée R. Hagesteijn, and Pieter van de Velde. Studies in Human Society, vol. 1, pp. 1–10. E. J. Brill, Leiden.

van Binsbergen, Wilm and Peter Geschiere, editors
1985   *Old modes of production and capitalist encroachment; anthropologi-*

cal explorations in Africa. KPI, London, Boston, Melbourne, and Henley.

van Binsbergen, Wim and Reini Raatgever
1985   Introduction: emerging insights and issues in French Marxist anthropology. In *Old modes of production and capitalist encroachment; anthropological explorations in Africa*, edited by Wim van Binsbergen and Peter Geschiere, pp. 1–38. KPI, Ltd., London, Boston, Melbourne, and Henley.

Vivens Vives, Jaime
1969   *An economic history of Spain*, 3rd ed. [1964], translated by Frances M. López-Morillas. Princeton University Press, Princeton.

Voltaire, François-Marie Arouet de
1963   *Essai sur les moeurs et l'esprit des nations* [1756], 2 vols. Garnier Freres, Paris.

Wachtel, Nathan
1971   Rebeliones y milenarismo. In *Ideología mesiánica del mundo andino*, edited by Juan A. Ossio, pp. 103–142. Instituto de Estudios Peruanos, Lima.

1973   *La vision des vaincus; les Indiens du Pérou devant la conquête espagnole*. Editions Gallimard, Paris.

1982   The *mitimaes* of the Cochabamba Valley: the colonization policy of Huayna Capac. In *The Inca and Aztec states, 1400–1800; anthropology and history*, edited by George A. Collier, Renato I. Rosaldo, and John D. Wirth, pp. 199–235. Academic Press, New York.

Wallace, Dwight T.
1986   The Topará tradition: an overview. In *Perspectives on Andean prehistory and protohistory; papers from the Third Annual Northeast Conference on Andean Archaeology and Ethnohistory*, edited by Daniel H. Sandweiss and D. Peter Kvietok, pp. 35–48. Latin American Studies Program, Cornell University, Ithaca.

Wallerstein, Immanuel
1974   *The modern world-system; capitalist agriculture and the origins of the European world-economy in the sixteenth century*. Academic Press, New York.

Weber, Max
1951   *The religion of China; Confucianism and Taoism* [1915], translated and edited by Hans H. Gerth. The Free Press, Glencoe.

1958   *The protestant ethic and the spirit of capitalism* [1904–1905], translated by Talcott Parsons. Charles Scribner's Sons, New York.

1978   *Economy and society; an outline of interpretive sociology* [1922], edited by Guenther Roth and Claus Wittich, 2 vols. University of California Press, Berkeley, Los Angeles, and London.

Webster, David L.
   1976   On theocracies. *American Anthropologist*, vol. 78, no. 4, pp.
          812–828. Washington.
Wedin, Ake
   1966   El concepto de lo incaico y las fuentes. *Studia Historica Gotho-
          burgensia*, VII. Almqvist & Wilksells Boktryckeri, Uppsala.
Weir, Glendon H. and J. Philip Dering
   1986   The lomas of Paloma: human-environment relations in a
          central Peruvian fog oasis: archaeobotany and palynology. In
          Andean archaeology; papers in memory of Clifford Evans, edited by
          Ramiro M. Matos, Solveig A. Turpin, and Herbert H. Eling,
          Jr., Institute of Archaeology, University of California, Los
          Angeles, Monograph XXVII, pp. 18–44. Los Angeles.
Wheeler, Jane and Elías Mujica
   1981   *Prehistoric pastoralism in the Lake Titicaca Basin, Peru, 1979–1980
          field season*. Final project report submitted to the National
          Science Foundation.
Wickham, Chris
   1984   The other transition: from the ancient world to feudalism.
          Past and Present, no. 103, pp. 3–36. Oxford.
Willey, Gordon R.
   1953   Prehistoric settlement patterns in the Virú Valley, Perú. *Bu-
          reau of American Ethnology Bulletin* 153. Washington.
   1971   *An introduction to American archaeology*, vol. 2, South America.
          Prentice-Hall, Englewood Cliffs.
Willey, Gordon R. and John M. Corbett
   1954   *Early Ancón and early Supe culture*. Columbia Studies in Ar-
          cheology and Ethnology, vol. III. Columbia University Press,
          New York.
Williams, Raymond
   1980   Base and superstructure in Marxist cultural theory. In *Prob-
          lems in materialism and culture*, pp. 31–49. Verso, London.
Wilson, David J.
   1987   Reconstructing patterns of early warfare in the Lower Santa
          Valley: new data on the role of conflict in the origins of
          complex north coast society. In *The origins and development of
          the Andean state*, edited by Jonathan Haas, Sheila Pozorski,
          and Thomas Pozorski, pp. 56–69. Cambridge University
          Press, Cambridge.
Wittfogel, Karl A.
   1957   *Oriental despotism; a comparative study of total power*. Yale Uni-
          versity Press, New Haven.
Wolpe, Harold
   1980   Introduction. In *The articulation of modes of production; essays*

from *Economy and Society*, edited by Harold Wolpe, pp. 1–43. Routledge and Kegan Paul, Ltd., London, Boston, and Henley.

1985   The articulation of modes and forms of production. In *Marxian theory and the Third World*, edited by Diptendra Banerjee, pp. 89–103. Sage Publications, New Delhi, Beverly Hills, and London.

Wood, Ellen M.

1988   *Peasant-citizen and slave; the foundations of Athenian democracy*, Verso, London.

Zagarell, Allen

1986   Structural discontinuity–a critical factor in the emergence of primary and secondary states. *Dialectical Anthropology*, vol. 10, nos. 3–4, pp. 155–177. Amsterdam.

Zárate, Agustín de

1947   *Historia del descubrimiento y conquista de la provincia del Perú y de las guerras y cosas señaladas en ella, hasta el vencimiento de Gonzalo Pizarro y de sus secuaces, que en ella se rebelaron contra su majestad* [1555]. Biblioteca de Autores Españoles, tomo 26, pp. 459–574. Ediciones Atlas, Madrid.

Zuidema, R. Tom

1964   *The ceque system of Cuzco; the social organization of the capital of the Inca*. International Archives of Ethnography, Supplement to vol. L. E. J. Brill, Leiden.

1973   The origin of the Inca empire. In *Les grandes empires*. Recueils de la Société Jean Bodin pour l'Histoire Comparative des Institutions XXXI, pp. 733–757. Bruxelles.

1983a   Hierarchy and space in Incaic social organization. *Ethnohistory*, vol. 30, no. 2, pp. 49–75. Durham.

1983b   The lion in the city: royal symbols of transition in Cuzco. *Journal of Latin American Lore*, vol. 9, no. 1, pp. 39–100. Los Angeles.

Index

Aclla (chosen women), 76, 81–82, 111, 113
Administrative system, kuraka's role in, 78
in Inca state, 66, 75–86
officials, 75–86. *See also* 'Apo; Runakhipukamayoq; Tokoyrikoq; Toqrikoq;
resettlement, 77–78
state cult, 74–75
Africa, 3
Agricultural economies
commercial, 147–51
and productive system, 16–18
landscape, 10–11, 18
Alcaviszas, 53
Almagro, Diego de, 124–128, 132–135, 137, 140–141
Amazon Basin, 31–32
Ancasmarca, 53
Ancestors cults, 39
Andean landscapes, human construction of, 10–11
Andes Mountains, 9–10
ecological diversity, 9
'Apo (prefect), 75
'Apu Mayta, 54, 58–60
Archaism, 35, 105–6
Archaeological evidence, 6, 12–13
state formation, 26–27, 30–31
resistance, 105–6
Aristocracy
in Spain, 143–44
and encomenderos, 136–47
Articulation, 6
of modes of production, 30, 158–59
state role in, 29–30
Artisans, 99
in productive systems, 99, 108–10.
See also Commodity production, petty
"Asiatic" state, 158.
See Tributary mode of production

Assassination, 63, 92, 95, 111–12
'Ataw Wallpa, 95–97
allies in civil war, 120–21
destroys mummy of Topa 'Inka, 95–96
kidnapped by Spaniards, 3, 122–28
relation with Pachacamac, 123–24
successional dispute and civil war, 95–97, 120–28
Ayar Cachi, 46
Ayarmarka, 53–54
Ayllu
description of, 56–58
Inca state, 55, 64–65
land, 56–58
productive system, 65
religious practice, 74
See also Panaqa
Ayacucho, 36
Aztec state, 131, 166

Biological Reproduction and state formation, 82
Bolivia, 114–16

Cacique, *See* Kuraka
Cajamarca, 73–74, 93, 122–28
Calca, 60
Calendar, agricultural ritual, 56–57
Cañaris, 113, 121–22, 137, 141
Cañete Valley, 31, 108, 110–11
Carangues, 111–14
Caribbean, 3, 130–31
Casma Valley, 26
Cayambis, 111
Census
Inca census taker, 76. *See also* Runakhipukamayoq
inspector, 76. *See also* Tokoyrikoq
mit'a labor, 76–77
tax and conscription, 76–77
Central America, 127
Centralization

in Inca state, 59–86
in Europe, 129–36, 143–44
in colonial state, 151–56
Chachapoyas, 108, 111, 122, 137
Challkuchima (war leader), 120–28
Chancas, 59, 61–64, 69–70, 72–73
Charcas, 114
Charles, 129–35, 138–40
Chicha (maize beer), 81–82, 99
Chile, 127, 140–41
Chimor, Kingdom of, 73–75, 107–8
  destruction of ruling class, 78
  branch oracle of Pachacamac at
    capital, 89
Chincha Valley, 31, 43, 90–91
  branch oracle of Pachacamac,
    89–90
  merchants, 108
Chiriguana, 107, 114–16
Chiqui Ocllo (secondary wife of Topa
  'Inka), 92–93
Cimarron communities, 141
Civilization
  as class and state formation, 2, 27
  rise of Andean, 28–41
Civil war, 62–73, 93–94, 116–28, 145
Class
  definition of, 4–5
  distinguished from estates, 55,
    64–65
  exploitation, 96–97
  formation, 2, 22–26, 116
  producing and non-producing, 4–5
  See also Estates
Class and state formation
  in Andes, 26–41
  in frontier areas, 79–80, 87–88,
    96–97, 116
  theoretical considerations, 20–26
Climate, 9–10
Cloth
  as plunder, 136
  for ritual use, 89
Cochabamba Valley, 94, 114
Colla, 60, 117–19
Colonial state
  civil unrest, 136–44, 149
  crisis of 1560s, 144–51
  encomenderos, 149
  formation of colonial society,
    151–56, 163–65
  mining, 147–48
  problem created by Spanish
    immigration, 142–43, 149

rebellion in, 156
regional economies, 147–49
Spanish Crown, 151–56
Colonialism, 129
Columbus, Christopher, 130
Commodity production
  state involvement, 108–110
Communal mode of production
  definition of, 13–21
  Conchas social formation, 16–18
  households as production and
    consumption units, 14–15
  La Florida social formation, 18–21
  Paloma social formation, 14–16
Conchas social formation, 16–18
Contradiction, 7, 24–25, 66
  culture, 70–72
Corregidores de indios, 153
Cortés, Hernán, 3, 131, 135
Crops
  failure of, 10
Cult, Inca state 74–75, 83–84
  appropriation of labor, 83–84
  calendar, 74–75
  ceque system, 74–75
  Coricancha (shrine), 74–75
  cosmology, 84–85
  landholdings, 75
  Temples of the Sun, 74–75
Culture
  contested terrain, 70–72
  contradictions, 70–72
  dominant, 70
  emergent, 70–72
  ethnogenesis, 31, 79
  oppositional, 70–71
  residual, 71–72
  resistance, 70, 105–6
  state formation, 70
Cuyumarca, 53
Cuzco, 46, 52–57, 122–28, 137, 139
  as Inca capital, 72–74
  education in, 78
  nobility in, 78
  religion in, 74–78
  rebuilding, 74
Cuzco Valley, 48, 50, 72, 74

Decimal system, 75–76
Deities. *See* Wak'as
Diseases. *See* Epidemics
Division of labor
  age-based, 14–17, 98–99
  gender, 14–17, 81–83, 98–99

social, 4–5, 22–26, 55, 64–65, 96–97, 116, 146–49
spatially and temporally organized, 16–19
Dominant ideology thesis, 33–34

Earthquakes, 9
Ecological zones, 9–11
Encapsulation and incorporation, 80–81
Encomenderos, 136, 140–41, 143, 146–47
  revolt of, 138–39
  tribute to, 132
  market activity of, 142, 146–49
Encomiendas, 132, 136–39, 146–47
Englightenment, 3
Entrepreneurs, 151–56. See also Encomenderos
Epidemics, 94–95, 141
Estates
  in class formation, 64
  definition of, 50, 55, 64
  differences between chiefly and nonchiefly, 50, 55
  distinguished from class, 50, 64–65
  transformation into class relations, 64–65
Ethnicity, 79
Ethnogenesis, 31–32
Exploitation, 7, 24–26, 65
  class formation, 96–97
  colonial state, 129–56
  encomenderos, 140–49
  Inca state, 65–66
  pre-Incaic states, 26–41
  plunder economy, 136–44
  resistance, 66

Ferdinand of Aragon, 129
Fortresses, 26, 110, 112

Gender, 81–83
  production, 81–83, 98–99
  technical divisions of labor, 14–17
Gold, 123
Grants. See Encomiendas

Habsburgs, 129–30
Herding, 83
Hernández Girón, Francisco, 140
"Hill of Silver," See Potosí, mines of
History
  Andean representations of, 43–45.

See also Traditions, dynastic
Horses, 123
"House of the Chosen Women," 76, 81–82
Huamachuco, 36
Huamanga Province, 125, 139
Huancavilcas, 111–12, 121
Huarco. See Cañete Valley
Huari state, 36–37
Huarochirí Province, 43, 88, 107
  branch oracles of Pachacamac, 89–90
Huayllacan, 53–54
Huno (unit of ten thousand households), 76

Ica Valley, 31–32, 105–6
Inca state
  appropriation of land, labor, and herds, 99–101
  constitution of ethnic groups, 79
  disintegration of, 94–97, 116–28, 145
  early society, 39
  encapsulated communities, 80–81
    transformation, 78, 81
  formation, 59–68
  frontier areas, 80
    border wars, 106–28
  imperial society, 69–86
  organization, 39, 66
  origin myths, 46–52
  pre-imperial society, 42–59
  succession in imperial state, 69
    transformation of class structure, 69–70
  successional disputes and civil wars, 59–63, 72, 119–28
  uneven development, 70
  weakness of, 66
  wealth of, 98
'Inka Roq'a, 47, 53–54
'Inka Urqon, 59, 62–63, 72, 119–20
Irrigation, 18
Isabela of Castile, 129

Jauja, 123–26. See also Wankas
Jewelry, 136

Khipu, 42–43
Khipukamayoq, 42
Kidnapping, 3, 48, 78, 102
Kin-civil conflict, 5–6, 50–51. See also Rebellion; Resistance

Kizkiz (war leader), 120–28
Knotted cords. *See* Khipu
Kurakas
  as Indian elite in colonial society,
    151–56
  as traditional leaders, 59
  in colonial state, 146, 151–56
  in Inca state, 77–78, 101–2, 157–58
  relation with encomenderos,
    138–47, 151–56

La Gasca, Pedro de, 139, 149
Labor as wealth, 98
Labor service
  communal, 16–20, 98–99
  tribute, 83
La Florida social formation, 18–21
Lambayeque Valley, 33–35
Land
  access to, 99
  of deities, 75, 83
  as wealth, 98
Land disputes, 142
Land tenure
  changes with state formation, 99
  dispossession, 142
  royal lands, 93, 96
  state lands, 75
  state cult lands, 75, 83
Law
  colonial state, 142
  Inca state, 103
Lima, 4, 137, 147–50
  administrative center, 147
  commerce, 148–50
Lloq'e Yupanki, 52–53
Looting, 26, 48
Lupaqa, 60, 117–19
Luque, Fernando de, 132–35
Lurín Valley, 32–33

Maize beer. *See* Chicha
Mama Anahuarque, 63, 86, 89
Mama Huaco, 46–47, 51
Mama Miqay, 53
Mama Oqllo, 46
Mamaq, 89–90
Manqo 'Inka, 46–47, 52
Manqo 'Inka, (16th century ruler),
  125–28, 137
Market system
  in Andean society, 108–110
  in colonial society, 146–56
Marriage
  political dimensions of, 102

state regulation of, 103
Mayta Qhapaq, 53–57
Merchants, 81, 108–10. *See also*
  Mindaláes
Mexico, 3, 131–32
Metals
  plunder of, 136
  and status, 136
Mindaláes, 109–10
Mining
  and labor service, 147
  in colonial economy, 147–48
  Indian control of smelting
    processes, 147
  Spanish control of, 147
Mit'a, 77
  colonial levies, 141, 153–55
  in Inca state, 77
Mitimaes, 77, 127, 153
  in Andean communities, 18–20
  in Inca state, 77, 102, 117–18
  in civil war, 121–22, 127
  in colonial state, 147–49, 153–55
Moche state, 33–35
Modes of production, 5–6
  base, 13
  communal, 13–20
  forces of production, 13
  relations of production, 13
  superstructures, 13
Myths
  of origins, 43–45. *See also* History,
    representations of

Nazca Valley, 31
Ninan Kuuchi, 95, 120

Orders. *See* Estates

Pacaritampu, 46, 50, 55
Pachaca (unit of one hundred
  households), 76
Pachacamac, 43, 88–92, 104
  branch oracles, 89–91
  branch oracles in borderlands, 108
  landholdings, 89–91
  oracle, 9, 88
  Mama Anahuarque, 89
  relation with 'Ataw Wallpa and
    Washkar, 123–24
  relation with Topa 'Inka Yupanki,
    89–91
Pachakuti 'Inka Yupanki, 52, 59–68,
  72–73, 86
  landholdings of panaqa around

Cuzco, 74
landholdings between Cuzco and Titicaca, 75
limits on Wiraqocha's panaqa, 85
relation with state cult, 87–88
Pacific Ocean, 10
Paloma social formation, 14–16
Panama, 132–35
Panaqa, 52, 56–57, 74, 86–97
Paqarina, 46
Paraguay, 4, 114–15
Pariacaca (deity), 88, 104
Pastos, 107, 111–13
Paullu 'Inka, 120, 137
Peasantry, 119
Philip II, 143–44
Pinto (rebel leader), 113–14
Pisco Valley, 32
Pizarro, Francisco, 122–28, 132–35, 137
Pizarro, Gonzalo, 138–39
Pizarro, Hernando, 123, 137
Plate tectonics, 9
Plunder, 3, 26, 59, 144
Plunder economy, 136–44
Potosí, mines of, 4, 146–48
Pre-and non-state societies
communal mode of production, 13–14
Production
for civil sphere, 81
for use, 14–20
spatial and temporal organization of, 17–19, 81
Pucará state, 31, 35
Pyramids, U-shaped, 17–21
and ritual practices, 18

Qhapaq Wari (son of Topa 'Inka and Chiqui Ocllo), 92
Qhapaq Yupanki, 53, 57, 73
father of Walpaya, 93
Quito, 122–28, 137
Quitos, 111

Raids, 26, 59
Ransom, 3, 123, 166–67
Rebellions, 117–28, 141
arms caches and threatened uprisings, 144
Reducciónes, 153
Representations of Andean peoples, 166
importance in social theory, 1
by Andean writers, 2

by Europeans, 1
Reproduction, 6
of Andean social formations, 11, 81–83. See also Biological reproduction; Social reproduction
Resettlement
by Inca state, 77–78, 102
Resistance, 6
armed, 106–28, 141
cross-class and cross-estate alliances, 119
cultural, 105–6
ethnogenesis, 31–33
sabotage, 141
theft, 142. See also Rebellions
Rimac Valley, 34
Runakhipukamayoq (census taker), 76

Sayri Topa, 140
Self-sufficiency, 14–21
Slaves, 133
alliances between native American and African, 141
descendants of African, 140
escaped slaves and resistance, 133, 140
native American, 140
participation in Spanish invasion, 140
resistance of, 141
Social reproduction
and production, 11
state formation, 81–83
Soto, Hernando de, 123–24, 134
Spain
as European power, 129–36, 143–44
Inca state, 129
Spanish Crown
colonial expansion, 129–36
colonial state, 143–44
commerce, 130–31
Spanish immigrants, 142–43, 149
Spoils of war
in Andean communities, 26–27
State formation, 2–5
as a crisis in social reproduction, 2–3
class relations, 2–5, 161–62
coercion and violence, 157
conquest in, 26–27, 160–61
control of labor, 33–36
control of trade, 37–39
construction of ethnic groups,

108–11, 125
cults, 39
    definition of, 2–3
    destruction of local ruling elites,
        78, 108–11
    and ethnocide, 27
    evolutionist theories of, 20–21
    expansion of imperial state, 72–86
    fragmentation of political power,
        162
    not a unidirectional process, 20–26,
        40–41
    reconstitution of class structures,
        96–97, 161–62
    religion in process, 67
    repression in, 26–27, 104
    resistance to, 65–68
    tradition, 67
    uneven development, 26–41, 162.
        See also Articulation; Kin/civil
        conflict; Resistance
State
    collapse of, 8, 116–28, 145
    definition of, 6
    failed, 2, 26
    Inca imperial, 69, 71–86
    mercantile, 37–39
    pristine and secondary in the
        Andes, 26–28
    strong tributary, 33–36
    spatial organization and uneven
        development, 26 ff.
    weak tributary, 25–26
    theocratic, theory of, 20–21
State systems
    Colonial state, 151–56, 163–65
    Inca state, 6, 71–97
    pre-Inca states, 6, 26–37
Succession to throne, 86–97
    disputes, 60–63, 72, 92–93
    gender in, 92–93
Surplus extraction, 7

Taki Onqoy, 156
Tarma, 43
Taxation. See Mit'a; Tribute
Temple of the Sun. See Cult, state
Teqzi Wiraqocha, 61
    subordinated to state cult, 85
    Urcos (shrine), 85
Theocratic state, 20–21
Tiahuanaco, 47–49
Tiwanaku state, 35
Titicaca Basin, 31, 36, 72–75
Tokoyrikoq (inspector), 76–77, 102–3

Toledo, Francisco de, Viceroy, 151–56
    administration of, 151
    and encomenderos, 152–53
    and mit'a, 153
Topa 'Inka Yupanki, 86–88
    as war leader, 74
    death, 92–93
    dispute over heir to throne, 87
    landholdings, 87–88, 91–92
    relation with Pachacamac, 74,
        88–89, 91
Topa Wallpa, 125
Toparáa state, 31
Toqrikoq (provincial governor), 75–76
Trade
    and mercantile state formation,
        37–39
    in Andean society, 37–39, 108–10
Tradition
    preservation of, 42–43
    dynastic Inca, 7, 45–67
Tributary mode of production, 24–26,
    158
    articulation with kin-based
        communities, 24–26, 30–31
    and tributary states, 29–30
Tumbes, 123, 133
Tumipampa, 93, 113, 121

Urubamba Valley, 60, 62, 72

Vaca de Castro, Cristóbal, 138
"Verticality," 16–21, 79–81
Viracocha, 48

Wak'as (deities and shrines), 102, 104
    and landed property, 74–75, 89–91
    and Inca state, 102
    and Spanish authority, 156
    and taki onqoy movement, 156
Walpaya, 92–93
    son of Qhapaq Yupanki, 93
Waman 'Achachi, 92–93
    succession dispute, 92–93
Wankas, 125–26, 137. See also Jauja
Waranga (unit of one thousand
    households), 76
Washkar, 95–97, 120–28
    allies in civil war, 120
    successional dispute and civil war,
        120–28
Wayna Qhapaq, 72, 92–97
    dispute over succession, 92–93
    appropriates land and labor for
        panaqa, 93–94

death sparks civil war, 94–97
Wealth, 98
Weapons, 26–27
Weaving, 81–82
Wika-k'iraw, 54, 58–60
Wiraqocha 'Inka, 54, 59–61, 119–20
  civil unrest during his reign, 60–68
  limited capacity of panaqa to

accumulate wealth, 85
  shrine of Teqzi Wiraqocha, 61
Witchcraft, 93
Yana (male retainer), 76
Yawar Waqaq, 54, 58, 60

Zinchi Roq'a, 46, 52, 55